THE BELIEVER AS CITIZEN

ISAAC HECKER STUDIES
IN RELIGION AND AMERICAN CULTURE

THE BELIEVER AS CITIZEN

John Courtney Murray in a New Context

Thomas Hughson, S.J.

Paulist Press
New York/Mahwah, New Jersey

TO MY PARENTS

Cover photo by Craig Callan. Cover design by Tim McKeen.

Copyright © 1993 by the Wisconsin Province of the Society of Jesus

Library of Congress Cataloging-in-Publication Data

Hughson, Thomas, 1939–
   The believer as citizen :   John Courtney Murray in a new context /
Thomas Hughson.
     p. cm.—(Isaac Hecker studies in religion and American culture)
   Includes bibliographical references.
   ISBN 0-8091-3412-8 (pbk.)
   1. Christianity and politics—Catholic Church—History of doctrines—20th century.   2. Sociology, Christian (Catholic)
3. Murray, John Courtney.   4. Catholic Church. National Conference of Catholic Bishops. Economic justice for all.   5. United States—Religion—1960-   I. Title.   II. Series.
BR516.H775   1993
261.8′0973—dc20

93-4655
CIP

Published by Paulist Press
997 Macarthur Boulevard
Mahwah, NJ 07430

Printed and bound in the
United States of America

Contents

Introduction: The New Context   1

1. Believer-Citizens: Identity and Texts   17

2. Believers as Citizens: From Historical to Hermeneutical
    Analysis of Tradition   40

3. Beyond Dogmatism: Discovering the People
    Behind *We Hold These Truths*   57

4. Remembering a Just Deed: The Maryland
    Experiment in Tolerance   77

5. Identity Reinterpreted: Church-State Norms as Principles
    of Self-Understanding   108

6. Free Exercise of Religion: An Option for the Poor   134

Notes   150

Acknowledgments

Many are the people to whom I owe thanks: members of the Martin, Febiger, Gramling, Hughson and Corsmeier families; Herbert Richardson; Most Rev. Donald E. Pelotte; David Hollenbach; J. Leon Hooper; Dennis McCann; Edwin Block; Stanley Harrison; Marvin Berkowicz; Donna Foran; Patrick Carey; Lawrence Engel; Paul Misner; Joseph Sheehan; Patrick Red Elk; Michael McNulty; James Ewens; Richard Abert; Daniel Gannon; Maria Moravski; James Flaherty; William Johnson; Martin Hosking; John Schwantes; Benedict Viviano; Lynda Brayer; Rebecca Kasper; William Clarke; Susan and Aled Jones-Williams; Jean Vanier; Gregory Lucey; Michael McCartan, Dana Kramer-Rolls.

Hospitable communities, too, deserve a word of thanks: the Pontifical Biblical Institute–Jerusalem; the Tantur Ecumenical Institute; the Jesuit communities at Georgetown University, Marquette University and the Jesuit School of Theology at Berkeley; the Miguel Pro Community in Milwaukee.

I wish to acknowledge the assistance of several institutions and their librarians: the Woodstock Theological Center Library; the Special Collections Room in the Joseph Mark Lauinger Library at Georgetown University; the Graduate Theological Union Library at Berkeley; the Tantur Ecumenical Institute Library; the Marquette University Library.

A grant from the Bradley Institute for Democracy and Public Values at Marquette University helped support my writing in the Spring of 1991, as did the Marquette University Jesuit community.

No individual, community or institution, of course, need accept responsibility for any of the views I have arrived at and have presented in this book.

Introduction: The New Context

Two Premises

One premise for this book is a particular reading of *Economic Justice for All.*[1] The pastoral letter was not a moral exhortation but a prophetic examination of the social reality of the United States. It presented poverty, powerlessness and marginalization as frustrations of divine creation, not just as violations of justice.[2] Within the larger framework of God's immanent action in history, it inaugurated a qualitatively new phase in American Catholicism, a *kairos* which is crisis and opportunity, death and rebirth. But whether the National Conference of Catholic Bishops initiated a renaissance in American Catholicism or not depends on what happens to their letter. How will the 25% or 28% of Americans who are Catholic[3] confront one-seventh of the nation living in poverty, one out of three African-American teenagers unable to find jobs, 7% of the labor force out of work, 75% of farms earning just 13% of agricultural income, and public policies detrimental to many developing nations?[4] How will this social reality qualify the futures of the 31% of Americans under the age of 30 who are Catholic?[5]

The answers, obviously, cannot be known at this time. On the one hand, younger American Catholics, especially, may fall into complete suburban captivity and a vortex of insecurity blocking out awareness of basic facts. In an essay critical yet supportive of the bishops, Victor Ferkiss stated:

> If, as polls indicate, the young no longer have faith in the Social Security system, if even beginning employees are concerned about pension plans and about Individual Retirement Accounts of their own, these attitudes tell us something about our nation. The insecurity they reflect means that no matter how affluent the majority may seem to be, they will not be easily moved by concern for those who are less well off.[6]

1

Were this insecurity to dominate, *Economic Justice for All* could be dismissed with a sad revision of Dives and Lazarus that would complain, "Dives, too, had his problems." Not every kind of justice will then have an appeal, though contracts made by a dwindling middle-class and an upper-level of the rich probably will not lose their moral cachet.

Of course, it could be worse. Andrew M. Greeley finds that "less than a fifth of the Catholic laity have even heard of the National Conference's much touted pastoral letters on nuclear weapons and poverty. . . ."[7] Complete oblivion to the social reality coupled with ignorance of a prophetic response to it could prevail over a frowning but adroit back-pedalling away from both. Yet, whether in any way due to the overall concerns in the pastoral letter or to something else, a preponderance of American Catholics expresses, according to George Gallup, Jr. and Jim Castelli, a willingness to have something done about some kinds of social problems, albeit in all too familiar (but what alternatives have developed?) ways. They report that approximately two-thirds of American Catholics support increased government spending on the following: Social Security (64%); health care (70%); aid for the homeless (67%); aid for the elderly (74%); the environment (63%); public schools (66%); AIDS research (71%).[8] These figures show at least a will open to social and economic justice. It may be that the Gallup poll does not get into specifics and does not allow for discrimination between what is due in justice and what might be offered in compassion. Or, it could be that *Economic Justice for All* rested on a fairly sound impression of middle-class American Catholics' incipient will to justice.

The case is not closed. This book provides one further response to the bishops, in line with their emphasis on the need for further discussion and research.[9] The second premise from which this response proceeds is a conviction, shared by many American Catholic theologians, that John Courtney Murray succeeded more than anyone else in explicating those dimensions of American Catholic identity most proximate to the public life of a pluralist democracy. John Courtney Murray[10] "had more successfully theorized about Catholicism in America than anyone in his Church since at least Bishop John Carroll."[11] His writings focused on the harmony between Catholic belief and American democracy. He gave special attention to the religion clauses of the First Amendment. His public career, including a significant role in the formation of the "Declaration on Religious Liberty"[12] at Vatican II warrants the judgment that "[n]o single figure in American history has had a greater impact on how American Catholics conceive of the relation between religion and politics."[13]

On the basis of that contribution he can be an unexpected tutor to those for whom this book was written, American Catholics pondering their country's social reality in light of basic agreement with *Economic Justice for All*, or disposed to do so. Unexpected, because nothing in his writings gives even a hint of anticipation that church-world relations, within which Vatican II situated church-state relations as a subsidiary part, would come to be so influenced by a reality learned in Latin America: the option for the poor.[14] And, unexpected, too, in how an option for the poor and a commitment to social justice can elicit new meaning from his texts. Latin American liberation theologies propose many analyses and strategies not, as John A. Coleman,[15] Dennis McCann and Charles Strain[16] have pointed out, germane to the social and ecclesial realities of North America. Yet liberation theologians' impulse to extricate the church from angelist concepts and modes of relation between faith and life cannot similarly be set aside.[17] Precisely here Murray's concept of a public consensus is pivotal for an American Catholicism reawakened to social justice.[18] For, Americans who are Catholic, have espoused the principles of democratic self-governance in a pluralist society. Murray can help show how to combine the procedural justice enshrined in the First Amendment's religion clauses with the substantive justice which is the goal of *Economic Justice for All*.

In a Populist Direction

Economic Justice for All mapped directions for an American exodus from the status quo to a just society. Movement, though, depends upon a functioning consensus about the destination. For that reason the National Conference of Catholic Bishops proposes a first step which reorients participation in American culture away from complacent adjustment to well-known difficulties and toward a renewed national self-understanding. Accordingly, states the pastoral letter, "[t]he first step . . . is the development of a new cultural consensus that the basic economic conditions of human welfare are essential to human dignity and are due persons by right."[19] Without this, any further steps will falter, lose their orientation, or cease. Renewal in national self-understanding becomes part of the journey and acquires also the significance of a guiding light for an arduous, fractious pilgrimage toward economic justice for all.

Beltway think tanks, whatever their value as sources of advice on more particular adjustments, cannot be expected to be Moses. Do citizens look to executive or legislative branches of government for cultural or moral leadership? The Supreme Court, arguably, has some claim, but not in regard to the economic conditions for human dignity. Most likely, and almost by definition, a consensus can be anticipated only as something arising from citizens in their "mediating structures"[20] rather than descending from elected officials, self-appointed guardians of the national interests or hired lobbies. A national consensus, to the extent that it operates, does so as a heritage held by the citizenry rather than as a body of esoteric knowledge possessed by experts. This may be regarded as an observation of common sense familiar to all.

What may be less familiar is that the case is similar, *mutatis mutandis*, in that mediating institution, the Catholic Church, to which between one-fourth and one-third of Americans belong. A Catholic initiative contributing to renewing America's self-understanding at large and within its members cannot proceed by *fiat* either from the chambers of the National Conference of Catholic Bishops or from diocesan chanceries. A consensus cannot be produced by some imagined central decision taken individually or collectively by bishops. This must have been fully clear to the bishops because their text never projects them as the sole or primary agents renewing the cultural consensus within the church or in society as a whole. Nor do they portray American Catholics as a vanguard whose conversion to social and economic justice will lead by example. The pastoral letter, to the contrary, presents a challenge simultaneously to American Catholic citizens and to their fellow citizens.[21] A Catholic contribution to a new cultural consensus can only emerge from American Catholics at large, in their families, friendships, parishes and dioceses, local organizations and institutions. For the church, no less than for the state, that crucial first step toward economic justice occurs at the grass roots, however much the bishops may encourage it, or not. This, too, belongs to the realm of common sense.

Renewal of an element in cultural consensus has one aspect which reopens a perennial American discussion on the relation between church and state. For, when it comes to economic justice and an option for the poor, a relatively simple, informal, unofficial, popular gathering of thoughts and conversations, agendas and commitments at the local level of the church already contains church-state implications prior to any kind of public activity in the political sphere. They follow from the fact that a just social and economic order depends to some significant extent on how these believers, in their capacity as citizens, want our government to act. In addition to their social and economic activities, Catholics convinced by their own analysis and *Economic Justice for All* on a need for economic justice have a relation to the state in virtue of their humanity and its exigence toward a political ordering of society.[22] *Economic Justice for All* states this humanistic tradition when declaring that, "it is the responsibility of all citizens, acting through their government, to assist and empower the poor, the disadvantaged, the handicapped, and the unemployed."[23] A renewed cultural consensus on economic justice, if accepted and promoted by members of the Catholic Church, has repercussions for their participation in American democracy.

It goes almost without saying that asking whether or not citizens should have any authority in the economy is a false question. Norman Birnbaum explains why:

> In fact, of course, through politics, the American financial and industrial elite exercises larger influence on government economic policy no matter which party is in power. That pressure does not by any means take the form of demanding an end to, or serious diminution of, government intervention. It consists, rather, in giving that intervention (Federal Reserve policy, fiscal structure, the administration of anti-trust and the policies of regulating agencies) a content favorable to the private sector. . . . The actual question is not whether we should have government intervention but of what kind and with what end and through which instruments.[24]

And the further question is, who will decide on the kind, end, and instruments of government intervention? Will it be citizens, including those with little or no economic power, acting through democratic processes?

Or will it continue to be those citizens controlling enormous economic power and exerting influence through lobbies? Gary J. Dorrien's analysis of present practices accounts for a weak influence from ordinary citizens.

> Federal economic planning in the United States presently subsidizes the most powerful corporations and business interests in the country, largely on the basis of what has been called the logic of the broker state. Since the giant corporations in the United States have the most means to lobby for assistance, they are also the chief beneficiaries of government loans, grants, import quotas, tax breaks, bailouts, price supports, indirect subsidies, uncollected taxes, and socialization of expenses and losses.[25]

His argument for economic democracy and a new species of decentralized democratic socialism includes the following observation:

> Reports by Congress Watch and the Congressional Budget Office have estimated that U.S. government subsidies, bailouts,

and other forms of corporate welfare exceed $100 billion per year. Moreover, even these studies usually omit most indirect subsidies, such as corporate income from government programs and regulations, which, if added, would push the true figure for annual corporate assistance to at least $140 billion.[26]

It is necessary to balance this with the benefits such "subsidies" eventually bring to workers, managers, stockholders and consumers and through them to the common good. But, this does not change an absence of citizen influence, and accents the need for some kind of political role for citizens without economic power. The option for the poor in *Economic Justice for All* is a mandate for some manner of shift toward economic democracy. Moving in a populist direction, in order to "expand economic participation, broaden the sharing of economic power, and make economic decisions more accountable to the common good,"[27] takes place through change, first of all, in the cultural consensus.

John Courtney Murray: Where Are the Wise?

Consensus, but not a manipulated public opinion, begins in the grass roots. There the fate of *Economic Justice for All* is being decided. So the local scene, played out in "mediating institutions," is a situation where Murray's practical wisdom has much to teach and much to learn. There is, consequently, a basis for an approach to Murray focused more on the local, grass-roots manifestations of national problems and directed to believer-citizens of ordinary station and low political profile. Both J. Leon Hooper's and Robert W. McElroy's books excel in relating Murray's thought to problems in the "politics of the nation."[28] Their application of his wisdom concentrates on the national, even federal, dimension of public life and policy discussion.

And yet, the category of "public discourse"[29] can be repatriated from the realm of elected officials discussing national problems with lobbyists to the reality of citizens facing national affairs at the local level in a "politics of interest" within a "politics of community."[30] "Public" need not be that which newspapers headline, nor "discourse" limited to debates in Washington. Murray's texts can have meaningful application among those ordinary believer-citizens whose reality he expounded. After all, Murray's Aristotelian-Thomist[31] background provided a basis for seeing that discourse about *ho polis* (the city) takes its rise in homes, among friends, between families, among colleagues, in neighborhood and parish-basement meetings, in community organizing and community service. Both the political order and public discourse originate, according to Aristotle's *Politics*,[32] from local, prepolitical society. The organizational principle of subsidiarity thus becomes a hermeneutical principle for locating public discourse in its roots.

This brings a friendly amendment to Murray's cognate concepts of "public consensus" and "public philosophy."[33] Applying his texts involves understanding and interpreting them, not presupposing that their meaning can be received as ossified and clear, then simply applied to new circumstances. New circumstances can amount to a new interpretative situation from which to engage Murray's texts in a dialogue which enters into and affects their meaning. This is the case with his idea of consensus. Beginning from *Economic Justice for All* and an option for the poor, for example, can rebalance Murray's tilting of America's "public consensus" toward the highly-placed.

In Murray's view each generation of Americans inherited a "public philosophy" from the Declaration of Independence, the Constitution and Bill of Rights, along with the intervening grasp and application of them. This "public philosophy" was content which people grasped and affirmed in an act of "public consensus." Entry into this common content and act was by citizenship, not by wealth, social status, formal education or association with the powerful. Americans drew upon its reserves and developed it generation by generation when defining the nation's purpose or determining courses of action toward it. At least, that was what Murray thought happened over the long haul and in widest perspective.[34]

However, and precisely because he wanted "not merely to maintain the existing consensus in the United States but to reclaim and revitalize it,"[35] he concentrated on those who, he considered, developed it. And that, according to his analysis, was not the people at large but an elite of wise and honest citizens primarily in the academic, ecclesial and legal communities. Ability to renew and apply the natural-law heritage in new circumstances made them unofficial sages in a "complex process of moral discernment."[36] They initiated thought on how to apply the tradition of reason to new problems.

Yet, according to Robert W. McElroy, "Murray's theory of the public consensus was not wholly an elitist one," because "he maintained that the masses in the United States had been more faithful to the tradition of reason than the 'wise and honest' had been."[37] Fidelity in maintenance, however, was not competence in working out increments to the national consensus. For this the three aforementioned protagonists of cultural development were essential. J. Leon Hooper finds an even more decided movement in a populist direction in Murray's later writings. Murray struggled to extricate principles of justice in the "public philoso-

phy" from an ethical relativism into which their connection to a changing social consciousness seemed to plunge them.[38]

His resolution was a distinction between the basic principles of
natural law, with their immediate implications for conduct, and their
further specifications by different societies, each with a diverse "human
reality",[39] in varying phases of growth or decline. The American people,
like people everywhere, had access to the basic principles but, as elsewhere, depended on the wise to work out the further specifications
which applied them to complicated situations. Yet Murray's recognition
of "the problem of historical flux did not permit him finally to locate
those 'wise' in any particular, identifiable social group."[40] He declared
that "all one can say is that they are men who have a 'care' but who are not
'interested parties' (in the usual sense of the latter phrase)."[41] Two lawyers, Jeremiah Black and Louis D. Brandeis, exemplified that combination when they acted for the national good rather than private interest.

For the most part, the wise is an elite, but an anonymous elite.
Neither elected nor appointed office, nor membership in a particular
institution or group qualified a person or a group. In Hooper's analysis,
Murray came to accept their dispersal throughout the population as un-
sung (but apparently well-positioned) sages who allowed love for truth to
guide their use of reason. Their common trait being "the ones who can
reasonably argue in the public forum for their own judgments."[42] They
were not isolated from the rest of the population because their wisdom
about public affairs passed to their fellow citizens. Their authority was
not coercive, certainly. They communicated and persuaded. The people
listened and adjudicated by moving, or not, to a common public opinion.
And there Murray came to the end of his populist theme.

Murray rested the final decision in "the *people's* abiding sense of
justice"[43] when they listened to the wise and decided, or not, to do
something about it. Thus, Hooper observes, when it came to moving
from deliberations to decisions on national matters, it was "the people,
not the wise, who directly validate the moral content of legislation and
other social institutions."[44] The wise helped the people form their minds
on complex issues. Murray envisioned no oligarchic rule or aristocratic
authority. And yet, the passivity of the people presents a problem. Theirs
was to listen and to learn but not to speak from struggles or suffering.
Like docile pupils before a lecturer, they absorbed the way the wise had
worked out the further implications of reason on their behalf. Diligent,
they went forth to apply the new findings to problems of the day. They
had effect on the political order by heeding what they learned from the
wise, then going forth to mass their voices into a public opinion demanding the attention of legislators. Murray had been a professor[45] but this

doctrine gives little evidence that the wise might actually learn something from the people the way teachers often receive insight from their students.

Murray's argument was, and remains, somewhat controversial. What *Economic Justice for All* does is to situate his argument and the controversy over its validity within a new framework in which all citizens, not only the well-off or well-educated are recognized as essential in society and as possessed of a right to participation in society, economy and democracy. This makes Murray's analysis of a populace passively absorbing the findings of the wise a problem. The problem is that passivity is an end to dialogue. In Murray's analysis, dialogue flourished in public discourse when, it turns out, the wise debated among themselves on national affairs. The wise had dialogue, the rest listened and learned, perchance to act.

Confining the principle of active dialogue to the circle of the wise, who could argue their views, who had access to a public forum on national affairs, committed public discourse to an implicit standard for admittance. Those who were in a position to engage national purpose and policy in the full light of civil society entered the circle. Those who, for one reason or another could not, might at best perform their citizens' chores by agitating legislators. Where did the poor, powerless, and marginalized fit? Had they nothing to say? Murray's central theme of "public consensus," then, can be read as limiting the formation of America's public consensus to those powerful enough to make their case effectively.

Too, his work as editor, author, professor, consultant, public speaker kept him linked to people in the upper echelons of church, state and society.[46] Rereading Murray from an option for the poor must contend with his own social location among the religious and political elite: consultant to the Public Affairs Office of the U.S. High Commissioner of Germany Bishops; a *peritus* at Vatican Council II; recipient of a telephone call from Kennedy's campaign staff; participant in the Center for the Study of Democratic Institutions; visiting professor at Yale University; association with Clare Booth Luce. That location favored conceiving national issues in their federal rather than local aspects: Congress; Supreme Court decisions; the White House; those associated with those at the top of the government. Ecclesiastical affairs, likewise, were subject matter for communication with high-level ecclesiastics. Murray, though popular in certain church circles, renowned for clear and cogent articles on matters important to believers in the pews, and not without a humane common touch, is not remembered for work on the grass-roots level of church or nation.

Murray's concept of "public consensus," then, was doubly limited in location: to the federal rather than local level of public discourse; to those with strong rather than faint political, economic and social voices. There was certainly nothing resembling the "hermeneutical privilege of the poor"[47] in his idea of democracy. Whatever crumbs of wisdom the poor could accumulate, apparently, were to be eaten in the privacy of their homes, not shared. Whether or not the National Conference of Catholic Bishops went beyond Murray's concept and consulted with poor, powerless and marginalized people to any great extent in preparing *Economic Justice for All*, their option for the poor has a central position in the final text. And there it leads American Catholicism, and John Courtney Murray's work no less, in a populist direction. Interpreting his work in reference to an option for the poor and social justice opens up his otherwise cramped principle of dialogue and brings his practical wisdom into dialogue with the lives of more people.

Every Believer-Citizen Is a Person: Beyond Paternalism

Murray could have wished no better fate than this kind of interpretation. It gives expression to one of his principles. It explicates some of the positive meaning of citizens dependent upon the wise for developing the "public consensus." They were active in holding the heritage, and might unpredictably become wise on one or other issue on the nation's agenda. He, better than anyone else, renewed Pope Leo XIII's and Pope Pius XII's emphasis on the person who is at the same time member of the church and citizen in the state.[48] His retrieval of Catholic church-state teaching gave new force and meaning to Pope Leo XIII's creative adaptation of the ancient Gelasian doctrine on this point. The whole of that teaching and the conduct of those relations had one goal—to facilitate life for the persons joined simultaneously to church and to state.

It was Murray who gave an American application of Pope Leo XIII's insistent embrace of the principle that church met democratic state above all within those who were both believers and citizens. Against a richly embroidered tapestry replete with tableaux depicting kings and popes, bishops and princes, emperors and clergy, Murray followed the founders of the Republic in placing the believer-citizen in the foreground. This person, by definition the holder of the first office in a democracy, is the one in whom the church encounters the democratic state. The encounter is not between the citizen and a bishop or pope, nor does it take place between a representative of the Vatican and a representative of our government.

In keeping with the nature of a democracy, and in respect for a church existing in all her members, the meeting has become an internal copresence in every person. Participation in church by faith, baptism, and practice met participation in the state by acceptance of citizenship and its duties, along with the public consensus underlying the rule of law and Constitution. Correlating these two participations, which are also responsible modes of activity—while allowing primacy to faith and the spiritual—is the ordinary, normal mode in which church and state relate in a democracy. American Catholics would be turning their backs on both papal teaching and John Courtney Murray were they to persist in imagining that church-state relations were first of all in communication between bishops and political figures, or between the United States Catholic Conference and congressional staffers.

Each American Catholic comprises a church-state relation. Conducting church-state relations, consequently, falls to every believer-citizen as an irrevocable prerogative and an unavoidable act. The believer is "church" by participation, and as representing that participation. The same person, who is also a citizen, is the "state" by participation, and as representing a citizen's informed judgment. The relation between "church" and "state" begins, then, in the consciousness and conscience of those persons who are at once Christians and citizens. Its conduct, however informal and piecemeal, involves correlating the thinking, deciding and acting proper to each, with due respect both to the priority of a relation to God through the church, and to the independence of the political order from the church.

Appropriation of that church-state relation, guided by Murray's teaching, can be incorporated into the point of departure for a new reading of Murray. The problem of how a new cultural consensus fostered among and by American Catholics comes to be in the first place, and becomes effective in the second, is inherent in the consciousness and conscience of a person heeding *Economic Justice for All.* The basic and comprehensive nature of the task of renewing the cultural consensus on the requirements of human dignity make this task, arguably, that which will define how Americans conceive of their relation to American democracy for the foreseeable future. An American Catholic option for the poor and an orientation toward structural transformations for the sake of social and economic justice imply more than such traditional flash points as aid to private education, morality in media, an American ambassador to the Vatican. It is as fundamental as right to life issues, since at stake is the right to the realization of human dignity and a corresponding social obligation toward conditions making that possible. Recourse to John Courtney Murray becomes a necessity. However, since his work did not enter into the problematic of social and economic justice to any great extent, his practical wisdom can only be regained by acknowledging a distance between the problematic he faced and that outlined by *Economic Justice for All.*

With Humanistic Qualifications

How can a dichotomy between Catholic faith and American social reality be reviewed and resolved, if not by believers accepting again their share in divine love—a love demanding a foundation in truth and justice? This acceptance, with knowledge of how deeply structures permeate and surround subjectivity, and moving beyond a postclassical but still purely contemplative humanism, receives Vatican II's insight into the bond between the church and the whole human family. It was not with an aesthetic consciousness mediated by and aimed at art or philosophy that the bishops of the world declared:

> The joy and hope, the grief and anguish of the people of our time, especially of those who are poor or afflicted in any way, are the joy and hope, the grief and anguish of the followers of Christ as well.[49]

Instead, solidarity with "those who are poor or afflicted in any way," is already contained in that union with Christ which is faith. Actual, too, in hope, labors and sufferings shared between, for example, the poor and the church in El Salvador, Haiti, Guatemala, the Philippines, India, South Korea.[50] This solidarity goes beyond even the contemplative magnanimity in Cicero's eloquent, *Nihil humanum mihi alienum est* ("Nothing human is foreign to me"). For scripture reveals the Lord's committed service to those whom Israel's prophets called the "anawim" and to those hungry, thirsty, naked, homeless, imprisoned with whom Jesus identified himself (Matthew 25:31–46). This defines solidarity in terms of active service.

And yet a contemplative humanism,[51] with suspicion for anything that might turn out to be a feckless changing of institutions incurring irrecoverable loss or, worse, shackling freedom in unexpected ways, can accompany an option for the poor. To action toward means and quantitative indices of well-being it brings vigilance protective of questions about ends and qualities. It can keep an option for the poor from forgetting that the "poor" are persons, imaginative, cultural, ends-in-themselves, whom no amount of economic justice achieved will relieve of their own ambivalence. It can guard civil and political liberties from infringement by a movement toward social and economic justice. Likewise, it can remind an option for the poor, which could decline into lethal bureaucracy, about the innate dignity of every person and about the competence of the marginalized to discuss public policies affecting their own destinies: to be poor in America is not to be stupid or uninformed on many social realities. Humanism, in fact, does dilute militance. In that sense this book is, indeed, halfhearted. Unlike the socialism Oscar Wilde impugned for leaving no free evenings, the social transformation it espouses does not depend on a crusading vanguard propelled by an all-consuming agenda derived from absolute knowledge of personal, social and historical reality.

In line with a humanistic propensity, then, an option for the poor will be approached more as an interpretation than as a norm, a matter of self-understanding more than of duty, virtue, or obligation (though these, when properly apprehended, it is). It takes its rise from a tradition of "incarnational humanism,"[52] is open to American secular humanism on many items on the social justice agenda, sees Catholicism within the one church of Christ, and considers Christian faith indissociable from social justice. At many points the hermeneutical philosophy of Hans-Georg Gadamer will come to the surface.

An Inquiry in Practical Theology

This book will engage in practical-theological dialogue with the texts of John Courtney Murray. The objective will be to apply their practical wisdom to social Catholicism in America after *Economic Justice for All*. There will be no attempt at economics, political science, or sociology, though themes properly treated by them will enter the argument at times, often as already interpreted. Practical-theological analysis, something of a fledgling in its new form,[53] differs from historical-theological or social-ethical study of Murray. A main principle of interpretation will be Hans-Georg Gadamer's disclosure of the internal unity among understanding, interpretation and application of tradition and texts. Consequently, chapter 2 draws a distinction between historical and hermeneutical consciousness, yet conceives a dialogical retrieval of Murray's meaning as the fulfillment of such valuable historical work as Thomas T. Love's *John Courtney Murray: Contemporary Church-State Theory*,[54] Donald E. Pelotte's *John Courtney Murray: Theologian in Conflict*, Gerald P. Fogarty's treatment of Murray and Americanism in *The Vatican and the American Hierarchy from 1870 to 1965*,[55] and Charles E. Curran's chapter on Murray in *American Catholic Social Ethics: Twentieth Century Approaches*.[56]

Social ethics, rather than practical theology, may seem the more obvious interlocutor in a dialogue on social Catholicism. Again, a practical-theological approach relies also on such social-ethical reflections as those by David Hollenbach in "Public Theology in America: Some Questions for Catholicism after John Courtney Murray," and "Theology and Philosophy in Public: A Symposium on John Courtney Murray's Unfinished Agenda,"[57] Charles E. Curran in *American Catholic Social Ethics*, John A. Coleman in *An American Strategic Theology*, J. Leon Hooper in *The Ethics of Discourse: The Social Philosophy of John Courtney Murray*, Robert W. McElroy in *The Search for an American Public Theology: The Contribution of John Courtney Murray*, and Todd David Whitmore in "From Religious Freedom to the Conditions for Witness: Developing the Heritage of John Courtney Murray."[58] In some distinction from social ethics, practical theology places practice among its formative principles in dialectical relation with theoretical knowledge. Moreover, practical theology complements a focus on normative understanding with attention to a cultural and theological preunderstanding in the identity of a person or group that partially draws the threshold beyond which ethical deliberation begins and that sustains the decision-making.

The subject matter has practical-theological aspects. Practical theology originates in something approximating what David Tracy described as "personal involvement in and commitment to . . . a particular praxis movement."[59] It will be presumed that *Economic Justice for All* arose from episcopal and lay involvement in social ministry; likewise the letter leads to further, and more clearly determined kinds of involvement. While nothing as definite as a "praxis movement" characterizes reception of the letter, its option for the poor is already a preliminary moment of practice that many American Catholics have tended toward. The document has what Dennis McCann and Charles R. Strain refer to as "the distinct focal concern" of practical theology: "to reflect critically and to shape the praxis of a religious community."[60] This describes the general nature of the letter's purpose and its organizing, pastoral objective.

John Courtney Murray's work has practical-theological aspects insofar as his active participation in American civic debate was a practice through which he tested his thought, as Hooper has shown. Like Ernst Troeltsch, Walter Rauschenbusch, John A. Ryan, Paul Tillich, Jacques Maritain and the Niebuhrs, McCann and Strain count him among the "precursors of the new practical theology"[61] because he, too, had an awareness of how religion and society change in their relations. He, like the bishops, reflected critically on how American Catholicism conducted itself in order to shape that practice. As well, his reflection carried the meaning of that practice into the life of Catholicism at Vatican II.

Unlike the method proposed by McCann and Strain, however, this book derives an understanding of interpretation from Hans-Georg Gadamer's hermeneutics rather than from the critical theory of Jürgen Habermas. With that comes a preference to follow a path through questions and answers arising from a particular subject matter rather than to carry out the prescribed procedures of a formally methodological set of tasks, be they ever so brilliantly thought through. Nonetheless, close affinities with some points in the McCann-Strain logic of investigation do appear. Their installation of a theory of interpretation[62] corresponds to the pressing beyond historical consciousness in and of Murray's texts in chapter 2. Their principles of a "form of life"[63] and a theory/praxis dialectic[64] can be found in the recovery of a pretheoretical way of life synthesizing Catholicism and American democracy shown in chapter 3. Their reconstruction of the "essence of a tradition" is a way of understanding the search in chapter 4 for the proto-practice of a post-Constantinian Catholicism in seventeenth-century Maryland. Their principle of "critical memory"[65] is latent in the observation that emergence of a right to liberty in religion did not expand the perceptions of those who held slaves. More could be done on this. Finally, their adopting of Habermas' idea of praxis as "truth-dependent socialization"[66] does not veer so far from Gadamer's principle of social dialogue, especially when placed in a democratic context under the impulse of an option for the poor.

1 | Believer-Citizens: Identity and Texts

PART ONE: IDENTITY AND CHANGE

A New Consensus Is a Cultural Transition

Economic Justice for All engages in prophetic not moral discourse insofar as it presents new possibilities for personal and political self-understanding instead of urging greater determination toward familiar tasks. It addresses a fundamental question of fidelity to God's work in history[1] rather than staying with the issue of Catholic adherence to well-known norms. It elicits change in self-understanding along with whatever moral conversion might be attendant upon consent to the requirements of justice. The pastoral letter places moral obligations within a larger framework of participating in cooperative renewal of creation. The premise is that poverty and economic injustice are not "the inevitable result of the march of history, of the intrinsic nature of particular cultures, but of human decisions and human institutions."[2] That is why the first step toward a just social and economic order occurs in the realm of culture, decisions, and identity.

The bishops lay out nothing less than a new way of being an American and a new way for Americans to understand themselves in history. They state that, "[t]he first step . . . is through development of a new cultural consensus that the most basic economic conditions of human welfare are essential to human dignity and are due persons by right."[3] This step takes Americans beyond their familiar, ingrained respect for political and civil conditions of human dignity. The bishops instigate, therefore, a new moment in the synthesis between being Catholic and being American. That evolution in identity is also the starting point for this inquiry into how John Courtney Murray's achievement can be broken away from attachment to an earlier moment in that synthesis and brought to bear on its successor.

And taking up this task means conceiving Murray's contribution as capable of development. His idea of culture will be accepted, then some

17

particulars in its content modified. Robert W. McElroy states that "[c]ulture, in Murray's mind, was the formative principle of society . . . the heritage of ideas, customs, and traditions that marked one society from another."[4] For Murray, a people's consensus on moral values animates the core of their culture. He argued that, "[c]ulture, then, means man's effort to be fully human, and hence his effort to bring spiritual order and spiritual purpose into his life."[5] And J. Leon Hooper has shown in detail how Murray conceived culture centered in a people's consensus.[6] McElroy's public theology and Hooper's social ethics have elucidated what American Catholicism has to learn from Murray in this regard.

But Murray saw something besides moral values and moral consensus in the core of culture. There was also identity or self-understanding, a basic act of interpretation, by which a people defined itself and in whose context a people formed a consensus and made its decisions. There were, as Murray put it, "these truths" which the Declaration of Independence spoke about, and which Americans had assimilated into their cultural tradition. There was the fact of a national self-understanding accompanying, to some extent resulting from, and guiding the whole process of arriving at a national decision.[7] Murray took up the relation of culture to the political order of decision and action, so he inevitably highlighted the moral content in culture and its consensus. He did not, however, detach culture from an intellectual heritage of rational truths. He understood the existence, sovereignty and finality of God as rational truths, not moral postulates.[8]

We Hold These Truths, for example, described Leo XIII's idea of a western cultural heritage, a *patrimonium generis humani*, as "a heritage of essential truth, a tradition of rational belief."[9] It went on to affirm that, "It was to this patrimony that the Declaration of Independence referred: 'These are the truths we hold.' "[10] Murray saw this affirmation of truths as "the first utterance of a people."[11] It was not an abstract utterance, made in a vacuum, for "[b]y it a people establishes its identity, and under decent respect to the opinions of mankind declares its purposes within the community of nations."[12] These truths belong to the core of American culture. Losing our grip on them, Murray proposed, was the dissolution of American culture, because it was the deterioration of a people's self-understanding. Without that cultural core, he argued, America begins to lose its self-identity because, "[s]elf-understanding is the necessary condition of a sense of self-identity and self-confidence, whether in the case of an individual or a people."[13] A kind of national insanity would ensue upon complete loss of the cultural core. That would portend danger for other nations.

The national consensus was cultural before it became political. And *Economic Justice for All* addresses that prepolitical consensus when it sets forth matter for a "new cultural consensus."[14] And that is to say that American Catholics, no less than others, stand before a new possibility in self-understanding, a new act of social interpretation. The novelty can be located primarily in an option for the poor, though also in the norms, policy recommendations and "New Experiment in Democracy." For Americans to accept the proposition that "the basic economic conditions of human welfare are essential to human dignity and are due persons by right,"[15] they have to reinterpret their culture, not just deliberate on specifications of human rights. This entails an inescapable realization that the pastoral letter presents American Catholics with the special theme of reconceiving their synthesis between being American and being Catholic. If both being American and being Catholic each gain in meaning, then their correlation necessarily has to be rethought, unless bifurcation between the two, or confusion of the two, is to displace a synthesis. When the bishops declared that "[a]s individuals and as a nation, therefore, we are called to make a fundamental option for the poor,"[16] they concluded from the principles that "[t]he common good demands justice for all,"[17] and that this means, "the poor have the single most urgent economic claim on the conscience of the nation."[18] Their argument was ethical and in that respect affects the moral consensus at the core of American culture. But the framework of biblical and rational truths, the principle that persons have innate dignity, and the national self-understanding into which they bring the argument all touch the truths in the core of American culture. The option for the poor, that is, engages the American identity as well as challenges the American conscience. And for that reason, again, a special theme arises within American Catholicism because the extant American Catholic synthesis is brought under review and opened to a new possibility.

An Option for the Poor Affects a Relation with the State

Economic Justice for All incorporates a fundamental option for the poor that contains unexplored implications for Catholic church-state thinking and conduct. Latin American in provenance, universal in significance, the bishops begin to apply it to the United States, and in so doing to modify its meaning. It represents an orientation toward an alternative to the status quo. The alternative, however, is not socialism. In that sense, William E. Murnion is correct in noting a major difference between the American and Latin American constructs.[19] But if the option for the poor as a principle is universal in meaning, truth and value, then it will be able to enter into many specific syntheses rather than emanate from Latin America uniform in all applications. The alternative actually outlined is a future phase in the evolution of capitalism and it does not yet exist in the concrete.

To describe *Economic Justice for All* as merely reformist or as a pragmatic tinkering with superficial details that will not face fundamental malfunctions is to underestimate the kind and difficulty of change required in advancing toward a just order. The changes involve cultural and social as well as political and economic shifts. But they are not, it is true, substitution of some other kind of political or economic system. And yet, while detached from socialism, the option remains a motive and horizon within which to conceive and initiate structural changes. The bishops have not endorsed a privatized concept of poverty and injustice; they see them resulting from institutional arrangements and from unjust decisions in an institutional context. The letter is about something besides conversion of hearts, though that, too. Is it the case that "the policies the bishops propose—full employment, the eradication of poverty, support for the family farm, and global interdependence—are more radical than the majority of Americans, including the Catholic laity, are now likely to accept"?[20]

Standard Catholic objections to socialism, though, may not concern many of its objectives as much as they refuse to accept a state monopoly on authority over all modes of social existence as well as some of its political and economic means. And to the extent that it relies on a cultural substructure, including an allegedly comprehensive knowledge of history, society, and persons which functions as a kind of revelation, it will not begin to be plausible. This reaction to socialism does not, however, touch in the same way an approach that contains a first-order commitment to democracy, that "emphasizes decentralization of authority, mixed forms of social ownership, and the necessary role of the market,"[21] and that does not seek to define the culture at large or ultimate destiny of persons. In this regard, it helps to notice that the alternative to socialism in *Economic Justice for All* is not a prolonged, slightly ameliorated status quo. Nor is it the present American economy simply reformed according to its own already entrenched principles. The alternative is the present economy opened up to the common good of American society in new ways. The crucial issue is less whether the government should decrease or increase intervention into economic activities, than whether or not the economy serves the good of society, and to the degree that it does not, how to bring about change so that it does. Still, Murnion's observation that *Economic Justice for All* presents policy proposals based on economic rights nowhere chartered in the U.S. Constitution, and that cultural trends do not seem headed toward an amendment securing those rights,[22] brings attention back to a cultural consensus as the first step toward economic justice.

In *Economic Justice for All*, the option for a determinate category of persons within American society specifies both a respect for our common humanity and the common good of American society. The basis for the preference in the option, of course, is the need of the poor and their relative lack of access to social and political influence. A turn to the poor opposes, not the wealthy primarily, but complacent support for all that sustains the American status quo. It has the breadth of a "preferential solidarity with the poor" which "speaks not so much to how the church relates to the poor in terms of compassion, identification or service but more to how the church relates to society at large and to the social structures which influence our life."[23] But it is not fixed in details of tactic and program, because its modes vary, although "the option for the poor should always be seen as part of the wider transformation of the structures of society which keep the poor, poor."[24] This kind of awakening to structural factors in economic injustice involves, it is clear, informal but actual change in how people see themselves in society and how they see society.

Promoting a consensus among American Catholics on an option for the poor and social justice has the dimensions of a cultural transition. Consequently, it involves changes in the American Catholic synthesis. In seeking to understand and to advance those changes, theology has a legitimate role to play because the synthesis was originally formed and now changes before a horizon of faith. That role can be defined as a contribution from what John A. Coleman calls "an American Catholic theology rooted in the unique experience of Catholic America," a theology aware of "the structural limitations and possibilities of the American Church as the conditioning context for an American Catholic theology."[25] One of those situational realities that conditions any and every American Catholic approach to social justice is, of course, the First Amendment religion clauses along with a tradition of laws, convictions and outlook applying them.

Transition to "Politically Significant" Social Ministry

Whereas Vatican II's "Declaration on Religious Liberty" removed the last vestiges of a putative doctrinal basis for a claim to establishment, the council's "The Church in the Modern World" gave theological principles for a social ministry to the dignity of the human person and the unity of the human community. In combination, pointed out J. Bryan Hehir,[26] the former text depoliticized church-state relations while the latter plunged the church more deeply into mission "religious in nature and finality" but in its consequences "politically significant."[27] Signs of that political significance abound in Latin America, in the Philippines and in Poland. In the United States, the bishops have adopted an "activist" role in public policy debate on abortion, nuclear strategy, equity in the economy and U.S. policy in Latin America.[28]

Nonetheless, the church is more than our bishops, and most of us relate to national issues in the family, neighborhood, social clubs, economic enterprises, schools, and cultural organizations which mediate between the individual and the state. Believers who participate in their family life, their neighborhood, who support their schools, clubs or cultural organizations, who work in a company, firm, union or farmers' cooperative are citizens who discuss and vote on political principles which are held within an overall way of life marked, if not thoroughly permeated, by the light of faith. The impact from faith, despite a so-called other-worldly quality, is to support more active participation in social and political life.

Inasmuch as "the general thrust of postconciliar Catholic thought has been to fight against narrow, 'churchy' conceptions of the religious task and the pervasive privatization of religion,"[29] to that extent "this position contains a strong animus against any attempts to segregate the Church from participation in the formulation of the moral aspects of political questions or to relegate it to the sacristy."[30] Postconciliar Catholicism does not encourage passivity in believer-citizens. Social and political activism is one answer to Coleman's question, "[w]hat scope, beyond worship and catechesis, is allowed to the Church for action in education, welfare, health, the media, and the world of work and economics?"[31] While commitment to social justice affects each of those spheres, the "world of work and economics" has many of the most controversial political implications.

A grass-roots group organized from churches in a city, such as Milwaukee Inner-City Churches Allied for Hope (MICAH), for example, may want changes in local and state policies regulating lending institutions, or in stipulations on minority hiring by construction firms under contracts involving public money, or other municipal and state policy changes. Their activism is a form of the free exercise of religion. Free exercise of religion under the First Amendment can be more than expressing opinions. Free exercise can become public activity with political significance. And that means that church-society relations begin to surface within the prepared context of church-state relations.[32]

At the least, the cultural consensus on human dignity spoken of by the bishops has to deal with the fact that the "separation clause is sometimes used either in the church or in society to argue against the legitimacy of religious witness on social issues."[33] Long before the National Conference of Catholic Bishops embarked on their prophetic social ministry in letters on nuclear weapons and the economy, Bishop James S. Rausch had commented that, "the separation clause, while rightly preventing any special privilege for the Church, cannot be used legitimately to silence or stifle Christian evaluation of the policies of the state."[34] That understanding of the First Amendment—protection against favoritism and discrimination alike without a silencing of the religious voices in the nation—is inherent in *Economic Justice for All*.[35]

Nor does that understanding come close to being a peculiarly Catholic reading of the no-establishment clause. James E. Wood, Jr., for example, points out that, "[i]n spite of the constitutional provision for the separation of church and state, the courts have never denied the rights of churches to be involved in the body politic."[36] He cites the Supreme Court case, *Walz v. Tax Commission of the City of New York* (1970):

> Adherents of particular faiths and individual churches frequently take strong positions on public issues, including as this case reveals in several of the briefs *amici*, vigorous advocacy of legal or constitutional positions. Of course, churches as much as secular bodies and private citizens have that right.[37]

The First Amendment protects that right to advocacy and he notes that

> even the most ardent separationist groups, such as the American Civil Liberties Union, the American Jewish Congress, and Americans United for the Separation of Church and State have strongly defended the right of advocacy on the part of churches in their efforts to influence public policy.[38]

Free exercise of religion can be more than worship, catechesis, Bible-study, and education; it can be organized activity and advocacy by churches or church-based groups on matters of public interest, including economic justice.

Vatican II similarly recognized that

> included in the right to religious freedom is the right of religious groups not to be prevented from freely demonstrating

the special value of their teaching for the organization of society. . . .[39]

That "demonstration," presumably, extends beyond argument and discourse to decision, to action, to organization and in general to a free exercise in practice. Edwin S. Gaustad, in fact, reported that, "we would urge that 'free exercise' be more often understood as just that: namely the exercise, the activity, the engagement on behalf of religion."[40] He and his colleagues may not have framed their view of "free exercise" in terms of a Catholic variation on the social gospel but their position is open to it.

And so there are church-state implications of a traditional, juridical sort within the question: "What might be the role of the Church in the creation of a new consensus"[41] in the United States? Did episcopal entry into public debate, it was asked, "breach the separation of church and state? Is it appropriate legally and politically?"[42] More generally, and in reference to many kinds of public witness, David Hollenbach saw post-conciliar social ministry needing to address the question of "how to distinguish social mission from religious imperialism or theological triumphalism."[43] Vatican II's official renunciation of a theological or moral claim to establishment was not retreat into privatized religiosity. It clarified conditions essential in ecclesial freedom—which is more comprehensive than papal or episcopal freedom—to approach social problems in a pluralist situation, by means of dialogue and persuasion. This renunciation and freedom define in a first, general way, the kind of means commensurate with a ministry involving effort to "influence the public life of a local community, a nation, or the global economic and political order without imposing its theological vision through brute power."[44] In the United States this means proceeding with full respect for the First Amendment.

However, respect for the no-establishment and free exercise clauses is also prejuridical insofar as it belongs to an accumulated heritage of self-understanding or national identity. In the diffused but occasionally acute memory of America's founding, Catholic Americans have developed a practical synthesis between being Catholic and being American. Frequently no more than a background knowledge, it serves as the preunderstanding with which Catholics approach public life and policies. There it can facilitate or impede a social ministry moving from an option for the poor to economic justice for all. There it is an implicit self-definition of what it means to be an American Catholic. In addition, then, to ethical norms and deliberations on decisions which might eventually affect the juridical order, or which need discussion in direct reference to it, there is another kind of political significance that reaches into the cultural and personal realm of self-understanding. The issue raised by the pre-understanding is not whether an option for the poor is good, not what kind of moral norm binds conscience to justice, but whether or not, and how the option may be true and authentic to American Catholicism.

The Personal Aspect of Political Significance

Yves Congar, notes Hehir,[45] saw Catholic tradition on church and state shift at Vatican II from the context of a juridical to an anthropological church and world relation. In that context, an anthropological element in church-state relations, one already taught by Pope Leo XIII and emphasized anew by Murray, can be brought into relief. The centrality of the person who is believer and citizen, while not identical with a philosophical turn to the subject, represents a Christian personalism not a liberal individualism.[46] Arising from recognition of the intrinsically social aspect of human nature, it asserts that institutional structures of social life are means to the actualization of persons. Persons, belonging to families and civil societies, who are citizens of a state, do not have their identity as instruments to the accomplishment of institutional ends. Leo XIII had presented the person primarily as the passive beneficiary of harmonious relations between church and state.[47] Pius XII, Murray explained, developed Leonine teaching by explicating the role of the person as the goal of church-state relations, above all by acknowledging that the citizen is a person who is " 'the root and end of social processes'."[48] Murray incorporated and amplified Pius XII's notion of a person who is an active believer-citizen.

This anthropocentric quality in church-state relations has been underplayed in studies on Murray, perhaps because Murray remained relatively constant in his interpretation once he arrived at it in 1948 within his analysis of a more debated principle, the indirect power of the church in temporal affairs. In moving beyond Robert Bellarmine's concept of church-state relations (by way of deepened apprehension of John of Paris' application of Thomas Aquinas),[49] Murray showed that a democratic state recentered the church-state encounter in the life, activity and consciousness of the ordinary citizen. Instead of the panoply of pope-emperor, pope-sovereign, bishop-prince dealings in imperial, monarchical, or ducal states, church met the democratic state within the one person, the plain citizen who was a believer and also the first officer in a democracy. Moreover, the believer-citizen was not simply a passive recipient of two kinds of obedience, to church and to state. Because, as Pope Pius had taught, the believer-citizen is first of all a person, she was the "responsible artisan"[50] who was the agent responsible for harmonizing civic rights with Christian faith.

Thomas T. Love summed up Murray's argument for an indirect relation between church and state because of the new reality of self-governing citizens:

> In modern governments, argued Murray, as the Church-state problem has emerged through history and modern political forms have evolved, the concept of the "indirect power" has been clarified, for "the church no longer, as in medieval times or in the classic confessional states, directly confronts the 'temporal power' in concentrated, centralized form" such as the person of the king.[51]

Instead, Love continued, "the Church comes into actual relationship with the state only indirectly and incidentally."[52] The church, as an organized institutional presence in a society, and the state as the political organization of that society meet, says Love citing Murray, " 'inasmuch as the two powers have a common subject or (what is the same thing) inasmuch as the one man is a member of [the] two societies.' "[53] As a consequence, explains Love, "because the same man is both Christian and citizen, the two powers meet indirectly as they seek indirectly to serve him in different respects."[54] The *topos* for church-state relations in a democracy is the believer-citizen.

The immediate practical effect is to shift the church's influence in a society to the activity of citizens who are Christians. Love concludes that the "individual Christian who is also a citizen is the one who participates in shaping the political affairs of the world. . . ." and for that reason, "it is only through the citizen that the purely spiritual power of the Church indirectly has repercussions in the temporal order."[55] This principle of the centrality of the believer-citizen serves to define the limit of any exercise of ecclesiastical power in fostering sacred objectives in the temporal order of a society organized democratically. But that was not the full meaning in the church's turn to the citizen, not for Leo XIII and not for John Courtney Murray.

There was also the principle that church-state relations had their goal in the good of that person.[56] The goal of church-state relations differed from the finality of either church or state. Each had, and this was essential to Leo XIII and Murray, a proper end or goal. The church was instituted to be instrumental in the eternal salvation of all humanity. The political organization of any society was aimed at the temporal, penultimate goods of justice, freedom, peace, etc. The relation between them, located first of all within the people who were believers and citizens, headed toward the good of these persons. Leo XIII, however, had a paternalistic vision of Christian citizens as an illiterate multitude incapable of much in the way of political activity, while Murray followed Pope Pius XII into a properly personalist idea of the citizen. Murray stated that in general, "[t]he medieval starting-point is the Church and its perspectives are social; the modern starting-point is man, and its perspectives are those of the human person."[57] For, according to Pope Leo XIII and John Courtney Murray, Catholic tradition places the primary relation between the church and a democratic state within the consciousness of persons who are believer-citizens.

Church-state relations are, in the first instance, a simultaneous participation by one person, in the church by faith and baptism, and in the state by citizenship. Each involves duties, responsibilities and action. Murray insisted that a relation between the two was "not constitutive of the being of either...." Neither was part of, or instrument for, the other. Rather, the "relation is in the order of action ..." and "implies a dynamic relatedness of distinct purposes and of distinct lines of action toward those purposes, under respect of their proper hierarchy."[58] The hierarchy of purposes kept the spiritual end of eternal life superior to the temporal end of the good life. Believer-citizens coordinating the "distinct purposes" and "distinct lines of action" constitutes the first, interior moment in relations between church and state.

Helping people coordinate them is the first objective for Catholic doctrine on church-state relations. Reception of *Economic Justice for All*, with its inciting of a new cultural consensus anchored in an option for the poor, impinges on church-state relations in their anthropocentric dimensions.

The Faith-Justice Link Is a Church-State Relation

There is no need to decide first on the precise ways faith involves a predisposition toward and actual link with social justice, nor on the list of culturally diverse modes people have found to actualize it. *Economic Justice for All* typifies rather than departs from Catholic social teaching when it situates concrete decisions in social and economic life within the perspective of faith in God. "Followers of Christ," state the bishops,

> must avoid a tragic separation between faith and everyday life. They can neither shirk their earthly duties, nor as the Second Vatican Council declared, "immerse [them]selves in earthly activities as if these latter were utterly foreign to religion, and religion were nothing more than the fulfillment of acts of worship and the observance of a few moral obligations."[59]

Catholic social thought, the letter reminds readers, "insists that human dignity, realized in community with others and with the whole of God's creation, is the norm against which every social institution must be measured."[60] Catholic social teaching, a theological link between faith and justice, and the inseparability of evangelization from promoting justice will be presupposed here.

The inquiry will hold to the much more particular subject matter of how, in American democracy, social Catholicism involves an anthropocentric relation to the state. In the consciousness and self-understanding of believers the faith-justice link discovers an inextricable church-state dimension. Even before specific decisions confront the church or individuals, there is a preunderstanding which comes with participation in Catholicism and in American democracy. The achievement of American Catholicism is to have produced an original synthesis from the two participations, an originality not fully grasped, historically, either by European Catholicism or by American Protestantism. Nevertheless, that preunderstanding underlies the process and product of *Economic Justice for All*. The preparation, content, and an anticipated dialogue on it all presuppose a Catholic faith which has long since taken the First Amendment's religion clauses as conditions of its existence. With regard to specific moral decisions this original synthesis is a preunderstanding which is also premoral. And in it Catholic faith, with a disposition toward seeking justice, already encounters the state insofar as the believer also has the memories and heritage of an American citizen.

This first moment in church-state relations, and a second moment when moral decision-making by believer-citizens coordinates the link between their faith and their will to social justice, are interior to persons. Both moments, obviously, are anterior to and immanent within public, external, juridical church-state relations. Interiority, however, is not privacy. A person exists in and through participation in social realities. Both faith and justice are attributes of public offices. Baptism, the sacrament of faith, confers readiness to partake in public celebration of the eucharist and other sacraments. Confirmation and eucharist lead faith into Christ's messianic mission to all creation. The faith that enlightens, strengthens and guides a will to social justice, is not a private, idiosyncratic religious subjectivity but ecclesial and, indeed, ecclesiastical.

Moreover, according to the idea of the state in social Catholicism,[61] justice is something for whose sake the political order exists. The person enters into reference to this goal of the state by becoming a citizen. To be a citizen is to hold the first kind of public office in a democracy and to become an agent for justice. Sometimes, it seems, discussions on faith, justice, and an option for the poor, overlook the fact that while the church properly teaches, motivates, and engages in certain kinds of action to promote social justice, it is the state which properly brings it about. Citizenship is already an orientation to justice and to action for the common good through political means. An option for the poor by the church and by persons who are believers, then, specifies and gives determinate, practical orientation to the self-understanding of persons in whom faith already has a relation to justice. This institutes a new moment in the church-state relation interior to persons who are believer-citizens.

The option for the poor in *Economic Justice for All* has, then, internal and external dimensions in its relation to the state. But only two receive formal consideration by the bishops. The pastoral letter, in fact, speaks principally to moral interiority insofar as it seeks to educate the "responsibility of all citizens, acting through their government, to assist and empower the poor, the disadvantaged, the handicapped and the unemployed."[62] Of course, insofar as this "responsibility" is a moral reality which includes value judgments on social goals and on political means to them, it has public effects through citizens' activity as voters or participants in public debate. The letter speaks mainly, it seems, to this interior moment since it does not, as Murnion notices, help organize the poor politically nor does it address the moment of self-understanding in church-state relations. And yet, it could be said that the faith-justice link, and its concretization in an option for the poor is, and not so incidentally as might appear from *Economic Justice for All*, a church-state relationship.

Receiving Is Reconceiving

American Catholics cannot overcome their own faith-life split, much less make a major impact on public opinion and policy, without first coming to more clarity on how the faith-justice link and an option for the poor take place within their own common experience and singular tradition of constant aversion to the establishing of any church or religion by any state. The practical outlook of American Catholics has been formed in continual, positive regard for the First Amendment. How can American Catholics receive Catholic social doctrine, including *Economic Justice for All*, without a dialogue between American Catholic self-understanding and postconciliar commitment to solidarity and social justice? John Courtney Murray is party to the dialogue insofar as he formulated crucial themes in American Catholic self-understanding precisely as a way of adhering to the American Proposition. And, the option for the poor in *Economic Justice for All* enters a dialogue with Murray because it represents a new phase in being an American Catholic. It is reasonable to expect that, just as American Catholicism offered its tradition of religious liberty to Vatican II, so too that same tradition will have something to say to an option for the poor.[63]

To some extent, American Catholics will receive an option for the poor when, and only when, they can develop an indigenous version arising from within the experience and self-understanding of this church as a proponent of the First Amendment. There is, be it only under the heading of "custom," a kind of authority inherent in an original, lengthy, local tradition in which American Catholicism has realized itself in an unusual, post-Constantinian mode. Reception, as writings on the subject insist,[64] is not passive; it involves active, dialogical assimilation of general and universal values or ideas. An option for the poor, as a result, will awaken with a kind of moral spontaneity in American Catholic consciences, only if it has found itself at home in an American Catholic self-understanding formed by, among other things, the First Amendment. Otherwise, it remains entirely possible that American Catholics will add to their social teaching's unwelcome attribute of being the best kept secret, the unenviable distinction of being also, once learned, the least effective knowledge.

Reception of *Economic Justice for All*, that is, occurs within an interpretative situation different in some respects from the American Catholicism for which Murray wrote. American Catholicism in the 1990s has a question addressed to it by the pastoral letter: Will we form a new cultural consensus in favor of economic justice? This raises a new question about Murray's texts. Are they applicable to an ecclesial presence in society once that social mission has begun to center in the social conditions for realizing human dignity? Can they still educate American Catholics on their role as citizens once citizenship begins to be an orientation to social justice?

Before Vatican II, Murray articulated the essential principles informing the church's mission in the temporal order, insofar as that mission touched the state. After Vatican II, he recognized that the church-state problem had become an element in the whole of the church's relation to society. The goal Vatican II set for that mission was to protect and to promote the transcendent dignity of the human person and to help build the human community. Has Murray's wisdom in response to one context of church-state relations any application to another? Is the content of Murray's texts recognizably open to further use? Granted that they have exemplary status in the history of American Catholicism, is their content still effective? How can readers gain wisdom from Murray's texts in a new situation? The following section will present some considerations expressing doubt that learning from Murray can simply start from the available bibliographies, select some or all texts, then finish with clarity on their content.

PART TWO: ENTER HERMENEUTICS

Murray's Texts: Distance and Access for Americans

The new situation, it might be granted at this point, contains grounds for a new interest in, and new questions for, Murray's work. An option for the poor and a commitment to social justice is an exercise of religious liberty by American Catholics which has implications affecting church-state relations. Yet, both church and state present themselves differently in the 1990s than they did when Murray wrote and his original readers read. These later modifications surround and inform believers and citizens so that they are not in all respects the same as Murray's contemporaries.

An initial interest in and openness to Murray's writings from within the actual interpretative situation has to pass through, acknowledge the influence of, and let itself be tested by the "temporal distance"[65] stretching between it and his texts. Readers have to achieve rather than presuppose access. Too much has intervened since Murray completed his work for subsequent readers to ignore the question about whether they share a common ground with the texts. Between the texts and later readers pondering *Economic Justice for All*, or open to an option for the poor, there is no smooth pathway. Insights (into the structural features of economic injustice, for example) may have been gained and have passed into habitual knowledge while others (a faith-understanding cognizant of divine providence, for example) may have vanished. Americans, in general, and American Catholics have undergone changes tantamount to an informal education since the 1960s. Texts and the interpretative situation of readers cannot be presumed to be in uninterrupted continuity. It would be fruitless to gain outworn applications by ignoring that.

On the contrary, it is essential to take those differences into account. Failure to acknowledge what lies between readers today and Murray's texts goes beyond merely inattention to the circumstances which were their original context. It would be simply naive to presuppose that nothing has changed and that, therefore, readers today have been formed in the same way and by the same realities that prepared people to understand Murray during his lifetime. No adjustments would then be necessary outside of saying that x, y and z occurred after Murray, as if they were exterior to, and not interior to, reading his work and learning his principles. Still, a sufficiently critical yet not actually defini-

tive presupposition on the full adequacy of historical consciousness of
Murray's writings could prescind from "temporal distance." This would
seem to bypass the present interpretative situation by moving to the texts
and then back toward self-understanding and choices in the present
without referring to any actual starting point, such as an option for the
poor or, contrarily, well-satisfied resistance to it.

Hermeneutical consciousness realizes, however, that matters entirely outside the progress of knowledge internal to church and state
shape the starting point for inquiry into Murray's texts, affect Murray's
subject matter, form his readers, as well as make possible and demand
reappropriation of his content. A series of illustrative changes can indi-
cate the significance of "temporal distance." American citizens, for example, have changed their views on Russia and the former Soviet Union.
The end of the Cold War, which set the international context for many
of Murray's writings, has made an American role in the world, formerly
clear to most Americans, an indeterminate superpower status, despite
claims to have defined a "new world order."

We Hold These Truths, however, analyzed many features of democracy and citizenship in reference to the Cold War and the threat of Soviet
communism. American policy lacked and needed a moral doctrine to
guide it, Murray argued. His contrapuntal, somewhat grudging admiration for the way Marxism-Leninism gave theoretical organization to
Soviet policy put piecemeal American fits and starts in an unfavorable
light. Dogmatic Russia was, he wanted readers to realize, all the stronger
when compared to pragmatic America. But internal instability in the
Soviet Union, Poland's Solidarity movement, and Mikkhail Sergeivich
Gorbachev changed that premise in Murray's book by introducing pragmatic change into the Soviet system. When Americans no longer look
eastward in dread, his analysis will seem misguided. Consequently, his
"Doctrine and Policy in Communist Imperialism: The Problem of Security and Risk"[66] no longer sounds a credible warning against a danger-
ously pragmatic mentality and has little meaning in promoting a self-
understanding equal in doctrinal clarity, though opposite in content, to
dogmatic Marxism-Leninism. Not to consider this would be to leave
intact Murray's admonitions against a pragmatic mentality.

Further, American citizens have witnessed more instances of public
deception by American presidents. President Eisenhower's public assurance that the United States did not fly spy-planes over Soviet territory
may well have seemed an isolated lie and not something whose premise
was that citizens and Congress had no need or right to knowledge of
what their government did on their behalf. There is no evidence that it
was a factor in Murray's subject matter or his readers. Subsequently,

though, President Johnson's deceptive explanation of the Gulf of Ton-kin episode seemed of a piece with the illegal way President Nixon's agents subverted the electoral process at Watergate, and still later, with the lack of accountability with which President Reagan's underlings conducted the Iran-contra affair. Deceit and manipulation of the citizenry began to look like part of presidential policy, or at least a practice against which presidents held no strong convictions. A government of the people, by the people and for the people depends, of course, on citizens and elected officials alike making informed judgments. Murray's worry about America's future focused on an eroding "public philosophy," whereas today many wonder what difference such a public consensus can make if deceit of the public has become the signature of so many recent presidents.

Like most Americans Murray, too, was riveted on the east-west conflict. In that context he did not deal with American relations to developing nations, and did not examine American policy, principle and performance along the north-south axis. His writings did not address, for example, U.S. policy in Latin America. American Catholics since Murray's time have seen congressional approval of foreign aid to Latin American regimes best known for egregious violations of human rights. Bifurcating democracy into a domestic wing adhering to ideas and values known by and accepted by U.S. citizens and a foreign wing supporting ideas, values and practices contradictory in theory and hostile, in fact, to the principles from which constitutional government took its rise was not something on Murray's agenda. This leaves his position unclear in regard to many aspects of foreign policy proximate to the international side of *Economic Justice for All.*[67]

Again, the civil rights movement and many of Dr. Martin Luther King, Jr.'s, prophetic measures figure more prominently in the self-understanding of American Catholics after 1967 than was possible for Murray's texts. For that or some other reason he did not treat resistance to injustice perpetuated under the will of the majority. Although he upheld a right to selective conscientious objection on the basis of a citizen's application of the just-war ethic,[68] it may seem today that he let slip the lesson of resistance in Henry David Thoreau's conscientious putting of justice ahead of majority rule. Murray criticized "political modernity"[69] for building democracy on the freedom on individual conscience and "totalitarian democracy"[70] for abandoning truth and value outside citizens and state. Yet an exemplary force in the deeds and writings of Henry David Thoreau and Dr. Martin Luther King, Jr., cannot be discovered in his texts.

Both Thoreau and King identified universal values which American law or policy violated. Both made justice normative in civil disobedience in obedience to a higher law. Many American Catholics could find Murray's approach too easily compromised by satisfaction with an unjust status quo. He did, however, identify and criticize a tendency in political modernity toward a state monopoly on authority. His guidance on how to prevent, resist or recover from the monist impulse to vest supreme power and authority in a state was in the form of renewing the natural law ethic and the church-state difference. Locating transcendental truth and power in the authority of the state could occur, he argued, in a democracy. A totalitarian democracy differed from fascist or communist totalitarianism by accepting as a final authority "the self-conscious free individual, armed with his subjective rights whose ultimate origin he may have forgotten but whose status as legal certitudes he cherishes."[71] What to do if a majority of such free individuals in a democracy might wish to eliminate any alternative moral authority to the state, or to persevere in injustice was not his forte.

Another perspective which enters into the "temporal distance" separating readers of *Economic Justice for All* from Murray's texts can be seen in the way the pastoral letter remembers America's origin and development. It is altogether more alert to the tendency toward national self-deception as a source of resistance to change. The following passage makes Murray's picture of America seem, on the whole, a little too innocent about social as distinct from individual history:

> The American experiment in social, political, and economic life has involved serious conflict and suffering. Our nation was born in the face of injustice to native Americans, and its independence was paid for with the blood of revolution. Slavery stained the commercial life of the land through its first two hundred and fifty years and was ended only by a violent civil war. The establishment of womens' suffrage, the protection of industrial workers, the elimination of child labor, the response to the Great Depression of the 1930s, and the civil rights movement of the 1960s all involved a sustained struggle to transform the political and economic institutions of the nation.[72]

This ambiguity in American history has particular meaning for American Catholics who, unless succeeded by some other group, were the last to let go of what W. Halsey described as "American innocence."[73]

Other Americans had their confidence in "the structure of values which characterized nineteenth century intellectual and cultural expressions" shaken by "currents of thought and the flow of events in the twentieth century."[74] Neo-Thomism served to buttress belief in an obviously rational and predictable cosmos, in a moral order inherent in the universe, in progress and a didactic rendering of cultural forms. World War I had ended Protestantism's "special identification with American life."[75] For American Catholics, on the other hand, the post-World War I era was one of "rapid movement from immigrant poverty to middle class respectability."[76] This inclined them to believe the promises of an American dream with enthusiastic vigor until "an unexpected wave of confusion" in the 1960s dispossessed them of their innocence.

The 1960s began for American Catholics "like the century had begun, full of confidence in reform and enthusiasm for ideals" and then Vietnam "provided the very real presence of ambiguity, despair, confusion, and irrationality."[77] Vietnam did to American Catholics something like what World War I had done to American Protestants. "During the 1960s," says Halsey, "the experience of a century converged upon Catholics to explode the structure of innocence they had preserved since World War I."[78] Nor was a monolithic, post-Vatican I, Catholic Church a haven for solace, because Vatican II brought the church into unsettling proximity and dialogue with modernity. Halsey may see the loss of innocence in too comprehensive a way. To have changed from strong to weak trust in American government is more specific than the cosmic kind of shift Halsey describes. Coming to grips with modernity was not necessarily immersion in nihilism.

Murray was not immune to this specious innocence, according to Halsey, and his "thought was definitely shaped in the post-World War I context of the Catholic survival of innocence."[79] This context injected a soupçon of triumphalism into the view that American Catholics had inherited the role of guardian over America's foundational truths and values. It does not, however, explain the truth and meaning in many of Murray's positions. To the extent that American innocence prevented Murray from dwelling on the failures of democracy in regard to the native peoples of North America, the African-Americans, women, and the structurally poor and marginalized in the United States and its client states, to that extent American Catholic readers may wish to claim the bits and pieces of wisdom gained from losing that innocence. And that is why, or partly why, reading his texts in dialogical readiness to hear the truth and to test for the truth cannot put aside what has become more clear since his death.

Murray's Texts: Distance and Access for Catholics

Catholic Americans participate in a church which, in the United States as elsewhere, has been anything but transfixed in immobility since

Vatican II. American Catholics have heard about, witnessed, and experienced changes in liturgical worship, in pastoral governance, in spirituality, in relations with other Christians, with Jews and with other religions, in their way of being in history, in certain instances in mode of magisterial teachings, and running through all, a renewed appreciation of the laity. But American Catholic experience and reception of Vatican II had barely gotten underway in Murray's day. His contributing presence at Vatican II, consequently, does not exempt his writings from being reviewed in the light of postconciliar assimilation of the event, charism and documents of Vatican II.

The self-understanding of the church contained in the documents of Vatican II and in postconciliar developments has moved decisively away from a definition primarily in terms of institutional structures. A question can be asked, in light of this shift, about the idea of the church in Murray's church-state teaching. In particular, it is important to know whether or not Murray incorporated an institutionist ecclesiology while redrawing church-state relations. Institutionalism is an ecclesiological error which, Avery Dulles has shown, differs from "acceptance of the institutional element in the Church."[80] Institutionalism "defines the Church primarily in terms of its visible structures, especially the rights and powers of its officers."[81] It can be understood as synecdoche forgetful of the difference between part and whole.

Robert Bellarmine's statement that the church is a society, "as visible and palpable as the community of the Roman people, or the Kingdom of France, or the Republic of Venice,"[82] had misled some into concluding that the visible structures by themselves are the church, or are that for which the church exists and acts. Was Murray, in determining church-state norms with increased precision thereby propagating institutionalism? Church-state contacts, tensions, conflicts and issues have lent themselves to emphasis on visible structures because so often action and thought in the area of the church's relation to a government have involved the highest authorities of church and a state. From Pope Gelasius I's letter to Emperor Anastasius in 494 C.E. through Pope Innocent III's standoff with Philip the Fair in the fourteenth century, to clashes between Pope Pius IX and the forces mobilizing after the French Revolution, the juridical and institutional side of the church has been the front along which states have arrayed their own juridical and institutional realities.

Even had post-Reformation Catholicism opted to take its stand in Aquinas' priority of the invisible, New Law of grace over the external institution and had not instead anchored its self-understanding in a defense of visible structures and offices, church-state relations still would seem bound to lead inevitably into preoccupation with the institutional element in the church. This was surely true for Murray's church-state teaching. But was his concentration one of respect for the institutional element or a mistaking this for the whole reality of the church? If the latter, the church side of his doctrine could well be irreparable. It would not only lag behind but remain opposed to a postconciliar tendency to take church-as-communion to be the paradigm which other models partially present. This, in turn, would impede moving into a theology of the local church, a fatal blockage for church-state teaching once the local church becomes, as Hehir states, the primary "social actor"[83] in the church's social ministry.

The issue is critical. If Murray cemented four essential principles—duality between church and state; primacy of the spiritual; independence of the temporal; finality toward cooperation in the persons of the believer-citizen—onto an institutionalist foundation, it becomes unclear how they can be extended into postconciliar church-state relations. The primacy of the spiritual in an institutionalist model could be taken to mean, for example, and was so understood by Innocent III, a superiority in juridical power or an ideal of juridically subordinate political power or an ideal of establishment. If in *Lumen Gentium* the church registered a shift in paradigms from institution to mystery and people of God, then continued recourse to the church as a *societas perfecta* over and against every political order becomes problematic.

In general, Murray, indeed, presupposed and invoked a post-Vatican I ecclesiology emphasizing papal primacy and the institutional element of the church. However, neither Vatican I nor Murray lost sight of the finitude of any faith-understanding of mysteries of faith, and on that basis remained open in principle to fuller understanding of the mystery of the church. Murray incorporated the Christocentrism of Pope Pius XII's *Mystici Corporis*[84] into his ecclesiology in a way that subordinated the institutional element to Christ as living center and not only as historical source. Integrating mystical body ecclesiology into a predominantly institutional ecclesiology gave Murray another way to relativize the visible structures besides their subordination to Christ as head. He taught, in accord with Pius XII, that the Holy Spirit, not an office or structure, was the ultimate principle of unity and life in the church. This meant that he did not conceive the church as a *societas perfecta* in oblivion to the difference between a "moral" union of persons around common truths and objectives and a "mystical"[85] union of persons joined by the indwelling of the Holy Spirit in all. The church by its nature was a mystical communion and a moral union, while in contrast, a state by its nature was strictly a moral community. His presentation of the traditional church-state principle that the spiritual had primacy contained, then, the primacy of the unique and *sui generis* mystical communion to any and every state.

The church as mystical body, though, is also a moral community insofar as the faith, hope and charity of its members are graced human acts uniting members of the church in a common assent to revealed truth, common practice of a way of life and common orientation toward the future. Here, too, the church surpassed that state insofar as grace and faith surpassed nature and reason. What may be most significant about this part of Murray's ecclesiology is the absence of conflict between it and, for instance, Joseph Komonchak's postconciliar ecclesiology emphasizing the self-realization of the church.[86]

In fact, Murray's 1937 dissertation analyzed Matthias Scheeben's theology of faith in such a way as to appreciate Scheeben's inclusion of the role of affective will in the act of faith but also to criticize the limited, authoritarian concept of that affect.[87] Faith, argued Murray against Scheeben's reading of Vatican I, cannot be limited to or even primarily identified as obedient assent to divine revelation in an overall genre of divine command. Faith was essentially, and understood as such by Aquinas, a fundamental volitional and intellectual act of orientation toward God that completed, fulfilled and actualized a relation to God as last End and Supreme Good, as well as to God as Truth. Though undeveloped, with this principle Murray pointed to an aspect of faith by which it is self-realization in and through the grace of faith which touched mind and heart. This is far from an unnuanced version of the position Dulles designates revelation-as-doctrine and seems to be compatible with Komonchak's principle of ecclesial self-realization. In these respects, at least, Murray's ecclesiology cannot be relegated to institutionalism or to a preconciliar position incapable of further development.

Conclusion

Catholic social teaching has long affirmed that "government has a moral function: protecting human rights and securing basic justice for all members of the commonwealth."[88] The first part of the state concerned is, of course, the citizen. "[E]very citizen," the bishops say, "has the responsibility to work to secure justice and human rights through an organized social response"[89] in "all the groups that compose society."[90] But, in addition, government has the obligation "to guarantee the minimum conditions that make this rich social activity possible, namely human rights and justice."[91] Consequently, "it is the responsibility of all citizens, acting through their government, to assist and empower the poor, the disadvantaged, the handicapped, and the unemployed."[92] How believers can carry out their civic responsibility while making an option for the poor has become a new form of the church-state problematic for American Catholics. This places believer-citizens in a new situation that is not identical with the one within which Murray wrote.

Conditions internal to both American democracy and to post-Vatican II American Catholicism are grounds for opening a new inquiry into John Courtney Murray's writings. What readers cannot do is simply pick up where Murray left off as if the interpretative situation remains what it was in 1967. Nor can it be a matter of formally and informally extending the agenda immanent in Murray's work because his texts are a completed *oeuvre* which attained the chief objectives for which it was undertaken. His wish in 1966 to set aside church-state issues and to ponder again the mystery of the Trinity[93] followed, it is assumed here, a completed trajectory and logic in his previous research. To that extent, his work was finished, though open to having its implications and applications drawn out.

The possibility of an option for the poor places American Catholics within a time of new self-understanding and choice, whose outcome cannot be predicted, and that redefines the situation in which readers engage his texts. There are many indications that Murray's teachings contain the kind of practical wisdom helpful in pondering and making an option for the poor. But, to read them in light of this new situation, with new questions and for the sake of social justice, is to admit the differences between his situation and ours. This kind of difference, which Hans-Georg Gadamer's hermeneutics refers to as "temporal distance," does not open an unbridgeable chasm between texts and reader. What has transpired since 1967, especially the church's hearkening to the needs of the poor and marginalized, along with a possibility of a social ministry to them, gives a new vantage point from which to read Murray and, as a start, to revise a judgment on his accomplishment made on prehermeneutical grounds.

2 | Believers as Citizens: From Historical to Hermeneutical Analysis of Tradition

The Dilemma

To assist the reception of *Economic Justice for All*, this chapter will extricate the work of John Courtney Murray from an interpretative dilemma. Then, Murray's pertinence to American Catholic self-understanding in a new context will appear more clearly. The interpretative dilemma, perfectly well-expressed in Charles E. Curran's *American Catholic Social Ethics*, chapter 5, "John Courtney Murray,"[1] consists in two judgments not easily reconciled. One is that Murray has presented the most impressive and valuable argument for harmony between being Catholic and being American, especially in regard to the First Amendment. The other is that, despite the clarity of his arguments, his role as a guide for American Catholics remains unclear and doubtful. Curran synopsizes Murray's work accurately and succinctly, singling him out as the most creative contributor to modern American Catholic social ethics. Then, his evaluation and critique take such sharp issue with so many specific positions essential to Murray's achievement (natural law, historical-mindedness, interpretation of Leo XIII) that the meaningfulness of Murray's writing falls into doubt and obscurity.

There are other problems in interpreting Murray's texts, to be sure. In an excellent study illustrating Murray's appeal beyond the borders of the United States, Francois-Xavier Dumortier elucidates two conflicting readings of Murray's texts. His analysis indicates that the meaning of Murray's texts is also at issue, and not only their meaningfulness or applicability.[2] Too, a critique of temporal/spiritual dualism has established itself in practical theology.[3] In its light, Murray's differentiation between sacred and secular orders of reality seems obsolete and, worse, ideological resistance to social justice. His dualism, however, represented resistance to and liberation from a monism whose principle was that one reality, the state, has competence and power to exercise undivided sovereignty over all sectors of social life. This critique of monism,

40

effective in clarifying the struggle of the church to defend its freedom against emperors and kings, gained universal significance in reference to the Shoah. For the Holocaust stands as an unnerving actuality casting a shadow across all subsequent thought about the authority of any state.[4] To the extent that Murray's dualism shares in a fundamental, though formal, source of resistance to the monopolizing of power in the hands of any state, it expresses resistance to the kind of premises and tendencies forcing their way to the Holocaust. This, along with this dualism's rejection also of the claim for state control of the forces of history made in the name of Marxism-Leninism and causing the deaths of tens of millions in the Soviet Union, demonstrates that Murray's dualism contains resistance to an omnicompetent state, and asserts the priority of society and human rights over any and every political organization. For these reasons alone, Murray's dualism cannot be dismissed peremptorily and without first examining how it shapes a mentality and practice on behalf of freedom. The cause of social justice gives no basis for uncritical rejection of something capable of preventing the kinds of regimes that have inflicted immeasurable suffering in this century.

A Hermeneutical Approach

This chapter will take a step toward renewing the meaningfulness of Murray's texts. It will concentrate only on a problem in his correlations of Catholic tradition with American values. The objective is to show that the role of practice can be recovered and renewed. This will help bring to the surface the moral dimension, still open to use, of Murray's texts in such a way that they can again help form self-understanding and conscience. They need not languish in a peculiar limbo between meaning (in their time) and meaninglessness (for subsequent times) in which Curran left them.

The approach will be indirect, somewhat tentative, carrying an admitted risk. The risk consists in placing John Courtney Murray's texts in the light of Hans-Georg Gadamer's hermeneutical philosophy. This can bring new awareness of the meaning and meaningfulness of Murray's texts while leading toward the overcoming of the limit Richard Bernstein has identified in Gadamer's hermeneutic. The risk must be admitted. Basic differences between Murray and Gadamer could be blurred, with the effect of upsetting the integrity of both positions by putting aside temporarily their respective and opposing first principles. Reading Murray's texts primarily in light of Part II in Gadamer's *Truth and Method*, for example, might falsify Part II by depriving it of momentum toward the universality of the hermeneutical phenomenon in Part III. This would leave the mistaken impression that Gadamer offers yet another technique for analyzing texts. Likewise, not directly confronting Murray's Aristotelian-Thomist metaphysics and ethics could seem to diminish Murray's linking of them and his tying both to statements on church-state relations and on religious liberty in *We Hold These Truths*.

Still, the risk is worthwhile. For there is common ground, not, it seems, in first principles (e.g., metaphysics and Aristotle's natural-law doctrine), but in a field of practical wisdom in which their respective and basic principles become, or give direction to, ways of deciding and acting. First and foremost, an orientation toward expanding the practice of freedom is common to the texts of each. No less, reflection on the centrality of dialogue to civilization and the political order characterizes the texts of both. And the respect each has for temporality in speaking, writing, acting and thinking is obvious to every reader. Their common ground extends also to acceptance of western humanism, and to a refusal to surrender citizenship to the language of science and technique.

Their affinity in an orientation and movement toward the practical-moral order makes the risk of muting the voices of their conflicts worth taking. Probably the nature of the risk is to postpone rather than to take up at the start confrontation between their oppositions. This admittedly makes the focus on their cognate interests and statements an interim measure. It also justifies delaying, for example, an argument over the issue of the universality of hermeneutics in Part III of *Truth and Method*. Until then, and under the condition of a temporary reprieve, Part II can undergo its own testing in dialogue with Murray. From Murray's side, his Thomist metaphysics and ethics—clearly unacceptable to Gadamer —will not suffer total eclipse if it is his creative application of them in American Catholic church-state relations (and religious liberty) that becomes, for the moment, the main issue.

This way of reading Murray's texts is nothing more than attending to his success in the universal phenomenon of understanding, as Gadamer analyzes it. Murray let a *perichoresis* among three moments—understanding/interpretation/application—occur in his mediation of Catholic tradition in a new hermeneutical situation.[5] In this way, his texts exemplify the universal phenomenon of understanding at the same time that their content teaches American Catholics how to let Catholic church-state norms inform their free, public and long-standing adherence to the First Amendment.

Reading *We Hold These Truths* in light of *Truth and Method* lets dual affirmation, of Catholic belief and of the American Proposition, be seen as an instance of the act of understanding, rather than as a feat of synthesis depending on a suspect finessing of Leonine doctrine, as Curran would have it. Gadamer shows how understanding, interpretation, and application belong together and are indissociable. *We Hold These Truths* presents a series of essays, it will be argued, in which traditional Catholic church-state teaching is understood inseparably from an interpretative moment in which Murray brings that traditional doctrine into dialogue with the American political order. In turn, this dialogue between tradition and a new situation becomes a way to appropriate that teaching in and for a new situation.

Text as Mediation

In *We Hold These Truths*, Murray's statement of Catholic church-state norms—and Vatican Council II vindicated him on many points—did not consist in his grasping and presenting them in an otherness due to historical consciousness of their ancient provenance and meaning, then repeating them to a new situation. Nor, of course, was it a matter of his treating them as if they were disembodied ideas suitable for, and quickly applicable to, any and all church-state arrangements.

Rather, his writing mediates the traditional norms, first of all, from within a dialogue with them that already participates in their meaning. From the onset their meaning is codetermined in the present. This is what Gadamer describes as a "fusion of horizons."[6] Murray's present was an American Catholicism shaped by a relatively brief but not negligible experience of living outside the legally privileged status typical of Catholic and Protestant Christendom in Europe. The novelty and practical character of American Catholic experience gave it, over time, a kind of moral authority all its own, operative as a preconception or, what Gadamer identifies as a "productive prejudice."[7] American Catholicism amounted to a new hermeneutical situation.[8]

Equally, Murray's best-known book of essays, each the reprise of earlier writings, allowed this new situation—Catholicism existing with no impulse toward legal establishment and in commitment to religious liberty—to gain a voice in dialogue with church-state norms accustomed to Catholic and Protestant establishments.

What Gadamer clarifies is that Murray's appropriation of Catholic tradition, so bitterly controverted during the 1950s,[9] was not a matter of compromising traditional beliefs by synthesizing them with American values. To the contrary, and in keeping with the meaning of the incarnation, he opened them to each other in an act of understanding that was a fusing of horizons.

An alternative was at hand: the horizon of American Catholicism was for practical purposes suppressed by Murray's opponents who repeated papal formulae to the end of discountenancing or merely tolerating the American church-state arrangement. Their anti-incarnational denial of the human novelty in the American experience amounted, as well, to withholding a gift, the lesson learned about religious liberty, from the whole church.[10] Murray's work helped bring this gift into circulation for the entire church.

Reconsideration of his achievement will involve shifting from reading his texts as specimens of historical consciousness to reading them with attention to their hermeneutical aspects. Because Murray's texts have not been studied in light of Gadamer, it should be acknowledged that this approach proceeds from a presupposition that their meaning and meaningfulness have such depth that no completely assured interpretation of them exists to serve as a standard for judging all other interpretations. And this absence of a definitive interpretation holds despite *The Problem of Religious Freedom,* in which he put his writings under the heading of "historical consciousness."[11] He gave readers what looked like the key to his message. This position, however, need not be taken as absolutely normative. A brief account of his book will explain why.

Drafted for the assembled bishops at Vatican II, this tripartite, 110-page book showed them how the proposed declaration on religious liberty "moved from the nineteenth century position as epitomized in the *Syllabus of Errors* to the position set forth in *Pacem in Terris.*"[12] Avoiding all pejorative terms for the rejectionist, traditionalist school of thought by calling it the "First View," Murray recounted the failure of dialogue between its proponents and advocates of the "Second View" (his own, that of the American bishops, and eventually, of Vatican II).[13] "The First and Second View do not confront each other as affirmation confronts negation," he wrote. Instead, "[t]heir differences are at a deeper level indeed, at a level so deep that it would be difficult to go deeper."[14] Presuppositions, not only nuanced views on religious liberty, were at odds. This was a division under a difference.

In fact, he stated, the two views anchored in their presuppositions "represent the contemporary clash between classicism (the First View opposed to going beyond the nineteenth century teaching) and historical consciousness (the Second View espousing the fact of a developing position)."[15] Murray's own writings, obviously, argued the "Second View." They, he let it be inferred, actualized "historical consciousness."[16] This statement, along with his close observation of and continuing reference to the contingencies of past actual church-state relations along with a disengaging of their basic principles, handed readers, it seemed, his own key to his achievement. This view, in fact, has come to prevail. But it is not sufficient by itself to interpret his texts, and for that reason, despite the apparently decisive authority of the author's declaration of intent and method, it cannot be the sole light in which to read his texts. This must be looked at in more detail.

In *John Courtney Murray: Theologian in Conflict,* Donald E. Pelotte signalized Murray's achievement as the victory of historical consciousness over a classicism enclosing his ecclesiastical opposition before and during Vatican Council II.[17] Pelotte, in what remains probably the best general introduction to Murray's work, described the reception of *The Problem of Religious Freedom* by the conciliar fathers in terms of its historical method. Taking up Murray's own line of thought, he pointed out that Murray's book had persuaded the bishops because it gave them "a clear and attractive analysis of the historical method and its application to the religious liberty issue."[18] This helped them decide to approve the "Declaration on Religious Liberty." Their vote expressed an advance beyond "classicism" into "historical consciousness."

Not, of course, that Murray had ushered the bishops into relativism. He insisted that a few, fundamental principles were coming into ever-changing modes of realization in contingent circumstances: 1) the transcendence of the church; 2) the independence of the political order; 3) the distinction between the church and any political order; 4) the goal of a harmony between the two, for the sake of the persons at once believers and citizens.[19] Murray did anything but belittle the value of permanently valid principles. He received them as objective truths. He was aware, though, of objective truth in a way which was "especially concerned with man's possession of the truth . . . with the conditions, both circumstantial and subjective, of understanding and affirmation."[20] This was the "historical consciousness" which Pelotte saw reigning victoriously in Murray's texts.

Unlike the First View, Murray was concerned "with the historicity of truth and with progress in the grasp and penetration of what is true."[21] His ecclesiastical opponents lacked this grasp of the historicity of truth. They could not admit that the church could develop in her understanding of the truths guiding her in relating to rulers and states. They locked themselves out of history by a methodological commitment to "a view of truth," Pelotte said, "which holds to objective truth, precisely because it exists objectively, 'already out there now' . . . apart from history, formulated in propositions that are verbally immutable."[22] This was "classicism."[23]

Pelotte portrayed Murray, in high contrast, as an expert in the school of history. History informed his theological method. According to Pelotte, "Murray envisioned this theological task first as an examination of the data of history and of the present historical situation."[24] This was "in order to determine what is permanent and what is relative in the Church's encounter with the state and with religious liberty."[25] Completing this, Murray proved capable of "[d]emonstrating through the historical method that his position was in continuity with authentic tradition. . . ."[26] Pelotte considered that Murray's commitment to historical method was essential to Murray's achievement.

How puzzling, consequently, must a reader find Pelotte's omission of this methodological option when the "Epilogue" explores the "import of Murray's work for future theological and especially ecclesiological discussion."[27] The role of history in theological method dwindles down to showing how "theology must be interdisciplinary" in order to respond adequately to human experience.[28] In fact, not historical consciousness nor historical method, but derivation from experience here becomes the avenue to future work in three areas to which Murray's accomplishment tends: development of doctrine; democratization of the church; and Catholic presence in American secular society. Nowhere does the "Epilogue" single out as an exemplary guide that historical mindedness which distinguished Murray's work. Is this because there is something problematic about this historical-mindedness in Murray's texts?

There definitely is when Charles E. Curran addresses Murray's contribution.[29] For Curran, too, historical consciousness was, along with natural law, a methodological presupposition in Murray's work. It enabled him, for instance, to distinguish between the permanently valid and the "historically and polemically conditioned" content in Pope Leo XIII's advocacy of the confessional state and church-state union. It gave him the conviction that church teaching could develop in understanding its relations to the political organization of societies.[30] It helped him appreciate the "shift from classicism to historical consciousness."[31] But, and here the problematic feature emerges, it left his writing open to all the charges Curran levels against it in a concluding assessment.

Curran acknowledged that, "Murray was one of the first Roman Catholic theologians to recognize the importance of historical mindedness and to employ such a concept in his methodology."[32] Then he faults Murray for failing to see that "[t]he natural as such and as distinguished from the supernatural has never historically existed."[33] Murray held a view of history, the state, social structures, and citizenship as if these were *natura pura* in the concrete.

It would take a lengthy investigation of Murray's theological texts and principles to ascertain whether he held a *natura pura* view.[34] More likely, despite the natural/supernatural unity in persons, he accepted the principle of methodological independence for history, philosophy, and political discourse, with the resulting tendency to emphasize their rights as those of "nature." It is clear, for instance, that he argued from histori-cal, philosophical and political grounds in order to emancipate ecclesias-tical discussion of church-state relations and of religious liberty from confinement to theology.[35] From these grounds he also rebutted a theo-logical reading of the First Amendment and proposed a political and legal reading. It is not at all clear that his language of "nature" ignores sin and grace.[36]

In any case, what Pelotte treated as an evident excellence in Murray's writings, though one not determinative of future follow-up has become genuinely problematic in Curran's analysis. He criticizes other facets of Murray's historical-mindedness: that he failed to let it deeply affect his notion of being and of natural law; and the opposite, that he capitulated to situationism in his refusal to adopt an ideal form of church-state relations, or to treat religious liberty as an absolutely normative civil institution.[37]

It can be noted that Murray wrote in 1965 that whereas religious establishment might be able to be justified as "useful for assuring the freedom of the Church" among a people whose law long recognized Catholicism as the common religion of that people, this could not be considered in any sense an ideal. In addition, he declared, "no argument can be made today that would validate the legal institution of religious intolerance" even as a "harmless archaism."[38] Consequently, in coupling intolerance with establishment, Curran makes the mistake of saying that, "According to Murray the institution of intolerance and establishment must be judged *in situ* and might well be valid *in situ....*"[39] To the contrary, and on grounds that are at once those of natural law and of history, namely the modern common consciousness of human dignity, Murray rejected any further justification for legal intolerance in religious matters.

One criticism, more than the others, shows how troublesome Curran found Murray's historical-mindedness: Murray's articles in *Theo-logical Studies,* though Curran never reproaches them as disingenuous, foisted a theory onto Pope Leo XIII. The pope's teaching on the tem-poral order had resisted church-state separation, had fostered church-state unions and had dismissed religious liberty. From this inhospitable, nineteenth-century soil Murray claimed his own advocacy of the First Amendment and religious liberty grew. Where Murray argued for a development of doctrine, Curran suspects something less took place. Something akin to a clever bit of finesse, prompted by Murray's inability to face the reality that papal teaching could be erroneous, allowed Murray to respect Leonine statements.

Thus, in saying that Murray's historical-mindedness "gives him a hermeneutical tool for dealing with past Roman Catholic teachings as illustrated especially in his creative interpretation of Pope Leo XIII,"[40] the terms "hermeneutical" and "creative" carry a connotation of putting words into Leo's mouth. For Curran to grant that "Murray's interpretation of Pope Leo XIII is ingenious in its distinction among the doctrinal, the polemical, and the historical aspects of the pope's teaching"[41] is to point out what will earn Murray an indictment for misrepresenting papal thought, though all to the good!

Murray had demonstrated that Leo XIII opposed the philosophy and polity of continental liberalism, but that this contained no condemnatory judgment on Anglo-American constitutional government, about which neither the pope nor the Vatican had any very good idea. Curran fully agrees with Murray's position of ignorance about Anglo-American constitutionalism but does not think that it permits Murray's reading of Leo to qualify as a development. For, he comments, "I do not think that Leo XIII would have recognized himself in the picture drawn by Murray!" Murray's ingenuity—not the subject matter of the Leonine texts, not Leo's ideas, not a tradition common to Murray and Leo—somehow contrived a conjunction between Murray and papal teaching, and then exceeded itself by managing to convince others of its validity.

Not, however, adversaries in Rome and in Washington. In Curran's estimation, Murray may have been ingenious, but he imposed his later theory upon the nineteenth-century pope, then taught the conciliar fathers that it differed from Leo's, not as truth from error, but as one phase of development from another. And all because "In no way can he be forced to say that Leo's position was wrong" since, "[i]n Murray's day there were practically no Catholic theologians publicly maintaining that the official hierarchical teaching could and did make mistakes."[42] In this analysis, Murray's hermeneutical skill consisted in an evasion of unacceptable facts, not in grasping the text, the subject matter and a new situation together.

Is not Curran's observation correct in noting the difference between Leo's self-understanding and Murray's doctrine? But, with this granted, is not this difference the very sign that appeal to the pope's intention or self-understanding by itself cannot suffice as the sole criterion for determining the meaning of the papal texts (or Murray's)? Curran, that is, has identified but undervalued Murray's "historical hermeneutic" precisely insofar as it exceeds the canons implementing historical-mindedness, including reconstructing authorial intention. Curran has posted a notice on authorial self-understanding in its difference from the meaning of Leo's texts. Far from undermining confidence in what Murray wrote, though, it draws attention to the advisability of reading Murray with the assistance of a more detailed consideration of the hermeneutic moment.

A Hermeneutic Moment in Murray's Achievement: From Papal Negation to Conciliar Affirmation of Religious Liberty

The art of interpreting begins when what has been handed down loses its qualities of obvious truth and familiar confirmation, when the text or other artifact appears as if at a distance, as somehow "other." "The true home of hermeneutics," said Gadamer, is situated in "[t]he place between strangeness and familiarity that a transmitted text has for us."[43] There the text is at once part of a tradition and already emerging from this proximity in meaning into "being an historically intended separate object."[44] Historical research, for example, clarifies the distance between the origin of and the reading of a text. Hermeneutical work begins in that distance.

Murray's major contribution to church-state doctrine began with an interpretation of Pope Leo XIII's teaching. Post-World War II ecumenism in the United States led him to the perception that the pope's teaching on church and state and on religious liberty was "between strangeness and familiarity." Leo XIII's repeated condemnations of church-state separation and his negative verdict on religious liberty had provoked understandable American Protestant reactions. How could American Catholics be trusted if the papacy had spoken so forcefully against principles all Americans recognized as contained by the First Amendment? Might they think of suspending religious liberty should they become the majority in America that they were in Spain?

In an encyclical to the Spanish bishops in 1882, Pope Leo had written: "[i]t will, first of all, be in place to recall the mutual relations of sacred and civil affairs, because many fall into contrary errors. Some are wont not only to distinguish political affairs from religion but completely to sever and separate them."[45] In 1884, the pontiff reproached the activities of the Masons. He pointed out that, "[a] lengthy and stubbornly laborious effort is being made to see that the teaching and the authority of the Church should have no influence upon society. To this end they publicly preach and contend for the idea that sacred and civil affairs must be completely sundered."[46] In 1892 Leo addressed the situation in France and objected to the "principle of the separation of Church and state—which is equivalent to separating human legislation from Christian and divine legislation."[47] These and other papal pronouncements raised new suspicions about Catholic adherence to First Amendment values. Ecumenical and interreligious cooperation with Catholics after the war could not proceed in America without some solid basis for assurance that Catholics were not assuming that religious liberty and nonestablishment were merely tolerable and not desirable.

Leo had presented "separation" as refusal to observe the New Testament injunction, "Give to God what is God's and to Caesar what is Caesar's." "From the moment the state refuses to give to God what is God's," Leo argued, "it refuses by necessary consequence to give to its citizens what they have a right to as men."[48] The consequence followed because, "like it or not, the true rights of man derive precisely from his duties to God."[49] And if the state, by separation from the church, isolated itself from a relation to the creator then it forfeited the ground from under its service to its citizens and so "misses the principal purpose of its institution,"[50] which is to protect and to promote human rights deriving from duties to the creator. "In consequence," Leo warned, "Catholics cannot too carefully beware of supporting such a separation."[51] French Catholics in particular ought not to put the church into the "precarious situation which it experiences among other peoples."[52] These and other denunciations of "separation" were prominent in Pope Leo's teaching.

A need to understand this sort of statement from the church's highest doctrinal authority—with the definition of infallibility in the background—belonged to the situation of American Catholicism. For American Catholics, whose whole experience of their religion had the obvious advantages of the religious liberty guaranteed by the First Amendment, the papal declarations entered that region Gadamer describes as "between strangeness and familiarity."[53] The strangeness was the distance from the experience of American Catholicism. The familiarity was the confident acceptance of papal authority, the recognition of the valuable purpose the pope sought to serve, and commonality in Catholic tradition.

A transmitted text, Gadamer points out, needs interpretative mediation rather than repetition when its place is somewhere "between being an historically intended separate object and being part of a tradition."[54] This was the place held by papal rejection of church-state separation and religious liberty for American Catholicism. No kind of teaching could be perceived as more traditional than that of a pope. At the same time, and influenced by the moral authority of their experience of nonestablishment as a self-evident good, the unusual content of the teaching made it "an historically intended separate object" requiring study.

In this condition of apparent conflict between being Catholic and being American, John Courtney Murray started to argue that there was, in fact, no conflict between the papal statements and the First Amendment. For the pope had not condemned what the First Amendment enshrined, but rather something altogether different. This put Murray in opposition to those who did not even perceive an apparent conflict be-cause they overrode the values of American Catholicism in favor of repeating the papal teaching, as if its import were completely clear, fully determined and absolutely uniform in application. He presented an alter-native to an American Catholic's assenting to papal doctrine at the cost of downgrading American church-state separation to an inferior condition in which it was a tolerable shortfall from a supposed ideal, legal establishment.

As a result, he was accused of contradicting the manifest content of Catholic teaching and of violating the reverent assent due to the papal magisterium. He responded with a series of five articles outlining the doctrines of Pope Leo XIII on church and state. They merit Curran's description of them as "historical hermeneutics." But their hermeneuti-cal aspect was not eisegesis as an escape from facing putative papal error. Instead, they joined understanding and interpretation of papal teaching to an appropriation by American Catholicism.

Where historical analysis, in the interests of objectivity, might try to prescind from an interpretative moment, he developed an "interpreta-tion" of Pope Leo's texts that brought their meaning and truth into relation with the American situation of their interpreter. More is asked of understanding, according to Gadamer, than accepting "the claim of historical consciousness to see the past in terms of its own being, not in terms of our contemporary criteria and prejudices."[55] This is not enough because it changes dialogue with a tradition into a strategy that, like an oral examination, seeks to know the "standpoint and horizon of the other person . . . without our necessarily having to agree with him. . . ."[56]

Were the truth of Leo's discourse not the primary issue, and were Murray's consent to that truth less than full, his five articles could have found safe shelter in a language of historical "objectivity." Murray chose, however, a language of engagement in an argument, not that of recording it. The goal for the first article, "The Church and Totalitarian Democ-racy," was innocuous enough; namely, to furnish a "background to a study of Leo XIII."[57] But, beyond that historical objective, it played a role in the tendency in all five articles on Leonine teaching toward an application which was "to make some sort of judgment on the American situation."[58] In this central article he proposed that, "[i]t will appear from what follows that Leo XIII condemned Continental separation for a variety of reasons, all of which were related to its root."[59] All the articles thoroughly supported Leo's condemnation.

Equally, all contributed to showing that "[t]his vitiating root is not the source from which the American concept of separation took its ori-gin."[60] And this historical conclusion, further, reached fulfillment in an interpretative judgment that "after full assent has been given to this condemnation [of Continental separation] as a matter of Catholic duty, there is still room for an unprejudiced examination of the American concept of separation."[61] Murray's argument throughout his five articles, then, accepted the pope's teaching as true but demurred on its applicability to American separation under the First Amendment.

To the degree that an historical analysis, by acknowledging "the otherness of the other, which makes him the object of objective knowledge,"[62] would be taken as the final norm, to that extent Murray was noncompliant with historicism. His reading of Leonine texts did not involve a "fundamental suspension of his [Pope Leo's] claim to truth," which Gadamer notes is a limit in "historical understanding" uncovered by hermeneutical reflection.[63]

In another aspect, too, Murray departed from what Curran takes as a norm for accurate rendering of the meaning of Leonine texts, authorial self-understanding and intention. Murray interpreted the papal texts not solely by reference to authorial intention but also in reliance upon participatory knowledge of the publicly accessible Catholic tradition shared with and enveloping both author and texts. His vocabulary of appeal to Pope Leo's own "doctrine," "concern," "task," "case," "concept," "thought," "understanding," "perspectives," and even "eyes," indeed, dots the five essays. The first essay by itself, nonetheless, fixes the whole analysis upon the meaning contained in the texts themselves, not toward recovery of an authorial subjectivity behind them.

Not that the pope was not a personality to be reckoned with. Rather, as Murray explained, the appearance of an encyclical was not an outburst of papal self-expression but communication in a known genre. As Murray said, and pointing more to the genre than to the individual author, "[i]n writing an encyclical the pope is not a scholar; he is exercising the Church's supreme prophetic and pastoral ministry."[64] This exercise has its traits, which are not those of a particular subjectivity. In reading an encyclical, consequently, "one does not look . . . for detailed analyses of systems of thought, for full-fleshed reconstructions of historical eras. . . ."[65] This is so, not for the reason that popes lack an educated grasp of the issues, but because their genre is "destined for all the faithful . . . [encyclicals] are done in the prophetic not the academic manner."[66] Accordingly, it cannot be said that Murray's reading of Leo XIII's texts proceeded from or was primarily directed to recovery of an authorial intention,[67] except, of course, insofar as this was the unifying meaning in the texts.

He was not attempting to regain by intuitive divination a self-understanding Leo had when composing his condemnations of church-state "separation." His interpretation started within the truth of the pope's texts, not in empathy with the act of their composition. Gadamer, as is well-known, analyzes the act of interpreting a transmitted text in such a way as to rule out appeal to authorial intention as the determinative criterion of meaning. His reason has to do with the finitude of reason within history: a later age cannot simply identify its understanding with that of an author from an earlier period.

Also, the "temporal distance" between earlier and later times is filled with events and ideas that are new possibilities for understanding the original text. The later reading could see more in the text than was recognized by its author or original audience. Further, the act of reading is an act of interpreting the meaning of the text in some dependence upon "the historical situation of the interpreter and hence . . . the totality of the objective course of history."[68] For these reasons, "the real meaning of a text, as it speaks to the interpreter, does not depend on the contingencies of the author and whom he originally wrote for."[69]

This can be amended and mitigated so that, in Murray's reading of Leo's writings, the *auctor solus* principle of interpretation is excluded, without rejecting a search for that unity in textual meaning which may be only imperfectly communicated, and might be provisionally conceived as an idea behind the text. Murray did not appeal, in alliance with romantic hermeneutics, to Leo's unconscious spontaneity, nor was he, in accord with what Gadamer treats as historicist norms, constricting the meaning in Leo's texts to the supposedly closed horizon of his period in the nineteenth century.

Rather, and as Gadamer's principle of the positive value in temporal distance between the origin and the subsequent reading of a text would suggest, Murray's exposition of Leo's texts has something to do with events after Leo's time. The temporal distance between the origin of the Leonine writings in the last quarter of the nineteenth century, and Murray's reading of them in the middle of the twentieth, entered into his interpretation of their meaning. This is noticeable in a small consistent moment interior to Murray's interpretation of Leo XIII within his larger argument that "separation" and "religious liberty" meant one thing in Leo's texts, another to Americans. Murray's interpretative perspective came from a tradition of politics alternative to the Continent's and arose from experience of Catholicism in America. This alternative to continental political and religious tradition created part of the need for a "translation" of Leonine teaching across the difference. In addition, there was a temporal distance between Leo XIII and Murray. As a result, Leonine texts were in need of interpretation if they were to be applied in mid-twentieth century America. Their distance from American reality was not solely due to the decades which intervened between Leo and the mid-twentieth century. It was due to a parallel development of that medieval heritage which on the Continent lost itself in varieties of state absolutism but which "reached the shores of America in secularized and Protestanized form"[70] in the eighteenth century to begin a second tradition, the American Republic.

Murray's reading of Leonine rejection of monism and of church-state norms was affected by World War II, and the ensuing Cold War. World War II revealed definitively the destructive nature of the disorder harbored in the principle of a monist political order which dissolved a dualist "Christian structure of politics"[71] by securing for the state alone an unlimited, undivided sovereignty. The common American term for such a political order came to be "totalitarian,"[72] and Murray introduced this into his analysis of Leonine teaching in constant redescription of the pope's enemy as "totalitarian." Murray did not settle for the "state absolutism" in summarizing the rule of dictatorial or tyrannical regimes. He drew instead a line between "monist" and "dualist" politics. Continental liberalism, fascism and communism all had in common a monist structure that was intolerant of any other social reality (e.g., the church) claiming its own authority from a source other than the state's concession of it and presuming to have truth and value of a sort not subject to the state's version of reason.

Then, borrowing J. T. Talmon's surprising turn of phrase, Murray argued that Continental liberalism was a "totalitarian democracy."[73] A democratic state monopolizing all power and authority, acknowledging no source for values above the human reason it represented collectively, regarding itself as conferring from its sovereignty all rights was a "totalitarian democracy." Here and in his constant redescription of Continental liberalism—the nemesis of Leo XIII—as "totalitarian,"[74] there occurred an instance of that "historical fusion of the past with the present" which Gadamer points out as the reception of a "classic" and then extends to any interpretative grasp of a transmitted text or tradition.

In a fusion of horizons that suppressed neither that of the papal texts nor that of American political life, Murray's vocabulary first specified and then relativized papal abhorrence at "separation" of church from state. This "translated" Pope Leo XIII's negation of "separation" into a post-World War II vocabulary familiar to Americans. And with the term "totalitarian," he was also able to identify the precise principle linking continental adversaries to the church with later regimes similarly claiming and exercising a monopoly of authority. In this way, the antitotalitarian lessons learned from the evils of Hitler's and Stalin's regimes entered into Murray's interpretation of Leo's texts. This, too, was how temporal distance enriched Murray's understanding of the transmitted text. The "separation" rejected by Leo XIII sprang from the same monist root opposed by the First Amendment and then inimical to the American tradition of liberal democracy.

"Understanding," Gadamer goes on to say, "is not to be thought of so much as an action of one's subjectivity, but as the placing of oneself within a process of tradition, in which past and present are constantly fused."[75] This is at once to enter into the meaning of the tradition and to mediate it by and to the situation of the interpreter. This is the fusion of horizons taking place, for example, in Murray's reading and interpretation of papal strictures against "separation" of church from state. History and culture introduce the differences between horizons. Overcoming the differences depends on a dialogue both sustaining the otherness and then bringing its truth and meaning into new language. This is to translate the text or tradition.

This means that in the fusion of horizons taking place in Murray's translation of Leonine teaching, he did not carry out above all an inquiry that moved into, reacquired and remained within the pope's horizon. In starting from his horizons and engaging the pope's, he accepted the instructive role of the difference intervening between Continental and American political traditions and the events between Leo's time and his own time. This exemplified what Gadamer speaks of as "effective-historical consciousness" as distinct from "historical consciousness." Effective-historical consciousness is the acceptance and exploration of the way awareness of past realities has been preformed by the totality of the past, including the temporal distance—replete with people, deeds, events, thoughts—between the text or tradition and its interpreter's own day. In Murray's case, that intervening temporal distance saw the foundational principle of Continental liberalism—indivisible, limitless state sovereignty—write its own destructive refutation in the language of human suffering.

What Curran regards as Murray's being conditioned by theology's unwillingness to admit error in the papal magisterium is actually Murray's success in performing an act of interpretation that kept intact a link between understanding Leo's confrontation with liberalism, interpreting his texts according to the future of their subject matter, and applying this in his own, American Catholic situation. His interpretation of Leonine teaching was also his appropriation of it within a hermeneutical situation, rather than from an imaginary Archimedean point outside and above all discourse, or removed from all prospect of deliberation for decision. His understanding of the Leonine position also disclosed new elements in it not visible to readers unfamiliar with the American Catholic experience.

3 | Beyond Dogmatism: Discovering the People Behind *We Hold These Truths*

Introduction

"What seems to me," concluded Gadamer in "The Philosophical Foundations of the Twentieth Century" (1962), "to be the most hidden and yet the most powerful foundation of our century is its skepticism over against all dogmatism, including the dogmatism of science."[1] An authority in a content accountable to no further thought or experience is the last thing readers expect to discover, or ever recall finding, in *We Hold These Truths*. Completely to the contrary, the author suffered an official ecclesiastical silencing of his argument that legal establishment of the church was not an ideal implied by Catholic faith or doctrine.[2] The nature of his argument was largely an appeal to experience and reason, not to theological premises, although his argument was situated within a theological horizon. The effect of his position was to draw attention to the shortcomings of the conventional, textbook teaching of church-state relations and to challenge its pretensions to dogmatic authority and doctrinal basis.[3]

His continual referring of the church-state issue to the contingent modes of its realization undercut a dogmatism which dismissed the differences between, for example, Anglo-American constitutionalism and continental liberalism on the meaning of religious liberty. His principle that ecclesial understanding of revelation, faith and creation developed, and that the church had come to a deeper realization of the right to religious liberty, overcame the resistance to moving beyond Pope Leo XIII's harsh words on it. On the whole, then, Murray's work seems to eradicate a dogmatism which obscures the way truth is learned, held, and deepened. Against that background, even raising a question about dogmatism in that work can appear to be impertinent ignoring of an episode of ecclesiastical conflict which marked Murray's thought as ahead of its ecclesial time.

Yet, a theme runs through *We Hold These Truths* that threatens to erect a prison of dogmatism around the book. It is a perspective that opens theology and the church's self-understanding and teaching to experience, history, and development, while at the same time closing the door against unconceptualized meaning in human action. Dogmatism does not lie in truths of faith, nor in asserting the truths underlying the U.S. Constitution, nor in identifying the essential structure and perennial norms in church-state relations, nor in propounding a natural-law ethic. Rather, the ground for a question consists in signs of fixation on the superiority and normative authority of theory as a director of practice. More than a few passages in *We Hold These Truths* bestow, without testing the principle, completeness of competence for initiating and guiding action upon doctrine and theory.

This species of dogmatism shields theory from the impact of experience in its negative moment of collision with human finitude.[4] Unbidden suffering can reverse expectations and pull the rug out from under security in possession of received truths and values. Experience contains, as Gadamer points out, recognition that suffering negates present convictions just as easily as it substantiates already possessed knowledge. This negative moment is a beginning for questions of a nonmethodical sort unlike those formed by the *status questionis* of formal research in a given field. Can Murray's book accommodate, listen to, the suffering of those who are poor, oppressed and marginalized in the United States, and that of American Catholics and others who opt for solidarity with them? It cannot if a dogmatism of theory rules out any receptivity from suffering and from action.

Indeed, by 1966, Murray's "The Issue of Church and State at Vatican II" resituated church-state relations within the broader church-world relationship. But it did not also recognize that Vatican II embraced a principle from which arises an unexpected question for Murray. In "The Pastoral Constitution of the Church in the Modern World," the council affirmed the church's solidarity with "the joys and hopes, the griefs and anxieties of [the people] of this age, especially those who are poor or in any way afflicted."[5] This principle of solidarity, especially with the poor and afflicted, is a willingness to open the church to unforeseeable experiences and to their possibly negative power to provoke. It can be read as a commitment to accept the negative moment in suffering and its questions into ecclesial self-understanding as an inevitable factor in pastoral activity and in theological reflection. The linking of "joys and hopes" to "griefs and anxieties" does more than present a balanced and comprehensive humanism. Its weight falls on the side of plunging into experience in solidarity with all brothers and sisters hurt by misery and oppression. This renders the church vulnerable to unanticipated learning, not just to further results from scientific research. Can the same be said about *We Hold These Truths?* If a dogmatism of theory means that its explanation of the harmony between Catholicism and American political life is over and done, finished once and for all, then implementation of its principles, but not action provoking further thought about them and interpretation of them, burdens its readers.

Here the question becomes most acute. An option for the poor is already a mode of what can be called praxis which beckons thought. Can readers whose option for the poor readies them to "evaluate social and economic activity from the viewpoint of the poor and the powerless"[6] and who can then bring that education with them to the text find there an irreplaceable practical wisdom, anymore?

Praxis and Murray

Murray did not use the term "praxis" in *We Hold These Truths*. He did not reflect directly on practice. He did explain at length the advantages of philosophical, moral, and political doctrines for reasonable practice. Does this amount to a dogmatism of theoretical knowledge? Before turning to his text for an answer, however, a preliminary discussion of praxis will present the problem in more detail and will present a qualified version of Gadamer's retrieval of Aristotle's praxis as an approach to Murray's text.

The problem is that Murray's book has symptoms indicating a theory/praxis relationship which is "classical"[7] in the worst possible sense of elevating theoretical knowledge to an unalloyed primacy which holds absolute command over a practice external to itself and which it prescribes down to the last detail. If "these truths" in the title of his book, which are the substance of a consensus supporting the Constitution and which the Declaration of Independence places before the world, ascended to become a "doctrine" or "theory" whose office was to exercise a unilateral supervision and command over the "American experiment," then the book inculcates that problematic and objectionable theory/praxis relation that Matthew Lamb calls "the primacy of theory."[8]

Lamb does not refer to Murray in his outline of the various theory/praxis relations finding their way into theology. He does discuss Jacques Maritain, however, as a representative of a Thomist variant on the primacy of theory.[9] He presents an "ascent to Being . . . complemented by a descent to action as one moves from pure speculation (knowledge for its own sake) to speculatively practical knowledge (moral theology and moral philosophy) which directs action from afar through practically practical knowledge (practical moral sciences) which directs action from nearby to prudence which directs action immediately."[10] If this was more or less Murray's presupposition Murray, too, might be expected to envision, with Maritain, "the temporal order of political and social institutions" in terms of Maritain's "new Christendom"[11] of pluralist democracy carried out by a prudent laity.

The possibilities are two. One is that Murray had been in substantial agreement with Maritain on a Thomist primacy of theory, had seen its consistent consequences for the temporal order, and had proposed a version of a neo-Christendom model of church-society relations that never suited American Catholicism and for that reason found no foothold in the United States.[12] In fact, Murray's arguments in favor of the no-establishment and free-exercise clauses of the First Amendment and his affirmation of harmony between American democracy and Catholicism refuted that kind of neo-Christendom model which was an implicit premise for post-Reformation confessional states. So, if Murray did hold a primacy of theory of the sort Lamb ascribes to Maritain, it did not dictate his vision of Catholicism's presence in the temporal order of the United States.

The other possibility is that Murray did not teach a new Christendom model of church-society relations, and yet held a primacy of theory. In this instance, some principle other than an unqualified primacy of theory would have formed his model of American Catholicism's relation to its social, economic and political milieu. As a matter of fact, Murray's vision of Catholicism's presence in the temporal order did not duplicate or imitate either a full-fledged new Christendom model or its descendent, the French Catholic Action model (1939–1960).[13]

According to Coleman, Maritain actually was one of the principal thinkers who contributed to the vision and praxis of this contextually specific and creative "strategic theology."[14] Catholic Action inspired the formation of the Christian Democratic parties, though not as a branch of the church. Murray never intimated in the least that a version of this would be a solution to secularization or to the citizenry's weakening grip on America's public philosophy. Coleman states, too, and on this point could agree with Lamb's interpretation of Maritain, that "the Catholic Action syndrome and the strategic theology which underpinned it still retained vestiges of the neo-Christendom ideal inasmuch as it fostered inordinate expectations for Catholicism's *directly political* impact upon its host society."[15] The assumption in the Catholic Action model was that "Catholics would be inserted into the political or economic order through the necessary intermediate buffer of an explicitly Catholic, even if not official Church, organization or party."[16] Precisely this assumption was at odds, Coleman points out, with "the American case" in which "citizens . . . directly insert themselves into the political order through secular political and economic organizations."[17] Murray, unlike Maritain, did not teach, advocate or lend support to anything resembling the premises or social reality of a Catholic Action model or an American variation on the Christian Democratic party strategy. Therefore, if he held a primacy of theory, this was not the main principle forming his position on church-state or church-society relations.

Comparing Murray with Maritain has detailed the kind of dogmatism at issue. The issue is how Murray could share in a primacy of theory without by that principle binding *We Hold These Truths* to a dogmatism prescribing a practice according to the neo-Christendom model of church-society and church-state relations. The import of the inquiry lies in its locating and identifying exactly why, in fact, Murray did not present that model when, from the same or similar premises, Maritain did. Upon this depends not only the accessibility of his book to readers starting from within a different situation in American Catholicism, but the possibility of dialogue with that book and not simply monologue from it. Few things squelch a dialogue between reader and text more than dogmatism, and few forms of dogmatism would be less significant to American Catholics convinced about social justice than one which ruled out from the start any meaning in praxis except that which theory put there.

Theory and Practice in *We Hold These Truths*

The following approach to and study of Murray's text will involve a qualified version of Hans-Georg Gadamer's hermeneutical appropriation of Aristotle's idea of praxis.[18] Hermeneutics, despite Gadamer's recurrent recourse to the exemplary significance of the phenomenon of play,[19] is humanism at work. Or, from another side, hermeneutics is everyone's daily practice of interpretation coming into self-knowledge and self-possession.[20] While not a strategy for social change, it does open up possibilities pertinent to social transformation. Attention to interpretation, for example, releases the poor and oppressed from just that overly restrictive description which omits reference to cultural, linguistic, religious and national specificity. The familiar phrase, the "Third World," adverts to certain important, and largely economic, features of domination and oppression, but in no way hints at the differences between, for example, northern Brazil and southern India, Ethiopia and Zaire. It also connotes something after, and less than, a "First World." There need be no presupposition that hermeneutics exists in unspoken alliance with the interests of a western bourgeois status quo. Richard J. Bernstein quotes Gadamer that:

> It is a grave misunderstanding to assume that emphasis on the essential factor of tradition which enters into all understanding implies an uncritical acceptance of tradition and socio-political conservatism. . . .[21]

This approach to Murray does not oppose itself to, nor completely identify with, Gustavo Gutierrez's sweeping affirmation of "the importance of human action as the point of departure for all reflection"[22] and a primacy of praxis in liberation theology. Nonetheless, in regard to theology, which was the horizon for *We Hold These Truths* though not a premise in its arguments, Gutierrez is surely correct to "recognize the work [sic: worth] and importance of concrete behavior, of deeds, of action, of praxis in the Christian life."[23]

Gadamer argues that industrialized culture and politics have transmuted Aristotelian theory/praxis into an opposition that deforms praxis by assuming that it is application of predefined theoretical knowledge.[24] However, Aristotelian praxis differed from *poesis* which was "knowledgeable mastery of operational procedures" and "production based on knowledge . . . that provides the economic basis for the life of the polis."[25] From this flows a deformity of praxis. Whereas for Aristotle, "praxis" was in a preeminent way "Aristotle's word for man's free activity in the realm of political life,"[26] "practice" has come to signify technique, whether of production, scientific experiment, technological implementation of knowledge or of other kinds.

The impact of this reduction of practice to technique has become all the more disturbing insofar as western rejection of tradition and loss of familiarity with shared truths and values inclines peoples to substitute science for prudential activity. In that cultural condition, deforming practice into technique leads to interpreting the ordinary activity of citizens deliberating matters touching the common good of society as a realm in which experts who possess the theories can better decide public policies which are akin to sociopolitical experiments needing proper techniques.[27] Gadamer's critique of this decline, part of his appropriation of Aristotelian praxis, brings to the surface but one way in which hermeneutics opens up concepts pertinent to social transformation.

It also sharpens the question about theory and practice in *We Hold These Truths:* Does Murray perpetuate that deformity of practice addressed by Gadamer and inimical to an effective option for the poor?

Does his text present human action as the concrete application of previously defined theory?

A Primacy of Theory in *We Hold These Truths*

Much in the book seems to reduce practice to technique and so to eliminate a possible understanding of action as practice. The whole volume revolves around the theme set forth by the title's borrowing from the Declaration of Independence, "We hold these truths."[28] In ensemble, their name is the "American Proposition."[29] All thirteen essays "explore the content, the foundations, the mode of formation, the validity of the American Proposition."[30] The American Proposition is the organizing idea under whose auspices Murray undertook "editing and collecting in this volume a series of essays that were done over the past decade."[31] In a broad sense, "these truths" comprise "a heritage of an essential truth, a tradition of rational belief, . . . its principles and doctrines are those of Western constitutionalism, classic and Christian . . . refined and developed in our own land to fit the needs of the new American experiment in government."[32] The Founding Fathers spelled out the foremost truths in that heritage and acknowledged them as "self-evident": "that all men are created equal, that they are endowed by their Creator with certain unalienable rights, that among these are life, liberty, and the pursuit of happiness."[33] That is the doctrine and theory of American democracy in its basic principles.

He commented that, " 'We hold these truths' meant something definite: 'There are truths, and we hold them, and we here lay them down as the basis and inspiration of the American project, this constitutional commonwealth.' "[34] The truths are oriented toward action, though, and are not simply for contemplation. They found, shape and guide a national action which has, as a whole and in its political dimension, the character of an "American experiment." The American Proposition directs the American experiment. Murray borrowed the term "Proposition" from Abraham Lincoln's Gettysburg Address and meant by it the natural-law truths as principles underlying and partially stated in the Declaration of Independence, the Constitution, and Bill of Rights. These fundamental principles are:

> —the idea that the government has a moral basis;
> —that the universal moral law is the foundation of society;
> —that the legal order of society—that is, the state—is subject to judgment by a law that is not statistical but inherent in the nature of man;

—that the eternal reason of God is the ultimate origin of all law;
—that this nation in all its aspects—as a society, a state, an ordained and free relationship between governors and governed—is under God.[35]

This is the content of the American Proposition according to Murray.

This content, and presumably Lincoln's term "proposition," has a relation to practice. To designate this aspect Murray turned to mathematics where "a proposition is at times the statement of an operation to be performed."[36] The American Proposition is truth but truth-for-action, "a theorem and a problem," "an affirmation and an intention," a "coherent structure of thought" which also is "an organized political project."[37] It is a composite of theory and practice that gives the American people their national identity and equips them for action in history. But it has an internal division between a sphere of theoretical knowledge of truths and another of practical implementation of them. Theory drives practice.

National action is, or ought to be, concrete application of the American Proposition's doctrine which organizes America's democratic institutions and guides their operations. The American experiment is the concrete application of the American Proposition which, ever needing remembrance and new applications, nonetheless "furnishes the premises of the people's action in history and defines the larger aims which that action seeks in internal affairs and external relations."[38] In each of the essays in Part One of *We Hold These Truths*, the American Proposition's truths function as the theoretical word producing the practical deed.

The four essays in Part Two similarly argue, one way and another, on the basis that the American Proposition is to be drawn down into concrete applications, in guiding determinations of the free-exercise and no-establishment clauses in the First Amendment. In its own particular way, the First Amendment, a great act of political intelligence, solved the problem of religious pluralism and social unity so well that it has become a "new doctrine." As an element in the American Proposition, and along with the rest of it, it exercises influence upon national action or practice, not directly but through the intermediate means of a secondary consensus in the American people. As occasions demand, the primary public consensus on the truths we hold, the public philosophy, is brought into a secondary level of consensus which responds to particular problems on the national agenda. This latter level emerges in public debate, including appeal to premises of a religious character, and belongs to the changing realities of American life. The decisions of the Supreme Court have a prominent role in bringing that consensus into our legal and institutional structures. Likewise, foreign relations is a field for concrete application of the public philosophy, though Murray doubted that "these truths" did, in fact, actually play a role in forming and carrying out foreign policy.[39]

Part Three carries a primacy of theory in the overall argument on behalf of a natural-law ethic that Murray posed in confrontation with its absence in American life, thought, policy and practice.[40] Governmental policies and personal conduct alike transpired in ignorance of this morality, evinced aversion to learning about it and refused to grant it doctrinal status. This flew in the face of natural-law principles continually and inescapably surfacing in practical deliberations. The heading of Part Three, "The Uses of Doctrine," set the line of argument from natural-law doctrine to its uses in concrete applications.

One of his most controversial arguments was that natural-law doctrine, filtered through Locke, indeed, but not entirely missing because of that, was part and parcel of the heritage influencing the thoughts, plans, and decisions of the Founding Fathers. More recently, he estimated, America had misplaced this tradition so that it no longer enjoyed common recognition or acceptance. The consequence has begun to appear in the form of confused governmental policies and blundering national practice. America's disorientation and uncharted course raises a question about "whether we at all hold these truths or any truths as determinatives of our purposes and directive of our policies."[41] Foreign policy seemed to Murray singularly without perceptible design or goal. So, perhaps "we have no use for doctrine—or perhaps even no doctrine to use."[42] In "the absence of an overall political-moral doctrine with regard to the uses of force,"[43] control of military forces proceeds without guidance by fundamental principles.

In Part Three, natural-law doctrine is a theoretical knowledge whose *raison d'être* is to be applied in practice. This could be conduct by an individual as a reasonable human being, or by the political order of society as an achievement by practical reason. In either kind of application, predefined, foreknown norms from natural-law theory determine actions which implement the known truths. Nor do the two final essays, "The Doctrine Is Dead: The Problem of the Moral Vacuum" and "The Doctrine Lives: The Eternal Return of Natural Law," give reprieve from the dominating sovereignty of theory. History and experience seem to teach theory because "the evolution of human life brings to light new necessities in human nature that are struggling for expression and form."[44] And a necessity for civil and political protection of the human right to religious liberty so emerged amid struggle and conflict. Its birth in the eighteenth century shows that natural law has "changing and progressive applications"[45] which earlier had not been known. The new legal and constitutional protections for religious liberty gave specification to basic natural-law principles. This seems to allow for the emergence of new meaning from action as if it were a kind of praxis bringing meaning to theory and not as implementation of prior theory.

But, it becomes clear from careful reading of Murray's text, new applications of natural law emerge in history. Incremental advances in theoretical comprehension of what befits human nature do occur. But practical interpretation preceded it. In the case of religious liberty, the step from old, Constantinian arrangements in one type or another of ecclesiastical establishment, to a new constitutional structure which divided the authority of the state from any church took place because enough practical insight had accumulated to guide new kinds of action and laws. Political and legal praxis contain meaning which theory grasps. This differs from a "practice" (i.e., technique) which implements prior theory.

No option, no orientation sums up the originality of Murray's achievement more than love for, understanding of, and struggle for freedom. Freedom in the area of religious belief and conduct, individual and ecclesial, but also freedom as the end for which a state exists, and the means par excellence toward it, were lifelong concerns and circumscribed the area of this major contribution. Other texts formulate his positions more technically and with more nuance, but *We Hold These Truths* contains a diffused, and yet leading affirmation of freedom of its own. Freedom is an element in action or practice, so that in this respect Murray begins to approximate what Gadamer means by practice.

At the beginning of *We Hold These Truths* he back-pedals away from answering a question of the day on freedom: what did the "free society" or "free government" mean as description of American society and political order? Instead of addressing American freedom, he turns toward American self-understanding and its essential principles. The actual condition prompting this redirection was that Americans' "essential affirmation that they are uniquely a people, uniquely a free society"[46] had lost a quality of self-evidence. As a way out of the resultant obscurity about the national identity, he preferred investigating "whether American society is properly civil" to the more obvious question, "whether the free society is really free."[47] His answer, shifting the focus away from the theme of freedom which *The Problem of Religious Freedom* and many of his essays handled, lay in "these truths" which define the basis of American democracy and the substance of American identity.

"These truths" are the doctrinal component of the American Proposition. Their content is a "public philosophy" and their act is the "public consensus." Definite and able to be itemized, they are a doctrine or theory with an aspect of practice because they liberate and civilize insofar as they ground social and political freedom. Their contradictory errors and falsehoods, such as a denial of divine sovereignty over nations and individuals, a separation of freedom from the obligations of conscience, and identification of a society with its state were premises for distorting social reality. In the twentieth century, such errors have lent themselves to building structures of oppressive totalitarianism.

Among these truths, the "first truth to which the American Proposition makes appeal is stated in that landmark of Western political theory, the Declaration of Independence."[48] It is an affirmation of the "sovereignty of God over nations as well as over men"[49] and it has an immediate political effect of limiting the sovereignty of the American state by placing it under that of the creator's, to which it owed respect, and by which it can be judged. This first truth negates any absolutizing of the state and thereby prevents a political order from, in principle, arrogating to itself a monopoly on values, power and norms for social life. The American Proposition conceives political community, Murray remarks, "as a form of free and ordered human life" which owed its existence neither to an utterly autonomous human reason as "the Jacobin laicist tradition of Continental Europe"[50] thought, nor to religious faith as some American Christians have imagined, nor, of course, to coercion.

Rather, the affirmation of divine sovereignty sees the political order as part and aspect of contingent, created human nature that can be known by reason. And yet, what reason could know, Christian revelation amplifies and clarifies when it divided what was Caesar's from what was God's. A fundamental affirmation of divine sovereignty is a truth that acts to block from the outset any claim by an American state that it is absolute, self-sufficient, omnicompetent or omnipotent in authority.[51] This places all human law under divine reason, divine law and divine judgment. The liberating effect is to protect human freedom from excessive demands by the political order. In that way the "first truth" adduced by Murray was foundational to American democracy, and served freedom by giving it a prominent position among the goals of the state as well as within their realization. America's political means—the rule of law, constitutionalism, sovereignty as political not sacred, the Declaration of Independence, Constitution, Bill of Rights—all recognized and gave legal, constitutional protection to something prior to themselves, namely the freedom and dignity of persons. That priority, moreover, was a principle integrated into the Declaration of Independence in its declaration that "all men [sic] are created equal." That was to acknowledge a dignity or worth in all persons insofar as they are created, not insofar as they are citizens. This made a natural priority of human nature and persons to political structures binding upon the foundational act and content of American democracy.

This priority was something implicit in, but gradually worked out from, the impact Christianity made upon the political order. Murray saw that impact to be the contribution of the dualism of church and state dividing the massive previous monism of the state. Distinguishing the realities and dividing the authorities of church and state constructed a situation wherein ecclesial, personal and social life came into its own reality as something prior to the political powers. Religious conscience was a primary reality which received a charter of independence from that division, though its individuated character was only slowly and imperfectly appreciated by church and by state.

Murray does more, that is, than propose "these truths" as the foundation for political structures giving scope to freedom and, though promoting freedom, similar to a theory or doctrine which free acts grasp and then implement. They, and the freedom they promote, are immanent and interior to the activities of those participating in them as citizens or acting on behalf of citizens. The truths and freedom are not foundations on which something separate, acts by citizens, rests because their nature is to be within those acts as horizon for and power to act. They are not an efficient but a kind of formal cause of practice, and for that reason civic action in *We Hold These Truths* has a first approximation to practice insofar as truth and freedom constitute participation in democracy. Murray's aversion to a direct treatment of "whether the free society is really free," and concentration on "these truths" in the American Proposition did not omit an indirect coverage of freedom.

One aspect of Murray's subject matter and, arguably, an implication in the text does not find a place in the foreground of *We Hold These Truths,* and yet it brings his treatment of practice closer to praxis. Bringing political institutions into existence that were commensurate with, were conditions for, and were favorable to the exercise of freedom was conflictual. The uprising against King George III, the Declaration of Independence, and the War of Independence preceded the drawing up of the charter for the new nation. This whole process, however, was not a simple matter of passing from fully defined theory through foreseen struggle to a known outcome as the practical implementing of the initial theory. It was not the case that a group of Founding Fathers sat down together to formulate, develop and refine a detailed plan in theoretical form, then subsequently decided upon a schedule for and mode of conflict with British monarchy, only to reach the Constitution as the legal practice and outcome that implemented the prior theory and design.

It seems more accurate to say that the rational passion for freedom from tyranny, in the people and especially in certain leading figures, intersected with and responded to King George III's oppressive measures. These, becoming less and less bearable in their assertion of authority without known limit, and without any form of consent, incited speech and thought onto an unexpected, though not totally unknowable path that eventually led to many unforeseen events and results. This is to vindicate a role for a rational impulse toward freedom that has not a conceptual character and cannot, therefore, be theoretical. An impulse toward, no less than an idea about, self-governance operated within the founding of the republic. Unrest under harsh measures was not an irrational feeling, a floating resentment seeking an outlet, but a lived response educated by memory, and a sense of the value in the principle of the consent of the governed. "These truths," then, which animated the Declaration of Independence were not necessarily held after the manner of a pure theory since they were inextricably tied together with that impulse energizing action toward ordered liberty which was as primary as the truths. It seems, therefore, as true to say that the truths mediated freedom to itself by means of institutions, as to say that freedom followed from putting the truths into practice.

When the full force of both the Declaration and Independence in the Declaration of Independence is allowed into the American Proposition freedom comes to view as an underived, nontheoretical constituent in a found practice. This means that Murray's American Proposition contains an implicit moment of nontheoretical appreciation for ordered freedom and for self-governance.

It can be read as an implication, too, in the principle that "the men who framed the American Bill of Rights" took their cues from the practical, legal tradition of England, rather than from a grandiose design for society which "believed the state could be simply a work of art, a sort of absolute beginning."[52] They "did their thinking within the tradition of freedom that was their heritage from England."[53] The core of the heritage was neither Locke's abstract state of nature nor social atomism, but "the medieval notion of the *homo liber et legalis*, the man whose freedom rests on law, whose law was the age-old custom in which the nature of man expressed itself, and whose lawful freedoms were possessed in association with his fellows."[54] This describes not so much the implementing of a fully known theory as a praxis guided by some basic truths about human freedom finding its way, generating new insights as it goes.

And when he discussed the "method of freedom in society" he meant citizens' uncoerced, spontaneous tendency to heed the "imperatives that stem from inwardly possessed moral principle."[55] This is the freedom as "free obedience to the restraints" of moral, and then of civil law that produces order in a democracy. This may be the nucleus of Murray's ambivalence toward practice as at the same time implementation of prior theory and an uncoerced freedom in obeying conscience. It may be that his position blends together two aspects of freedom, each with a distinct dynamic. Freedom as the end of the state is an objective toward which the political order and civil activity tend; a society freed by its own state for activities over and above political tasks is the goal. As an objective, it needs something that could seem like implementation of a foreknown moral principle. But freedom is also the means to the goal insofar as it is already exercised, under law and according to its own native power, which make it more like a formal principle interior to that exercise and something other than implementation of theory because of its underived coprimacy with "these truths."

A Logic of Praxis in How the "Public Consensus" Learns from New Experiences

There is tension, therefore, between Murray's tendency to locate meaning and truth entirely in a theoretical knowledge which, in relation to practice, has an unqualified primacy, and a tendency toward locating meaning and freedom in a practice whose content of freedom is coprimary with theory and whose content in regard to church and state can at times anticipate theory. Six specialized themes, only one of which can be examined here, support the conclusion that, though much in *We Hold These Truths* seems to reduce practice to technique, in significant ways Murray also treats action as meaningful freedom capable of containing new understanding. These themes are usually considered facets of historicity and will be familiar to any reader of Murray. Here they can be noted as indicators of how action in history is more than technical implementing of theoretical knowledge yet is reasonable and can be progressive.

These themes are:

1) the role of decision and action in the progress in western political institutions to rightful independence from the church;[56]
2) the importance of the religiously pluralist social reality to which the First Amendment religion clauses were a reasonable response;[57]
3) conduct of church-state relations sometimes in advance of an adequate doctrine;[58]
4) the development of the public consensus in America on the basis of new experiences;[59]

5) absorption of lessons from history into church-state doctrine;[60]
6) unreserved, lived acceptance of the First Amendment by American Catholics.[61]

In these respects, too, *We Hold These Truths* tends to treat practice as irreducible to technique. Because both the truths in the American Proposition and an irreducible moment of freedom are coprimary and mutually formative, it can be concluded that Murray worked with an unclarified dialectic between theory and practice. To some extent, then, action approximates practice as understood by Gadamer. The primacy of theory is paralleled by a capacity in practice to contain and express meaning prior to its theoretical concept. To that extent Murray departs from the "ascent to Being" and "descent to action" found by Lamb in Maritain. In Murray, an undefined kind of priority of action to thought admits some content in action or practice prior to, and the source of, theoretical knowledge of the same content. An actual but obscure mode of influence upon theory joined with a clear and professed movement from theory to practice is the theory-practice relation in *We Hold These Truths*. Finally, an unclarified theory/praxis dialectic is the reason Murray's concept of the church's social mission in America presented an alternative to, rather than a species of, Maritain's historical ideal of a new Christendom.

Of the six specific themes which likewise demonstrate that *We Hold These Truths* does not unequivocally reduce practice to technique, the ongoing development of the public consensus shows how Murray acknowledges, yet cannot give primacy to, practice. In "The Origins and Authority of the Public Consensus: A Study of the Growing End," he outlined and approved a proposal put forward by Dr. Adolf A. Berle in *Power without Property*.[62] Berle's idea helped Murray explain how the foundational truths affirmed by the Declaration of Independence and held in consensus by citizens were kept alive. Murray saw a principle of development for the content of the public consensus. Far from being a fixed deposit of truths "closed to all change and addition . . . complete and perfect, beyond need or possibility of further development,"[63] the consensus has the aspect of "an open-ended action" tending toward either growth or decline. If "these truths" are doctrine, they nonetheless are doctrine that can develop in a way similar to that development of Christian doctrine described by Cardinal Newman and applied by Murray to the church's teaching on religious liberty.

One of the most challenging new realities to confront "these truths" was "the great sprawling Thing known as the American economy."[64] Addressing and giving specific response to new realities moved the consensus along by applying its normative implications to new situations.

One of the ribs of the consensus was the rule of law. Though not by nature wrong or even problematic, "science, financial acumen, productive enterprise, and the skills of business management" have combined to produce an economy "which is now coming to be recognized as also a strange and new sort of polity."[65] The American economy has power to affect how people live. It exerts decisive influence on the political order. Distribution of its power, moreover, has not been wide but "concentrated in a relatively few great corporations—more exactly, in their managements, or concretely, in the hands of a few men who in effect direct the activities of the economic-political system, determine its forms, create and distribute its profits and select the path of future growth."[66] This phenomenon raised a question about the rule of law.

Was the power unlimited by law and tantamount to a new form of tyranny analogous to that of King George III? Murray asked, "Is this omnipresent power also somehow an omnipotence?" In reference to the Bill of Rights, he asked two specific questions. First, "How does this [economic] power establish its legitimacy, as all power must, if it is not to be indicted as a usurpation?"[67] And second, "Before what bench or bar may this power be summoned for judgment on its uses to know if perhaps they be not abuses, and therefore an exercise of tyranny?"[68] Berle's thesis answered that citizens themselves had the means to demand accountability from the economic system.

Their public consensus, applying the more basic consensus on truths and values foundational to America, acts through the instrument of public opinion which can demand political intervention in cases of demonstrable abuse of economic power. Berle defined the "public consensus" as

> a set of ideas, widely held by the community, and often by the (business) organization itself, and the men who direct it, that certain uses of power are "wrong," that is, contrary to the established interest and value system of the community.[69]

Berle's definition of the "public consensus" derived from and applied the content of those primary truths which Murray referred to as a "public consensus."

Berle, that is, located a secondary consensus applying primary truths to the task of determining the aims and plans of America at a given time. It consisted less in clearly defined, exactly stated precepts than in mainly unstated premises from which issued, on occasion and in regard to troubling cases, an empirically detectable public opinion. Public opinion, according to Berle, "is the specific application of tenets embodied in the public consensus to some situation. . . ."[70] The secondary consensus and public opinion, naturally, underwent change in the form of development due to solving new problems.

Berle explained how "students, writers, financial analysts, business-men, economists" work on the edge of the prevailing consensus to evalu-ate "the results of (particular business practices) for good or evil."[71] They arrive at an unofficial, informal convergence, a collective value judgment which enters into the public consensus. From there, it emerges as a criterion applied to specific practices by citizens at large in their own deliberation. They then put the pressure of public opinion upon political officials to correct a commonly perceived abuse. Public authorities, fi-nally, respond with legal measures designed to safeguard the good of the citizens.

Berle concluded, and Murray agreed, that:

> It seems that the ultimate protection of individuals lies not in the play of economic forces in free markets, but in a set of value judgments so widely accepted and deeply held in the United States that public opinion can energize political action when needed to prevent power from violating these values.[72]

Murray endorsed Berle's analysis of how America's foundational truths came into play in a process applying them to new cases.

But for Murray this was to integrate moments of both economic and political practice into the formation of doctrine. Neither American eco-nomic progress nor political use of public opinion proceeded purely from predefined theories. Economic progress had not occurred under the supervening tutelage of one particular reigning and comprehensive theory which dictated exactly how science, technology, financial acumen and productive enterprise were to act in cooperation. There had been an overall practice resulting from many far from completely coordinated initiatives flowing from piecemeal, *ad hoc* calculations. Murray saw and accepted that. He gave a more obvious welcome to Berle's explanation of how citizens of the nation retained some capacity to assert and to obtain justice in public policy in the face of colossal power to turn everything to the self-interests of the economic system.

This capacity was in a political practice in language and thought, taking rise in "careful university professors, the reasoned opinions of specialists, the statements of responsible journalists, and at times the solid pronouncements of respected politicians."[73] Their wisdom passed to citizens at large who called for public intervention. The direct effect was change in policy; the indirect effect was that the citizens modified their public consensus. They contributed to applying a new criterion. Change in regulating business practices in turn changed the prevalent consensus. Nonetheless, the movement was from the wisdom of experts to the practice of citizens. To this extent Murray persevered in a primacy of theory by locating the first movement toward evaluation of a new reality in thinkers and speakers whose theoretical reflection draws up a basic response.

And yet, in Murray's analysis, practice by citizens contains deliberation and initiative toward change, not resignation to passive compliance with the wisdom of pundits. Citizens possess an independent starting point for action in their own undiminished hold on and share in a primary consensus.

Concluding Critique: Despite a Theory-Praxis Dialectic, Repressed Practice Distorts Interpretation of How Catholic Acceptance of the First Amendment Occurred

Murray's ambivalence on practice in *We Hold These Truths* can be described as an unclarified dialectic of theory and practice. Neither was abolished; each had its contribution; each affected what the other was. This actual but incompletely conceived dialectic also can be understood as an instance of what Gadamer designates "application," in which theory and practice become codeterminative of each other. Murray was at once too wary of American pragmatism to permit a fuller account of an independent practice, and too versed in history, too committed to freedom, and too opposed to doctrinaire treatment of religious liberty and the First Amendment to stifle practice. Murray's position on the First Amendment fails to conceive and integrate the impact of practice on theory. This prevented clarity about the nontheoretical nature of Catholic acceptance of the First Amendment.

Here, in subject matter central to *We Hold These Truths*, we find practice obscured in its aspect of possessing meaning underived from prior theoretical doctrine. Two essays, "E Pluribus Unum" and "Civil Unity and Religious Integrity," address the congruence between Catholicism and the American Proposition, particularly the First Amendment. They treat the congruence as an absence of contradiction and conflict and a presence of harmony between Catholic and American theories. The common principles are: 1) "the sovereignty of God over nations as well as over individual men";[74] 2) "the tradition of natural law and natural rights";[75] 3) "the rule of law, the notion of sovereignty as purely political and therefore limited by law, the concept of government as an empire of laws and not of men";[76] 4) "the principle of the consent of the governed";[77] 5) "the principle that the state is distinct from society and limited in its offices toward society";[78] 6) "Acton's phrase, that freedom is 'not the power of doing what we like but the right of doing what we ought.' "[79] These principles in the American Proposition were amenable to American Catholic consciences in the sense that they were already in Catholic tradition. They needed only mutual recognition.

"Civil Unity and Religious Integrity" went on to spell out the principles on which Catholic consciences thoroughly integrated the First Amendment religion clauses: 1) The First Amendment is good law, and "the primary criterion of good law . . . is its necessity or utility for the preservation of the public peace, under a given set of conditions";[80] 2) the no-establishment clause affirmed the venerable distinction between the temporal and the spiritual orders, though "the ancient distinction between church and state had to be newly re-affirmed in a manner adapted to the American scene";[81] 3) the free exercise clause provides the church with "a stable condition of right and of fact within society";[82] 4) "the goodness of the First Amendment as constitutional law is manifested not only by political but by religious experience"[83] [of the church's freedom to perform its mission]. On these grounds Catholic acceptance of the no-establishment and free exercise clauses was principled and arose from conscience, not from expedient toleration adapting to what it could not avoid.

Catholic American consciences integrated the American Proposition in general and the First Amendment in particular, not only as a matter of historical fact, but did so on principle. What made this acceptance possible and, indeed, motivated it "was the evident coincidence," Murray concluded, "of the principles which inspired the American Republic with the principles that are structural to the Western political tradition."[84] His task was to explain the "coincidence of principles" and to do so by presenting them as truths in the theoretical order.

In "E Pluribus Unum," he wished to turn from the lessons of history and to explain the congruence within the coincidence of being American and Catholic. His success stating that "coincidence of principles" involves, however, obscuring the nontheoretical manner in which it for the most part occurred in the consciences of millions of Catholics. Not so many would have had defined and theoretical positions on natural law, constitutional limitation of government, the origin of the First Amendment, and the coincidence in moral principle between Catholicism and the American Proposition. Practice, aware enough of actual conditions and laws, appreciative of freedom without being instructed in natural-law ethics, was the nontheoretical reality in which Murray participated, on which he relied, and which he explained.

He honored, indeed, an American Catholic past marked by adherence to the First Amendment. "We have behind us," he recalled, "a lengthy tradition of acceptance of the special situation of the Church in America, in all its differences from the situations in which the Church elsewhere finds herself."[85] He commemorated this "lengthy tradition of acceptance" of the First Amendment, but just as quickly dismissed it in favor of theoretical explanation of its content. The "tradition of acceptance" did not lead him into its nontheoretical content. And for a clear reason, "for it is a question here of pursuing the subject, not in the horizontal dimension of history but in the vertical dimension of theory."[86] He wanted to specialize in exposing the theoretical reasons— "the vertical dimension of theory"—for harmony between Catholicism and the "American Proposition." He didn't wish to recapitulate the "tradition of acceptance"—"the horizontal dimension of history."

As a result, the role of practice in that "tradition of acceptance" dwindled first into "history," a stream of successive, contingent facts which thought explained systematically, finally to vanish inside theory. Murray buried the nontheoretical, practical content in the "tradition of acceptance." The meaning of "experience" as sense-experience hid the subjects of that experience, retiring from view, for example, the lay believer/citizens whose acceptance constituted in large measure the tradition. Consequently, the nontheoretical substance may be said to be located somewhere beneath or between the lines of Murray's text. Excavating that subject matter and returning it to view can keep *We Hold These Truths* open to the practice of Catholic laity, and an option for the poor.

4 | Remembering a Just Deed: The Maryland Experiment in Tolerance

A "Tradition of Acceptance"

Speaking to fellow Catholic Americans, Murray remarked that, "We have behind us a lengthy historical tradition of acceptance of the special situation of the Church in America."[1]

"Acceptance" was more than "coexistence within the American pluralistic scene"[2] by adjusting to unalterable external realities. It signified principled participation in the same national heritage as other citizens, a morally deliberate position whereby "American Catholics participate with ready conviction in the American consensus"[3] on the American Proposition's truths. The "acceptance," moreover, had such unofficial and universal life, such generation-after-generation force among American Catholics, that he referred to it as a "tradition." It was never merely one school of opinion, nor was it ever a bookish norm languishing in the pages of episcopal pronouncements.[4] Murray undertook to explain why and how the "tradition of acceptance" was a unanimous and collective consent informed by traditional Catholic doctrine.

But Murray headed into what he called "the vertical dimension of theory" instead of describing the "horizontal dimension of history."[5] This section will show that these alternatives hid from view the actual nature of that "tradition of acceptance." From 1776 onwards, but especially after 1850, this was a tradition of practice prior to, and not derived from, theoretical argument or doctrine. This pretheoretical reality had been developing in silent anonymity in millions of people who brought into harmony Catholic belief and a new way of relating to the state in practice and thought. After a stately "Republican interlude" (1776–1815),[6] tumultuous waves of immigrant Catholics entered upon, apparently without crises of conscience, a new way of life which integrated their Catholicism with the American consensus, including the First Amendment's religion clauses.

Murray's subject matter, then, was a legacy won by generations of

American Catholics who harmonized their religious tradition with their political condition. Murray did not perform an act of discovery or invention when he explained that harmony. Rather, the discovery or invention was the accomplishment of American Catholicism's unheralded millions. Relying upon an already achieved and all but unanimously cherished new practice of religious liberty, without the least impulse toward establishment,[7] Murray gave American Catholicism the advantage of clearly conceived theory. It would be incorrect, however, to imagine that Murray single-handedly performed the feat of solving "the problematic that confronted American Catholicism from its very beginning—Could one be both Catholic and American at one and the same time?"[8] No less, perhaps all the more, is it worth recalling that millions had decided the issue, unreckoned and unrecognized, before Murray thought it through so brilliantly. No confused picture of Catholic practice and thought demanded Murray's theoretical work. To the contrary, the massive and simple fact of his coreligionists' practice in all the solidity of its unanimity was the datum. The frantic and partisan polemic against his theory by a few American Catholic theologians was negligible and disconnected from this primary datum.[9]

The "tradition of acceptance" was active practice, not just accumulated experience. The practice occurred in the workplace, in cooperation with fellow citizens of other beliefs or none, in speaking in the public debate of the political community, in confident assurance that the First Amendment religion clauses were for the common good. At bottom, adherence to the practice of religious liberty rested on realization that "the consent given to the law is given on grounds of moral principle."[10] Taken for granted, as if its reasonableness were self-evident, "Catholic participation in the American consensus has been full and free, unreserved and unembarrassed, because the contents of this consensus . . . approve themselves to the Catholic intelligence and conscience."[11] But this approval was not necessarily a considered theoretical conclusion. It was enacted and lived. The active aspect of "Catholic participation in the American consensus" was a practice making visible an untutored application of Catholic tradition. Catholic moral sensibility simply found in the American political order something akin to itself, something worthy of honor, a constitutional-legal order recognizably deserving of consent from a spontaneous affinity not needing laborious arguments.

The tradition of practice whose meaning Murray expounded was uninterrupted and unanimous but mainly in the form of silent, unargued, nontheoretical, anonymous action. The conviction held by Catholic Americans from 1776 onwards embraced the American Proposition and the First Amendment as entirely compatible with their living of Catholic faith. A convinced harmony between Catholicism and American democracy informed Catholics' activities within the ordinary duties incumbent on American citizens, from paying taxes to voting to serving in the armed forces to serving in public office. Likewise, it was immanent in those activities by which Catholics elected to public office discharged their civic responsibilities. Their "acceptance" of the church's "special situation" in America was active, had the nature of practice primarily, and had an interiority not identical with a theoretical concept synthesizing elements from the Catholic and American traditions. Their "acceptance" was an acted-on, guiding, practical, enacted synthesis, not a theoretical one.

A. Counter-Practices?

Nor did a mid-nineteenth century option for organizing Catholic schools contravene the "acceptance." It was understood by Catholic parents precisely as an exercise of their acceptance of the First Amendment guarantee to liberty in religion. Despite this, some Americans perceived a critique of the public school as "un-American"[12] activity. The option for a Catholic school system was made in the first place because "Catholic lay people put a primary value on the need for religious instruction."[13] Although informal religious education at home remained essential, in the mid-nineteenth century there was "a shift from the primacy of informal religious education to formal religious instruction, from family to school."[14] The option for formal religious instruction took place within a form of Catholic church life and work that, from the War for Independence onwards, "depended on the voluntary support of a committed laity."[15] Even so, Catholic schools would not have been feasible without 40,000 religious women who, in 1900, as members of 119 congregations, 91 of which came from Europe or Canada, toiled on behalf of American Catholic families.[16] Too, episcopal authorization and promotion insured that the option for Catholic schools became an ecclesiastical mandate with the stature of official policy that, along with the moral authority of the bishops' policy, guaranteed access to collected funds.

Thus, Catholics' acceptance of their situation in America was not a feckless conformism or compromise of principle. Nor was it dissent from the ethos and institutions of American democracy. To be sure, initiative toward a separate school system did arise from what Catholics saw as a "quasi-establishment" or "voluntary establishment"[17] of religion that instituted Protestant hymns, prayers and Bible reading. This did not, they thought, respect the no-establishment clause in the First Amendment. Instead, it seemed to make the public school house an "established church of the American republic."[18] Critique of an institution that seemed to violate the First Amendment no-establishment clause took shape in a practice of dissent from, and construction of an alternative to, the public school system. Their hope for religious liberty and espousal of the free-exercise clause was active in their dissent and their alternative. It was practice expressing their constitutionally guaranteed right to free exercise of religion. Their objectives were an education not carried out in conjunction with religious practices contrary to their beliefs and, positively, in connection with Catholic faith and morals. They saw both as enriching American public life.

A second phenomenon that might appear to dilute the unanimity of the "acceptance" of American democracy was a culturally conservative reaction against *fin de siècle* "Americanism."[19] "Surveying the beginnings of the Americanist episode from the vantage point of one hundred years" said one scholar, "it appears as a case study in the relationship between Catholicism and American culture."[20] "Americanist" bishops, clergy and laity favored maximum assimilation in regard to the English language, relations with Protestant Americans, and American culture. They tended to see American conditions as uniquely and providentially suited to allow the Catholic Church to flourish. Bishop Bernard McQuaid and others who reacted against the "Americanism" of Archbishops James Gibbons and John Ireland, Bishop John Keane and Monsignor Denis O'Connell, felt more deeply, or at least appreciated in a different way, the values in European cultural, linguistic and religious mores.

According to one interpretation, opponents of Americanism "simply assumed Catholicism and the American way of life to be fundamentally at odds."[21] And so, the most they could hope for was "a kind of mutually advantageous truce between two hostile cultures" (Catholic and American).[22] This interpretation, however, exaggerates the degree to which American conservators of Catholic European religious mores were antagonistic to values and institutions in America. Conservative opponents, no less than progressive advocates of Americanism, were only too glad to leave behind the European custom of an established church. Criticism of Americanism never proceeded from opposition to anything conceived so broadly as the "American way of life."

Nor did dissent from America's charter documents or the ethos and the institutions of American democracy underline the critique of public schools. Opposition to "Americanism" was an unwillingness to acquiesce in customs, values and institutions infused with an obviously Protestant ethos. It did not even begin to touch matters pertaining to the foundations and structures of the political and legal orders. Those who protested an "Americanist" strategy they saw as an over-enthusiastic assimilation of American mores likewise held an unreserved commitment to the First Amendment.

This commitment, essential to what Murray called the "tradition of acceptance," was not necessarily enunciated in clear, theoretical terms because it was taken for granted as a common and principled practice. An historian of American Catholicism asserted that, in the case at least of the bishops,

> the fundamental principle of the separation of Church and State has always been accepted by the American hierarchy from the time of Archbishop Carroll to our own day.[23]

He went on to report that his research had not located

> a single instance where an American Catholic Bishop had given expression, either publicly or privately, to a view at variance with the statement of the chairman of the Administrative Board of the National Catholic Welfare Conference when in January, 1948 he said: "No group in America is seeking union of church and state; and least of all are Catholics. We deny absolutely and without qualification that the Catholic Bishops of the United States are seeking a union of church and state by any endeavors whatever."[24]

So much were bishops and laity agreed that further examination of the originating moment of episcopal practice in the person of the first American bishop, John Carroll, has the unexpected result of reinstating a primary role for lay Catholic practice in the "tradition of acceptance."

B. Origins of Practice: John Carroll

John Carroll imbibed the novelty of religious toleration as part of his Catholic faith and upbringing in a family that shared the Maryland Catholic tradition of religious tolerance. Long after Maryland's founding (1634), this conscientious practice "persisted at least among Catholics of Maryland up to the days of the Continental Congress."[25] Theirs was not theological compromise with that "denominationalism" which "especially among the mainstream churches of British origin . . . came to constitute a virtual ecclesiology."[26] Denominationalism repudiated the principle that any one church alone could be the true church though "none was denied the right to the Christian name."[27] This degree of indifference to ecclesial life, activity, structure and belief did promote political as well as religious tolerance by asserting a theological equality among all ecclesial bodies. This easily translated into equality of all before the law. According to denominationalism, no one church could propose on theological principle that it was, in an ultimate way, preferable to any other. Denominationalism did give an impetus to legal intolerance of any (Christian) religion.

The Maryland Catholics, on the other hand, practiced religious tolerance from another principle. They held that the Catholic Church was indeed the one true church, but acknowledged that this was a matter of the spiritual order which involved no basis for legal preference or constitutional establishment in the temporal order. The traditional Maryland principle was a practice expressing a difference between the spiritual and temporal orders. This was the Catholic practice that John Carroll presupposed when, before his appointment to the office of Superior of the American mission, he wrote to the Vatican advising that whoever was appointed should be an American. He wanted his fellow Catholics and fellow Americans to be free from any doubt about the kind of bond American Catholics had to the pope in Rome.[28]

The bond was purely of a spiritual nature and belonged to the spiritual, not the temporal, order. This meant that the jurisdiction of a pope in regard to an American Catholic invoked a kind of obedience utterly unlike that due to a European monarch by one of her subjects, unlike too the kind of obligation due to any political authority of whatever sort. The Catholic's obedience was, Carroll pointed out, to "the Pope, as Spiritual head of the church";[29] it was devoid of "any dependence on foreign jurisdiction"[30] in the temporal order. Carroll was convinced that the only kind of papal jurisdiction belonging to Catholic faith was

> that which being purely spiritual, is essential to our Religion, to wit, an acknowledgment of the Pope's spiritual Supremacy and of the see of St. Peter being the center of Ecclesiastical unity.[31]

This meant also that American Catholics were not enfeoffed to the pope as if they were living in the temporal order of the papal states.

Carroll had a heritage of pre-Revolutionary religious tolerance, that is, arising from a uniquely American (i.e., Marylandian) appreciation of practical implications in the difference between the spiritual order of religion and the temporal order of the state. It was the most natural and obvious thing in the world for this first bishop and resident Catholic, after 1776, to embrace religious liberty as "a fundamental right endorsed by the Revolution."[32] For example, Catholic opinion in Maryland opposed a bill before the state assembly in 1784 that would tax people for the support of all religious denominations. Most Catholic delegates to the assembly opposed the bill. John Carroll argued against it by appealing to that suffering of state persecution well-known to English Catholics and non-conforming Protestants, and then known again by Maryland Catholics and Protestant non-conformists after Virginia reestablished religious conformism on the conquered soil of Maryland. "[We] have all smarted heretofore," he reminded the delegates, "under the lash of an established church, and shall therefore be on our guard against every approach to it."[33] When consecrated the first bishop in America in 1788, his commitment to a practice like that prescribed by the First Amendment in 1791 was firmly in place and of a piece with that Maryland practice of tolerance his family had held as a part of Catholic tradition.

The "tradition of acceptance" to which Murray adverted had a conspicuous commencement in the practice of the first bishop in the new Republic, John Carroll. But, whereas Murray's essay situates this acceptance in the period following the founding of the Republic, his subject matter already had been in existence as a tradition of practice for one hundred forty-two years before 1776. And that heritage of Catholic, pre-Revolutionary religious tolerance was in the first instance a lay practice. In effect, Bishop John Carroll did no more than authorize a long-standing lay Catholic habit. He did not inaugurate a new and unfamiliar orientation suddenly needed as a way of adjusting to the First Amendment. Catholic religious tolerance dated to 1634 and the founding of Maryland. This was the proto-practice out of which the "tradition of acceptance" emerged. It was the beginning of that pretheoretical reality which became his subject matter.

C. Origins of the Practice: Calvert Maryland

The continuity between Maryland's religious tolerance and the First Amendment's religion clauses may consist above all in one excellence in the latter which Murray defended. He argued that "the constitutional clauses have no religious content" and consequently are not "articles of faith" but "articles of peace" which are "invested . . . only with the rationality that attaches to law."[34] The religion clauses contained the practical rationality of good law, not a theory of church or society, of human nature or of belief. What Murray did not advert to was that Maryland had enshrined that rationality in laws guaranteeing religious tolerance on the basis of a distinction between the spiritual and temporal orders, and their respective authorities.

The way in which the "tradition of acceptance" began was not in clear, written, theoretical synthesis of elements from Catholic tradition with some new political philosophy. It came about in the free, legal initiative of the Lords Baltimore, George and his son Cecil Calvert, in proposing legislation for tolerance of religion in seventeenth-century Maryland. This practice extended to the prudent polity of their resident governors who supervised the colony's political and legal activities. It received formal consent and informal abiding from norms of tolerance by the Maryland assemblymen, Maryland's chartered gentlemen-adventurers, from the yeomen and servants.

Maryland's short-lived and ill-fated experiment in religious liberty probably "contributed even less than Rhode Island's to the development of religious freedom in the American colonies."[35] But its failure to set a new standard and to gain permanence was due to forces beyond the Calverts' control. The rest of "the world was not ready for its extraordinary example of Catholics and Protestants living together in relative harmony while freely and openly practicing their respective religions."[36] Within Maryland itself, "Marylanders, and for that matter, English men and women, were not ready for broadly based religious toleration in the seventeenth century."[37] Nevertheless, the Calverts' "efforts to implement religious toleration cannot be diminished by its ultimate failure, for they pointed to the future."[38] There is no reason to deny that, whatever its fate as precursor to the First Amendment, it was a practice that founded a peculiarly New World kind of Catholic commitment to no-establishment and free exercise of religion.

To be sure, the "origins and nature of toleration in Maryland were once controversial historiographical issues."[39] Two lines of interpretation handled the known facts in conflicting ways. "The more popular interpretation credited the Calverts with founding religious liberty in the New World," while another "played down the importance of religious toleration, ascribing it to mere expediency on the part of Lord Baltimore (as if doing something expedient were bad)."[40] Not surprisingly, neither interpretation is entirely satisfactory.[41] While the former line exaggerates the debt of the Republic to the Calverts, the latter view ignores the inherent value in the institution of tolerance by concentrating excessively on inferred motives for it.

Consequently, it seems preferable to propose that the Calverts instituted a Catholic practice of religious liberty and church-state separation in seventeenth-century Maryland. Their initiative ended thirteen centuries of a Constantinian model for church-state polity and can be recognized as the proto-practice from which the "tradition of acceptance" emerged.

Before considering recent historiography, it will be well to note those features in the new polity and practice that justify stating that, "[p]rior to 1689, the religious world of Maryland was unique."[42] The central and obvious fact was that, "[u]nlike in Massachusetts and Virginia, religious toleration was the law of the land."[43] But if the existence of that law is an incontrovertible fact, controversy over its motives, ideas, values, objectives, plan and meaning make it advisable to set forth briefly the leading and indisputable aspects of Maryland's toleration.

First, Calvert policy from 1633 on broke away from the post-Reformation version of the generally accepted principle that "it was the duty of the magistrate (i.e., the monarch) to protect the true faith."[44] The *cuius regio, eius religio* settlement brought political and civil relief to Protestant-Catholic conflicts. This, however, introduced several practical consequences touching religion. Religion and political authority were joined in the person of the ruler, whose religion became normative for all under his rule. "In England as elsewhere in post-Reformation Europe, civil peace and political stability rested on the belief that the subjects' religion must conform to that of the ruling monarch. . . ."[45]

However, in England the sufferings of the Catholic minority educated it to a perspective novel in Catholicism and in England. And so, "[a]s a Catholic, Baltimore was also heir to a different perspective on religious uniformity than other Englishmen."[46] English (but not, apparently, other European) Catholics "rejected the dominant concept that the religious faith of the subjects must be the same as the rulers [sic]."[47] George and Cecil Calvert, the first and second Lords Baltimore, from the very outset kept their authority as proprietors separate from the religion of their settlers. This gave new practical scope to the ancient, Gelasian principle of the nonidentity of spiritual and temporal powers.

They did not seek to establish Roman Catholicism, to force it upon Protestant settlers, or, for that matter, to make worship a civil obligation for Catholic settlers. There were no penal laws infringing upon conscience, though there were penalties affixed to public intolerance in the forms of various kinds of derogatory speech, as well as for civil disturbances on the Sabbath. Though the royal charter granted authority to the Proprietor to erect churches and have them dedicated, the Calverts never exercised their prerogative, probably because the grant likewise required that its exercise accord with English ecclesiastical law. For a time, Catholic and Protestant Marylanders took turns using the same building for their religious services.

Although from 1634 to 1647 Calvert appointed Catholics as governors, in 1648 he chose William Stone, a Protestant. The assemblymen faced no test of religion as a qualification for this office, and the governors were enjoined to exercise their authority impartially. The two groups that seemed least appreciative of the novelty in Calvert's policy were the resident Jesuits and the Puritans. The former thought Maryland should offer the same arrangements for clergy that were common in European Catholic nations. The latter could not extricate themselves from thinking that tolerating Catholics was conniving in support for anti-Christ. Catholic laity, the Quakers, and some educated Church of England laity, seemed the most positively inclined toward the Calvert policy of toleration and no-establishment.

Interpretation of Maryland's toleration need not take the form of adding details to historiographical reconstruction of events in Maryland. Nor need it concentrate on refining an analysis of Calvert motives, plans, and goals. Rather, relying upon historical research, yet seeing its openness to hermeneutical fulfillment, interpretation can find a proper task in explicating three texts central to the documentary evidence for religious toleration. The advantage of this approach is partially suggested by historiographical neglect of genre. All three are legal texts on religious tolerance. After considering some recent historiographical analyses, attending to the legal genre will lead to the question of justice implied by the texts.

Documentary Evidence of a Proto-Practice of Toleration

1) Instructions from the Proprietor, Lord Baltimore, Cecil Calvert to the governors and councillors aboard the *Ark* and the *Dove* for the passage from England to Maryland, November, 1633 to March, 1634:

> His Lo[PP] [Lordship] requires his said Governor and Commissioners that in their voyage to Maryland they . . . be very careful to preserve peace and unity amongst all the passengers on Shipp-board, and . . . suffer no scandal to be given to any of the Protestants, whereby any just complaint may heerafter be made by them, in Virginea or in England, and . . . for that end . . . cause all Acts of Romane Catholiques to be done as privately as may be, and . . . instruct all Roman Catholiques to be silent upon all occasions of discourse concerning matters of Religion; and . . . treat the Protestants with as much mildness and favor as Justice will permit."[48]

2) From the 1639 Acts of the Maryland Assembly:

> Holy Churches [sic] within this Province shall have all her rights and liberties. . . ."[49]

3) From the Act concerning Religion passed by the Maryland Assembly in 1649:

a. Penalties for someone who blasphemes God, someone who will, "that is, Curse Him or deny Our Savior Jesus Christ to bee the sonne of God, or shall deny the Holy Trinity . . . shall be punished with death and confiscation or forfeiture of all his or her lands or goods";[50]

b. Prohibition of irreligious speech, that is, "uttering reproachfull words of Speeches concerning the blessed Virgin Mary, the Mother of Our Savior, or the Holy Apostles or Evangelists";[51]

c. Prohibition of divisive speech, that is, calling someone a, "heretick . . . puritan . . . Jesuite . . . Jesuited papist . . . Lutheran . . . Separatist, or any other name or term in a reproachfull manner relating to matter of Religion. . . ."[52]

d. Protection of religious liberty: ". . . noe person or p[er]sons whatsoever within this Province, or the Islands, Ports, Harbors, Creekes, or havens thereunto belonging professing to believe in Jesus Christ, shall from henceforth bee any waies troubled, Molested or discountenanced for or in respect of his or her religion nor in the free exercise thereof within this Province or the Islands thereunto belonging nor any way compelled to the beliefe or exercise of any other Religion against his or her consent. . . ."[53]

Historiographical Analysis: A Question of Evidence

The variety of positions on the meaning of the texts given above can be learned from consulting historians representative of three types of historiography: the religious history of America (Sydney E. Ahlstrom); the history of American Catholicism (John Tracy Ellis, James J. Hennesey, Jay P. Dolan); and the history of Maryland's toleration (Thomas O'Brien Hanley, John D. Krugler, Thomas J. Curry).[54]

Each historian explains the phenomenon of Maryland's tolerance by recourse to the same documentary evidence used by the others. Each places the texts against a different background, for instance, a Stuart tendency,[55] a Calvert policy,[56] a seventeenth-century penchant for struggling with religion,[57] a theory of church-state relations,[58] etc. This interprets the words and statements of each text as possessing, beyond their own literal content and implication, a less obvious meaning insofar as they represent or instantiate a larger reality for which they become evidentiary. The latter meaning is not so much located in the texts themselves as if part of the content, as in the relation of that content to an external framework.

In this regard, it can be valuable to notice that these legal texts do not analyze, argue, or state a philosophical meaning. They prescribe and proscribe actual behavior. As law, the texts enjoin practice rather than disclose a theory. Law has an aspect of command, and in that respect addresses leaders and the community for the practical effect of guiding deliberations, choices and activities. To begin with, then, the historians are examining evidence of how people could and did act, rather than only evidence for the legislators' minds and motives.

Sidney Ahlstrom places the 1633 text in relation to the "extremely liberal grant of proprietary authority" by a "Protestant king of England to a Roman Catholic convert" toward the purpose "that the founder's co-religionists might be free from the statutory disabilities they suffered in England."[59]

In general, although "the undeniably democratic implications of Cardinal Bellarmine's political philosophy" may possibly have influenced Cecil Calvert and Father Andrew White, who was superior of the six Jesuit priests among the first Marylanders, the policy of toleration was motivated by a search for "freedom for Catholics and a desire for profits."[60] That blend of motives leads to the conclusion that "the common tendency to bracket Maryland with these two other colonies [Rhode Island and Pennsylvania] as 'experiments in religious liberty' confuses as much as it clarifies."[61] Maryland's "toleration is best remembered," concludes Ahlstrom, not as one of the "holy experiments" but as "one more instance of English liberality during a century when France and Spain ruled their empires without the slightest allowance for deviation from Counter-Reformation norms."[62]

Ahlstrom reads the 1633 and 1649 texts as indications of royal liberality, not of a Calvert orientation toward religious liberty. What this interpretation fails to explain is any degree of difference between royal liberality and regal whim, on the one hand, and any difference between Calvert norms on tolerance and arbitrary willfulness on the other. Was Calvert policy, then, merely an inexplicably arbitrary extension of an equally inexplicable Stuart will? Or if liberality were a matter of policy, how was it elsewhere in evidence? Little is said about the intrinsic content of the laws for tolerance.

John Tracy Ellis identifies George Calvert's motive for undertaking Maryland's founding as a combination of fulfilling what Charles Andrews had described in an earlier day as "the sacred duty of finding a refuge for his Roman Catholic brethren" with the commercial aspects of his American colony.[63] An exclusively Roman Catholic colony did not turn out to be feasible. So Cecil, son of George Calvert "saw no reason why men of different religious faiths could not join in a business of this kind if all practiced moderation and good will."[64]

In general, Ellis reads the 1633 and 1649 texts as examples of a practical solution to a pressing social and political problem. The nature of the solution was not theory but a Calvert disposition and practice whereby the English, divided by religious loyalties, could cooperate nonetheless in social, political and economic matters. The two texts present to Ellis a mingling of principle (religious toleration for the sake of cooperation and social peace) with expediency (the need to prosper economically and to succeed politically). What this view leaves unexplained is the specific kind of practicality in the Calvert solution to the problem of religious pluralism. Why were the legal texts of 1633 and 1649 precisely "practical" rather than, by contrast, utopian or impractical, in an empire and amid colonies hostile to such intolerance?

Jay P. Dolan portrays Maryland's founding as "a joint effort of Catholics and Protestants to establish a colony where 'mutual love and Amity' would prevail among people of differing religious beliefs."[65] The 1633 text expressed "Cecil Calvert's concern for the religious sensibilities of his colonists,"[66] and its opening paragraph "clearly indicated the mind of Cecil Calvert regarding the place of religion in colonial Maryland."[67] The injunction to perform acts of Catholic religion "as privately as may be" meant that "religion was to remain a private affair" because "civil harmony was the primary consideration."[68] Not only that, but the motive for seeking "civil harmony" between Protestants and Catholics was success in the tobacco trade. "Maryland was established first and foremost," Dolan asserts, "as a commercial enterprise, with profit, not religion the primary impulse."[69] The primacy of economics debunks the primacy of religious or theoretical impulses, and paints a picture in "stark contrast to Massachusetts, where a religious outlook dominated."[70] "In Maryland," to the contrary, "religion was not to get in the way of man's other pursuits,"[71] notably planting, raising and exporting tobacco to Europe.

Dolan, then, downplays the 1633 and 1639 texts as failed privatization and lifts up the 1649 text as a forerunner of the First Amendment, all under the influence of a dominating impulse toward mercantile prosperity. All three texts, consequently, were tactics in an economic strategy to raise and export tobacco. They should be read, in that light, as instruments of commercial purpose. Still, Dolan's reading omits considering the nature of the texts as law and hence as within and for the sake of a political community. This is to suppress their legal genre, and to treat them as exemplars of a mercantile pragmatism. This blurs any distinction between the political and the economic spheres, since what governs the government is not, as the texts imply, law and the proprietor, governor and assembly, but the profit motive. Appeal to the profit motive to account for ostensibly political and religious matters leaves us with unanswered questions. Why did an unprecedented, religiously pluralist settlement three thousand miles away seem commercially feasible in the first place? Was trade in tobacco, or another colonial investment, the single avenue for increasing Calvert fortunes? Were there no alternative ways for them to act from a profit motive? If so, why this way? The argument from profit motivation ignores altogether, as Thomas J. Curry[72] points out, the greater economic ease the Calverts could have enjoyed had they not converted to Catholicism. That conversion seems impossible to explain on the basis of economic expediency, and it was in some way formative upon the founding of Maryland.

James J. Hennesey follows Andrews and Ellis in identifying the motive in George Calvert's project as religious: to found a haven where English Catholics could practice their faith. While an Anglican, he founded the earlier, unsuccessful colony, Ferryland, in Newfoundland; there "Anglicans and Catholics shared Baltimore's own house for worship services."[73] This "foreshadowed developments in Maryland's history."[74] The 1633 text by Cecil Calvert, in Hennesey's reading, authorized his father's kind of tolerant practice.

The text, moreover, accompanied by the royal charter, began to do what the charter required of laws made under its auspices. The requirement was that laws be "consonant to Reason and be not repugnant or contrary but (so far as conveniently may be) agreeable to the Laws, Statutes, Customs and Rights of Our Kingdom of England."[75] The unusual feature in Calvert's specifying of what was "consonant to Reason" and "agreeable to the Laws, Statutes, Customs and Rights of Our Kingdom of England" was its return to a fundamental of English law, the Magna Carta. In 1639, Hennesey observes, the Maryland Assembly enacted its law protecting "rights and liberties" precisely in language long familiar and venerable from its use by the Magna Carta.

The 1649 restriction of tolerance to those professing Christian faith resulted from the political influence and vote of Puritans who fled to Maryland after 1642, and from Puritan pressures in England, leading Cecil Calvert to draw up his Toleration Act in the first place. What Hennesey leaves without enough explanation, is why Calvert's 1633 edict of toleration was "realistic pragmatism."[76] Does "realistic pragmatism," expedient and somehow in contrast to idealism and purity of principle, account for the exact nature of the legal measures Calvert took? How does "realistic pragmatism" in religious tolerance differ from pragmatism in assuring uniform standards in weights and measures? Precisely what kind of pragmatism was religious tolerance?

Thomas O'Brien Hanley reads the 1633 text in light of a body of

Catholic thought on church-state relations that developed between the death of Thomas More in 1535 and King Charles I's chartering of Maryland in 1632. More's *Utopia*, with its nonestablished religion and freedom from coercion upon conscience, along with Cardinal Bellarmine's writings and the pamphlets by Robert Persons and Cardinal Allen, searched for the way to distinguish in thought and conduct between two obligations, one to divine faith and another to nation. Hanley sees this as an English Catholic theory which the Calverts put into practice.

Cecil Calvert's pamphlet, *Objections Answered*, distinguished a loyal subject's faith with God from a fidelity due to king and the law of the land. The former was prior and superior to the latter, as scripture and faith clearly taught. Calvert, or the more likely author Father Andrew White, argued that attempts by a political authority to coerce a subject's conscience contrary to its faith with God for the sake of conformity with human law, brought a grave disadvantage precisely to the political order. A person coerced to compromise on what is due to God will be thereby all the more readily disposed to break faith with obligations to human authority. The 1633 text "began putting all this theory into practice."

Because the 1633 text obliged the passengers, as well as the civil authorities, to observe a tolerant practice, it "implied the reverent regard for conscience and one's 'faith with God' to which More had become so sensitive."[77] As a norm and as practice for Catholics in political authority or under it, "the distinction of church from state" in thought and in practice was the bedrock for religious toleration. The shipboard directives of 1633 "were also to be the norms of conduct in Maryland itself."[78] In that respect, Calvert's law began one of the "historical traditions of freedom which are articulated from one generation to another,"[79] namely, the Maryland Catholic tradition of religious freedom.

Generally, Hanley reads the 1633, 1639 and 1649 texts as the application of theory (English Catholic thought) to practice. Hanley does not refer to recourse to legal precedent in applying the law to a case. Rather, and to the greatest degree possible, the meaning of the texts lies in theoretical truths in the minds of the lawmakers. A purely or primarily theoretical analysis of the toleration laws has not gained widespread support from historians. Further, a matter in need of much clarification is the fundamental issue raised by Gadamer's analysis of practice. It does not consist in simply implementing previously defined theory because it involves also a dialogical relation, codetermination, between the new situation and the received tradition. Hanley's approach scants the novelty of Maryland as a situation within which its lawmakers received English Catholic theories.

John D. Krugler interprets the three texts in reference to Calvert policy, which was less than a complete plan and more than an *ad hoc* reaction, and which made toleration "the foundation of the Calverts' overall strategy."[80] The strategy was to govern in such a way as to succeed in colonizing. The central role of toleration was as a device to prevent religious conflict from interfering with Maryland's commercial success. The Calverts did not colonize, insists Krugler, for the sake of religious objectives. They did not make toleration the *raison d'être* of Maryland. Instead, "the Catholic Lords Baltimore saw religious tolerance as a means to accomplish their goal of founding a successful colony, not as an end in itself."[81] Their institution of tolerance "was not so much a philosophical posture as a practical one."[82]

Toleration was a practical concession made to compensate for a disadvantage. The Calverts and their fellow English Catholics "were a distinct minority within Maryland," while the "majority of the settlers reflected traditional hostilities toward Catholicism."[83] Moreover, across the Atlantic, Cecil Calvert had to labor within the confines of a militant Protestant country."[84] Thus, "toleration was the *modus operandi* of the Maryland Design,"[85] because Cecil Calvert "recognized that the colony's survival depended on removing religious considerations from the political arena."[86] He installed toleration as an expedient, pragmatic measure to further his goals.

Calvert innovation lay in placing civil and political unity on some foundation other than religious and ecclesiastical unanimity. The Calverts opted to build unity through "loyalty to the head of the civil government,"[87] not adherence to a religious dogma. So Cecil Calvert legislated protection for liberty of conscience in religion as something to give Protestants "in return for their obedience to him and the civil government instituted by him."[88] This bargain likewise gained Catholic loyalty because it "insured the Catholics would be protected in their own religious worship" under a Protestant governor and majority. It was part of the "Calvert design" of "gaining the loyalty of Marylanders of differing religious affiliations and tying them to the proprietary government."[89]

The three texts evince astute, secular pragmatism in service of commercial success through whatever political devices were expedient. Though legal in genre, Krugler understands them as political techniques for an economic goal. Their content, accordingly, has its meaning primarily in light of known economic objectives. What this ignores is any further consideration of the political and legal nature of these techniques or devices. It is difficult to escape the overall impression that Krugler sees Calvert toleration law as essentially an irreligious measure in service of purely economic motives and goals.

However, contemporary analysis of religion does not demand that an action be deemed religious only in reference to manifest motives, contexts and goals.[90] Contrarily, an action need not be irreligious in the absence of explicitly religious motives, contexts and goals. A good deal depends on how a religious tradition conceives of and treats specific kinds of acts. For example, as Francis Schüssler Fiorenza[91] shows, washing, eating, manual labor, fasting, etc., can be either religious or not. Therefore, toleration of religion in Maryland could conceivably be irreligious (as the Puritans thought in regard to tolerating Catholicism) but is not necessarily so.

Definitions of religion by genus and specific difference fail to locate the pervasive, diffused and unofficial way religion can influence an individual or community and seek to single out some specifically "religious" quality. While it is true that modern theology has been busy trying to differentiate that quality from the aesthetic, the moral, the scientific and the political, it cannot be regarded as having succeeded in the attempt. And the failure stems from not realizing that religion is a complex reality in which many otherwise distinct motives, goals and contexts intersect one another and receive their meaning from how a religious tradition envisions divine presence and activity in the world. As Fiorenza concludes, "there is neither a common denominator nor a specific difference, but rather a complex set of crisscrossings and intersecting patterns that makes religious actions religious."[92]

The crisscrossing of economic, political, legal, social and private motives, goals and contexts in the Calverts' instituting of toleration did not, therefore, *ipso facto* remove it from the realm of the religious. The possibility is left open that toleration of religion could be in some sense religious, on the premise that spiritual-temporal differentiation in authority flows from the Christian vision of reality and that this difference was grasped by the Calverts in a new way as an organizational principle. This is a possibility that Krugler's interpretation does not examine.

Thomas J. Curry reads the three texts in reference to Calvert subjectivity. The minds, thoughts, intentions and temperaments of the Lords Baltimore explain the texts' existence and meaning. They intended to "make their colonial enterprises havens in some sense for their fellow Catholics."[93] To this end they had "plans for religious toleration" and were willing and capable of developing "innovative religious arrangements." They held, that is, a new ideal, English Catholics and Protestants living and working in harmony. Expediency and economics did not dominate their project because "the most expedient course for both Baltimores would have been to remain Protestant themselves and to settle Protestant colonies."[94] However, founding Maryland was neither a "triumph of Catholic-inspired idealism" nor "an undertaking in which Catholicism played only an incidental part."[95] Unfortunately, they joined their farsighted religious ideal to a feudal political structure and a manorial social system.

According to Curry, the Calverts' experiment in religious toleration proceeded from a largely silent but basically new grasp of church-state relations. Beyond a pamphlet, *Objections Answered Touching Mariland* (London, 1634), "neither Calvert felt any urge to expound his views on Church and State beyond the obvious import of his actions."[96] They preferred "privacy and restraint in the religious area of their lives"[97] and Cecil Calvert's instructions in 1633 obliged the governor, councilors and Catholic settlers so to act.

The effect was to bring about a *de facto* tolerance on the transatlantic voyage and in early Maryland. Eventually, however, and without educative theoretical arguments, it proved incapable of eradicating ingrained habits of mind that foreclosed the possibility of conceiving of tolerance as a reality compatible with Christian belief. It suffered from the absence of any known precedent in Catholic or Protestant Europe that might give an example.

Curry reads the three texts as weak, legal substitutes for a change in communal consciousness that was needed in order for the Calverts to translate a new insight into social and political reality. Only a changed common consciousness and a new consensus among the Marylanders could have given the law footing and stability. But this would have required the proprietors to "launch a hitherto unheard of campaign to demonstrate both the religious and the practical value of toleration."[98] The three texts are evidence for a practical failure which saw policy and law issuing from the proprietors without also arising from, or making inroads into, the consciousness of the community they sponsored and governed. A modern insight got lost in the trammels of a feudal structure of community and politics.

Hermeneutical Completion: The Texts and Justice

The three texts also can be read in light of their explicit and implicit subject matter. In so reading them, they become evidence for their content and in that respect are self-evident. Or better, they become evidence for that larger reality, toleration as justice, whose instruments they were. This is to regain the originality of the texts as laws for a particular society rather than starting from historiographical assignation of their role within a sequence of events upon which they apparently exerted only minimal effect.

One immanent feature in historiographical analyses of the texts is a concomitant prescinding from attention to one of the most obvious attributes of law—justice. Correlative to regaining the original genre and nature of the texts as law will be an initial and far from complete analysis of the texts in reference to just law. None of the historiographical analyses takes up the practical-moral dimension of the texts, and so cannot develop a full understanding of the texts as a prescription for practice which they were prior to their later status as records of a legal practice.

Hanley, Hennesey and Curry give most respect to the texts as laws, and Ellis approaches them accurately in discussing their practicality. Curry recognizes the legal genre, but regards law as a poor substitute for consensus on the value of toleration, and to that extent minimizes the applicability of the texts in their original context. The legal genre and nature of the texts matters least to Ahlstrom, Dolan and Krugler, whose explanations, consequently, cannot escape the charge of reductionism. Hanley's reading overemphasizes the role of theory and underestimates the novelty of the laws, while Hennesey allows an obscure pragmatism to distract from the kind of pragmatism that might be an appropriate quality of law. None, again, expressly dwells on the toleration texts as just or unjust law.

Instead, each of the historiographical interpretations refers the texts and the phenomenon of religious toleration in Maryland, 1634–1689, to some other, larger reality of the time which subsumes the particular texts and this specific phenomenon, and which texts and phenomenon represent. Texts are read in light of something which they exemplify: practicality and a desire for religious freedom for Catholics on the part of the Calverts (Ellis); English liberality by King Charles I (Ahlstrom); English Catholic theory (Hanley); realistic pragmatism, a desire for religious freedom, and the Magna Carta as a precedent for the Calverts and the Marylanders (Hennesey); the impulse for commercial profit (Dolan); commercial expediency (Krugler); ineffective intuition (Curry). None, be it noted, accepts an earlier view that the texts were evidence for a toleration that was an example, like Rhode Island or Pennsylvania, of a holy experiment in liberty.

An interpretation with consciousness of the need for and right of a text to be read in its power to address the reader, does not have to ignore justice as a larger reality in light of which to read the toleration laws. This is not to advance a legal hermeneutic, but only to draw the texts into the field of meaning immediately appropriate to them, leaving to others their thorough legal interpretation.

A principle uncovered by Gadamer's hermeneutical reflection is that a legal decision interprets and applies the received tradition of relevant law, with an openness to practice, to a new case. In "The Exemplary

Significance of Legal Hermeneutics,"[99] he considers a judge applying a
known and recorded law to a particular case. The judge takes cognizance
of original and subsequent applications of the law, but with something
more than a legal historian's detachment from a need to find its applicability. In grasping the applicability of the law in a new case, the judge
supplements the original meaning of the law with an act of understanding
and interpretation not identical to grasping it as a past idea, but wholly in
accord with the normativity of the original law and its availability to
future, unforeseen cases.

A judge does not perform, first, an act of purely historical recovery
whose content is allegedly objective, then attach to it a separate, second
act descending from the realm of meaning ascertained by objective
method into a subjective and dubious application. From the outset, the
judge's understanding of the law involves interpreting its original and
subsequent application in view of the need to render a decision in a
particular case. A legal historian, not interested in actualizing the normative side of the recorded law, understands its meaning and marks its place
in the history of law. By contrast, the judge's entry into understanding
and interpretation by way of the law's accessibility to application, is not a
deterioration from historical research to an inferior orientation to
application.

Instead, in Gadamer's analysis, the judge's understanding exemplifies what occurs less conspicuously in all understanding. He notes that,
"[w]hen a judge regards himself as entitled to supplement the original
meaning of the text of the law, he is doing exactly what takes place in all
other understanding."[100] The judicial act has exemplary significance by
being a recognizable moment of that appropriation in which all thought
opens onto the self-determination and practice of the knower. The
judge's decision has another quality from a technique by which she puts
already codified law through a computation to produce a result uniform
in application to all of a pre-given category of cases.

This principle allows the further inference that a judgment instituting a law, as an act of understanding in view of a decision about particular
circumstances, has also a moment of application. The instituting of new
laws of Maryland, no less than later application of them, emerged from a
dialogical relation between English legal tradition and the Calverts' unprecedented need for cooperation among religiously divided English people. Their laws proscribed public or private coercion of conscience. All
three texts applied English law in a new religious, social and political
situation. Their applications were of a piece, and amounted, in their
inconspicuous practicality and plain language, to a rupture with the Con-

stantinian alliance between church and state prevalent in Europe since
the fourth century.

The Self-Evident Legal Genre and Political Content
of the Texts

The identification of the genre can be only an approximation at this
point, but an approximation to the relevant larger reality: positive, written law. The shipboard rules of 1633 were not a farewell address spoken
extemporaneously, but a written text exercising prerogatives and authority granted by the king to the proprietor holding royal charter to a proprietary palatinate, namely, George Calvert and his successors. In 1633
his successor was his son Cecil Calvert, "His Lordshipp." The words
address and bind to their stipulations "his said Governors and Commissioners," not with the hope of educating them to sentiments of tolerance,
but with the authority of legitimate law obliging its observance by governor, commissioners and those whom they were charged to govern. The
1633 text is the promulgation of interim law for a proprietary palatinate
by its royally chartered proprietor. Interpretation has to take that fully
into account.

The political community governed under the law, both aboard the
Ark and the *Dove* and later, with the 1639 and 1649 laws, was a proprietary palatinate. A colony could be chartered to a private corporation like
the London Company, or under the auspices of the king, as in the royal
colony of Virginia. A proprietary palatinate was, though, more than a
colony, yet less than a kingdom. It was not an indeterminate political
concoction because it had a model, the Durham palatinate in the north of
England.

A palatinate did not simply extend the territory of the kingdom of
England, but left to the royally designated proprietor a large measure of
authority to rule and to make law, almost equivalent to that of the king
whose sovereignty was too distant, from the north of England or from
Maryland across the Atlantic, to be exercised effectively. The owner of
the designated territory was the proprietor, under the king. King Charles
I himself designated the scope of authority granted to the proprietor of
Maryland in declaring that, "[t]he Proprietor has authority over matters
criminal as well as civil, both personal and property, and those of a mixed
nature. . . ."[101] Cecil Calvert's shipboard rules were within this scope,
exercised as authority vested in him by King Charles, and gave some
norms of a civil sort. They pertained to governance in the civil matter of
the public peace as affected by manifestations of religion.

The 1639 Act for the Church Liberties was not enacted solely and immediately by the proprietor because he forwarded it to the Maryland Assembly for its approval and passage into law. The assembly was chartered for the office of "advise and assent" but took upon itself a measure of initiative unanticipated, yet eventually accepted, and thereby ratified by the proprietor. This act was also the promulgation of law in written form, however mixed its authority. In language and in rights asserted, it placed itself in continuity with, and under the aegis of, the Magna Carta without seeking by that to withdraw from the transatlantic jurisdiction of Cecil Calvert or King Charles. The initiative by the assembly was linked through the Magna Carta to the principle of consent by the governed, so famous a part of the medieval document's content.[102]

The 1649 Act Concerning Religion likewise promulgated law for Maryland, also under the shared authority of proprietor and assembly. The palatinate as the political structure of Maryland ceased to exist after military conquest by the Virginians in 1689. In 1691, King William III "vacated the Baltimore charter and made Maryland a royal province."[103] In 1692, the Church of England was established in Maryland. As a result, the three texts ceased to guide behavior and lost their practical meaning as norms for conduct. Maryland's legal practice of religious toleration became a short-lived experiment in church-state separation. The texts then became evidence for something. They had been productive of tolerance.

The three texts are best understood from the point of view immanent in them, rather than from the absence of legal effect they had after 1692. They were law for the proprietary palatinate. This can be made more exact in light of the concept of law. "Law" means "rules made in accordance with regulative legal rules."[104] All three texts state rules for conduct made in accord with the charter and the proprietor's authority. "Law" refers to rules made "by a determinate and effective authority, itself identified, and, standardly, constituted as an institution by legal rules."[105] All three texts issued norms made by the proprietor, or his heir. The 1639 and 1649 laws also were passed by the Maryland Assembly. 'Law' means rules for a "complete community,"[106] usually called the state; for the Calverts and King Charles it was the kingdom of England, and yet also the palatinate, which in a number of respects approximated a "complete community." In the opinion of Sir Edward Coke, its proprietor had quasi-regal power.

'Law' is "buttressed by sanctions in accordance with the rule-guided stipulations of adjudicative institutions."[107] On this count, the 1633 directives were less than law, since they did not buttress the norms with sanctions; the 1639 law made idolatry punishable, and the 1649 code meted out severe punishments for blasphemy, irreligious and reproachful speech.

The broader use of law in a community encompasses an "ensemble of rules and institutions . . . directed to reasonably resolving any of the community's co-ordination problems."[108] The rule of law aims at the "common good of that community."[109] All three texts brought certain free activities in regard to religion under the rule of law, and were ways of resolving problems in coordinating social, political and economic life in a pluralist community. The law, practice and institution of toleration was, clearly, for the common good of Maryland.

Laws act for the common good "according to a manner and form itself adapted to that common good by features of specificity, minimization of arbitrariness, and maintenance of a quality of reciprocity. . . ."[110] The specificity of Maryland's laws on religious tolerance was the way they modified the rule of law then enforced in England in order to adapt it to the end of social peace in a populace including Catholics, Anglicans, Quakers, Puritans and Jews. The laws minimized arbitrariness by requiring officeholders to carry out their responsibilities toward all with impartiality and by removing religious affiliation from among the qualifications for public office. Residents of the palatinate were related in reciprocity by the equality all enjoyed under the law, while reciprocity between rulers and people lay in the trust that could be put in political authority—often in fact not done—because of the absence of coercion upon conscience. These two reciprocities formed the political community on the grounds of English rights and liberties, not on the basis of membership in an established church.

This effectively separated church from state and was correlate to protection of the right to religious liberty. Because the three texts are written promulgation of law and partially institute a rule of law in an (almost) complete society, an interpretive reading of them as liberality (Ahlstrom); economic tactic (Dolan); pragmatism in regard to a balance of powers (Hennesey); theory made practice (Hanley); or even as a practical solution (Ellis); as commercial expediency (Krugler); or ineffective intuition (Curry), gives too little credit to their legality within the political context of a proprietary palatinate. After all, they were the written law of the land, even if often distrusted, disobeyed, and eventually rescinded.

As such, they can be read in regard to a primary attribute of law—justice. Unjust law impedes the realization of what is practically reasonable in service of the common good. The common good is a "set of conditions which enables the members of a community to attain for themselves reasonable objectives,"[111] whether of an individual sort or those values for whose sake they collaborate in the community. The texts helped implant a rule of law which provided conditions needed for members of the Maryland political community to attain their own diverse religious objectives and to realize in common their social, political and economic goals.

The alternative, found in England and in royal colonies, was a *de facto* rule of law which enforced not only external obedience to royal authority, but also internal conformity in matters pertaining to religion. The affliction endured from these laws was a lesson on their injustice remembered by English Catholics and Quakers in Maryland, though not, apparently, by Puritans. Insofar as the texts were just laws, and this is what the historiographical interpretations overlook, they were more than means to an end, though this they were. As just laws on a matter fundamental to human life in community, they were more than instrumental to that civil harmony consequent upon their observance and existing as a just social order. They had also an intrinsic value deriving from their admission of an already existing, innate right to inviolability of conscience. Rather than conferring this right by requiring the novel duty of tolerance, they protected it by separating the rule of civil law from the authority of any church. Instead of instituting one means or another by which to achieve social peace, as if they were equally prepared and willing to use any and all means such as bribery, suppression of all religion, or manipulation by threat from an external enemy, the laws were part of the common good because they were already just in advance of the hoped-for social harmony.

Because the Maryland laws on religious toleration in 1633, 1639 and 1649 were just in recognizing to some extent an innate right to liberty in religion (mitigated in 1649), they fostered civil harmony. This was their excellence: they were first and foremost just laws at a time when this particular area of justice was still not commonly acknowledged. Their justice lay in concord with what practical, socially-oriented reason needed to promote—a condition in which persons could realize their human dignity.

Maryland's Legal Initiative and Practice: Appropriated Tradition

The texts of toleration (1633, 1639, 1649) "apply"—in Gadamer's specialized sense of an appropriation receiving part of a tradition in a way that links it to the interpreter's situation and self-understanding, and which is open to practice—elements in England's and the west's political tradition. Their application of tradition took place in, and because of, a social reality fraught with the imminent possibility that religious conflict would disable Maryland. This religious pluralism in search of cooperation became, for the Calverts and those Marylanders open to it, a new starting point for interpreting the government's duty toward religion. They were in a new hermeneutical situation.

Reading the texts enshrining the toleration laws precisely as laws, involves dialogical engagement between the reader and their claim, implied by the legal genre of the texts and their force as law for the common good, to justice. Their meaning contains, as a consequence, continual connection not only to the circumstances in which they were composed, but also to what became evident to Americans and others much later— that toleration of religious differences is a just practice in accord with basic human rights. This is to read the texts in light of, and not despite, the "temporal distance" between them and ourselves. In between the texts and our reading of them looms the achievement of the First Amendment guarantee of the church-state difference as protection for the free exercise of religion.

Acknowledging this means reading the texts in light of subsequent vindication of the Calvert option for governmental respect for religious liberty on grounds of the spiritual-temporal difference. The Calvert option contained, it has become clear, a principle of universal justice insofar as it protected the human right to religious liberty. Taking account of human rights and their ground in human dignity likewise introduces into the reading of the texts an awareness that toleration exists in a society primarily in activity or practice. The laws do not ornament, but order society. As Hanley remarks, "[t]oleration is a practice, and its practice is limited or expanded according to how one understands the state and its legitimate scope and the church as well."[112] Toleration in practice flowed from its inscription in law. The texts have the character of presenting a dialogue with England's tradition of law and politics, but also with traditions of practice in the area of English rights and liberties. For the Calverts, the Marylanders following laws on tolerance, and Catholic Americans after 1776, the kind of understanding deposited in tolerant practice need not be understood as theory. In fact, tradition is transmitted largely by means of "tacit knowledge"[113] which can be practical in nature.

Religious tolerance in Maryland, and the texts obliging it, confront us with a new practice of justice. Though inscribed in documents as law, behavior according to them was not reducible to routine technique implementing a fully defined theory. The legal texts did not present theory. Nor was tolerance routine. In fact, Maryland's practice broke from antecedent and routine ways that European governments had interpreted the social role of religion and the religious responsibilities of rulers. Maryland's toleration, based in an effective application of the long-standing, Gelasian distinction between spiritual and temporal realms, was a new application and new practice. Even if Thomas More and Cardinal Bellarmine had taught a form of tolerance, this was far from a fully defined theory needing only technical implementation of a routine sort. Toleration, then, was rational practice.

The toleration laws applied received law in a new way codetermined by the new social reality. Calvert application refused to place the Catholic Church in the legal position of an established church and proscribed intolerant word and deed. The Catholic Church, as others, had freedom to act in society but lacked authority, as did others, to superintend the political or social orders.

The laws, especially that of 1639, reclaimed the content and authority of the Magna Carta's recognition of the church's "rights and liberties" as something prior to, not conferred by, the temporal power of the king. In doing so, the Maryland Assembly invoked and gave force to an ancient distinction which Murray referred to as the Christian contribution to the political order of reality, the nonidentity of temporal and spiritual powers and societies. This difference had replaced the ancient elevation of the government to the sacred and transcendent. The core of western political and legal tradition revolved around the distinction between God and Caesar. This was what Maryland's laws of toleration understood, interpreted and applied. The legal texts issued from codetermination by, on one side, the core of the western political tradition as mediated through the Magna Carta and, on the other, by the new social reality of religious pluralism in need of civil peace. Then, as now, the only avenue to peace was justice, and often, just laws. However fragile and short-lived, Maryland's toleration laws were novel prescriptions in which universal ideas and values received from tradition (temporal-spiritual difference) gained new application. They anticipated later American law and practice because Maryland's religious pluralism similarly anticipated later American pluralism.

In addition, as norms for conduct, the laws contained and communicated to Marylanders a deepened practical knowledge of justice. They opened up the possibility of a new social and personal self-understanding in regard to religion in public life. Maryland's political order, and individual persons, when guided by the toleration laws, were under the influence of an impetus toward freedom from the old Constantinian arrangement. Tolerance meant that religion no longer filled the office of supplying social and political unity. Though its religious reality was not doubted, its ecclesiastical structures were moved away from authority over structures and institutions of civil governance. This brought freedom, insofar as the government no longer placed a claim upon religious conscience. Maryland's government did not enforce religious doctrine or exercise. With this, a new kind of self-actualization or self-determination became available to Marylanders.

Their practice of tolerance was to act justly and in a new way toward fellow Marylanders and any who might come to join them. Moreover, churches and political structures both observed this new justice grounded in the church-temporal power difference. This brings readers of Maryland's toleration laws into solidarity with an earlier struggle for justice and freedom. Unless readers are to deny that liberty of conscience is a fundamental human right, whose violation affects something as universal as our common humanity, Maryland's laws of toleration and its practice of toleration cannot be denied the attribute of justice.

Maryland's Proto-Practice of Tolerance: Justice from Justice

Practice, in Gadamer's hermeneutics no less than in Aristotle's political philosophy, is free activity by citizens. But Gadamer understands practice to arise within the citizens' solidarity in appropriating freedom, and to be at the same time a commitment to extending freedom to all human beings. It is conduct freed from individualism and characterized by a human orientation, more discovered than produced, toward communication in action as well as in language. Gadamer joins the Aristotelian concept of practice as political activity by free men [*sic*] to the Hegelian principle of universal freedom as the movement of history.

Maryland's texts of toleration were practice in an obvious Aristotelian sense of enacting public norms for just conduct in the interest of the common good of the political community. In another sense they were, as norms (did they ever become habits?) immanent in those exercising tolerance, practice in Gadamer's fuller sense. They communicated an obligation to a new type of solidarity in a mode of conduct which placed members of the political community in equality with one another's right to religious liberty. In that way, they opened the door to solidarity with the struggle for universal human freedom.

This was especially true for the protection for liberty in the 1649 Act Concerning Religion. Its newness of conduct had a universal dimension in two ways. First, it rested on the ancient Christian affirmation that, in all cases and therefore universally, obeying God and conscience has priority over obeying Caesar and political obligations should the two conflict. Secondly, it gave a fundamental and universal human reality, which can be called intellectual freedom in the matter of God, actuality by enforcing its protection. Tolerant Marylanders, not all at all times, behaved in a new manner. Their conduct was practice in the sense of emancipatory change. They threw off the burden of government oppression upon groups and individuals for reasons of religious conviction; at the same time they lifted from government and its officers the weight of conformity to ecclesiastical authority.

Also, the laws of 1639 and 1649 were principles immanent in conduct that was not only just, but also self-governing. Both laws were enacted by delegates elected to the Maryland Assembly, as well as by the overseas proprietor and his appointed governor-in-residence. Participation in making the laws was a mode of self-governance. Self-governance does not guarantee just law, but does lend support to the view that institutionalized tolerance was conduct not shaped by some peculiar and extraneous precept derived entirely from idiosyncratic motives in the Calverts. The wider participation in law-making gives some degree of historical substance to the view that tolerance was the releasing of the innate dynamic of practical reason in search of freedom from the tyranny of unjust and arbitrary law, and of freedom to act according to conviction. This is to propose that the toleration texts had authority not simply from the chartered jurisdiction of the proprietor and his mandated assembly, as if all colluded in arbitrary exercise of authority, but also from reason and an appeal to human experience as a way toward a just exercise of authority. The failure of so many in Maryland to accept either the authority of the Calverts or of reason, does not, subsequent American history argues, demonstrate an absence of reason in the texts or in tolerant practice.

Calvert and Maryland tolerance can be best understood as an innovation in practical Catholic humanism giving novel realization to the traditional spiritual-temporal difference. It was not irreligious, because it arose from a Christian vision of the superiority of the reign of God to any human authority. It was in a certain sense secularization of law, though within the ambit of the gospel's division between God and Caesar, (acknowledging Caesar, too, to have office and authority from the divine order of creation) for the sake of a more adequate realization of the common temporal good of Maryland. It can be understood as a remarkable anticipation of human rights in the charter documents of the American Republic. Yet, it was by no means the advent of a comprehensive justice. The presence of slavery in Maryland shows that an advance in religious liberty did not lead to a profound grasp of human dignity except in the one sector wherein it suffered abuse in regard to full members of the civil and political community.

There is no avoiding the impression that this was a peculiarly

Anglo-New World type of practice, insofar as the route to universal freedom—far from a reality in the Calvert palatinate when it came to indentured servants and to slaves—lay through incremental advances in just legislation. This is less utopian than fashioning in advance a fully detailed design for an ideal society or state. Yet it may be more encouraging, since it demonstrates the competence with which human reason, beset by internal conflict and ignorance, can devise, nonetheless, piecemeal solutions possessed of momentum toward a just social order. Novel, practical and reasonable steps in justice can be taken, despite an unnerving absence of a grand design.

What recommends further pondering of the Maryland initiative in religious toleration, in reference to social justice, is that paradox in Gadamer's hermeneutics which perplexed Richard Bernstein. Bernstein says:

> When Gadamer tells us that practice is conducting oneself, and acting, in solidarity, that phronesis requires a type of community in which there is an ethos and a shared acceptance of nomoi, that practical and political reason can be realized and transmitted only through dialogue, he presupposes, at least in an incipient form, the existence of the very sense of community that such practical and political reason is intended to develop.[114]

The paradox is "that the coming into being of community already presupposes an experienced sense of community."[115] To advance from weak to strong communal life depends upon an existing possession of the experience of a strong common life. The conclusion from Bernstein, applied to western societies, is that groups or nations can only move from a strong experience of community to a deeper common life, but have no possibility of moving from atomized individualism to community. This says nothing, then, about how to make the transition from, for example, American individualism to conviction on, and action for, economic justice as part of a common good.

The Maryland initiative suggests a variation on this paradox and a hint toward a solution. Progress toward a just social and political order by means of just laws (1633, 1639, 1649) depended upon the prior existence of just laws (Magna Carta; royal grant of the proprietary palatinate; English rights and liberties) and just practice. In Maryland, the Calverts moved the political structure from already possessed and known just laws and practices, to new just law and practice. The transition was a new appropriation (which affected the traditional content of the Magna

Carta, etc.). The Calvert innovation was not a change that abrogated England's legal tradition, upon which the colony depended through the royal charter, in order to commence anew. There was no wholesale rejection of English laws or even all of its penal code pertaining to religious disturbances of public peace. There was a new appropriation of the spiritual-temporal difference that took the humble form of new legal restraint upon both civil government and ecclesiastical access to it. The restraint was legislated by that government and grounded in English legal tradition. Progress in the practice of justice, the Maryland initiative suggests, occurs in a new application of already received just norms. It cannot be assumed, consequently, that legal tradition does not contain undeveloped, powerfully transformative means for advancing justice.

This further suggests that progress in social justice, no less than political justice, will have aspects of restoration and of novelty. But the focus has to shift from legal to social tradition. Then, the question arises, does a principle in an option for the poor already exist in a latent, still unsatisfactorily determined manner, in some traditional American Catholic way of acting? Is there a practice of solidarity?

Surely both Gadamer and Bernstein are correct in circling around the absence of, and need for, solidarity in western societies. It would seem, in fact, that re-forming solidarity within and between majority and minority cultures and "races" is the precondition for movement toward social and economic justice in America. The commonness of a common good is precisely what is missing as an operative norm. But a grasp of the communal nature of conditions for realizing human dignity depends upon a prior experience and affirmation of solidarity among all Americans as participants in one society. Without solidarity as a lived experience, as practice and as principle, no perception of what is or is not due can be accessible to all in society. The actual alternative, evident everywhere, is a division of what is due to "us" from what is due to "them" because "we" and "they" have no adequate experience of solidarity in common humanity, much less in common nationality. Justice is intrinsically communal. Renewing our cultural consensus depends, then, also on renewing, or beginning, an experience of solidarity.

The First Amendment, Murray liked to point out, originated in 1791 as a reasonable, practical measure in law to insure social harmony in the populace which the Founding Fathers found before them. An origin from careful, learned, practical lawmakers piecing together a Bill of Rights, rather than from grand designs and doctrinaire theory, did nothing to diminish the universality of the human rights protected by the First Amendment's religion clauses. Practically-oriented reason proved able, with extensive debate over an exact formulation, to arrive at a social practice commensurate with our humanity.

This was an especially happy instance of what Gadamer terms "application," in which the "universal" (the English tradition of freedom under law, and the self-evident truths in the Declaration of Independence) and a "particular" (colonial social reality, making unity on the basis of religion undesirable and impossible) codetermined each other.

Conclusion

We Hold These Truths presupposes and adverts to a "tradition of acceptance" whose primary mode was practical, and whose inner nature was assent to new means for justice. The "tradition of acceptance," however, was a pathway which emerged from a proto-practice of religious toleration in the Calvert administration of Maryland, 1634–1689. The latter tradition was a practical synthesis of modes of conduct open to, but not necessarily deriving directly from, a theoretical synthesis of Catholic and American principles. Bishop John Carroll, no less than John Courtney Murray, was heir to a lay practice of religious tolerance and liberty that embodied a temporal-spiritual difference. And, it can be said, the millions of Catholic immigrants to America who actualized a new mode of Catholic faith in their unhesitating embrace of the self-evidently valuable First Amendment were the preeminent *locus* of that truth and value conceived theoretically by Murray. Theirs was a new synthesis, combining a new prudential moment of Catholic faith and a political prudence new to them. The resultant, operative self-understanding demonstrated and actualized something in Catholicism not lived or known elsewhere. To borrow and alter a Hegelian metaphor, theirs was the day's work over which the owl of Minerva flew in a theoretical dusk.

This means, of course, that Murray's theoretical concept of that synthesis did not arrest continuing movement in its practice. Grasping the truth and expressing the concept of the practice did not terminate development in it. The tradition of practice remained underway, unfinished, capable of future development. It may yet be seen that an American Catholic option for the poor is just such a development in practice.

5

Identity Reinterpreted: Church-State Norms as Principles of Self-Understanding

Introduction

The tradition of practice need not be understood as an objectified, distanced "history" now fixed forever in the past as an object for research. As tradition the practice which synthesized Catholic and American principles did not suddenly freeze in its tracks once Murray's theory clarified its inner logic. It has a present and a future. This is to affirm that continuing practice of the synthesis can sustain Murray's theory while at the same time giving grounds for reinterpreting it. An American Catholic option for the poor in social ministry crosses a threshold into a new moment in practice of the synthesis. Is this in continuity with the Catholic-American synthesis already achieved and cherished only to be clarified by Murray? How can new and old practice be grasped in their continuity so as to evince a trait of authenticity in the new?

The synthesis, moreover, was and is an element in the inculturation of Catholic faith in America. Murray's doctrine can be understood, consequently, as a contribution to the inculturation of Catholic faith in America. As instances of inculturation, both the practical synthesis and Murray's theoretical analysis of it will be regarded as open to further development by an option for the poor.

An Option For the Poor is a Cultural and Ecclesial Transition

The condition of the poor, an option for the poor, and a just social and economic order are culturally relative because no two societies are identical in every way. This is because social reality is also cultural reality. El Salvador is not Haiti, Brazil is not the Philippines, India is not the United States, England is not South Korea. Unjust social, political and

108

economic structures affect persons and families belonging to one nation or culture differently from those living in another. Unemployment among African-American teenaged males prevents movement out of poverty, and thwarts their hopes as it does unemployed men everywhere.[1] But the racism entering into that unemployment has peculiarly American nuances however much it resembles racism elsewhere and has commonality with affronts to human dignity everywhere.

But what is culture? To the extent that racism, economic oppression, disrespect for life, sexism, political oppression and militarism spring from choices by those with power to influence their societies or from complicity in institutionally magnified choices and solidified decisions, something prior to institutionalized economic, social and political structures causes oppression. Somehow, an underlying context of meanings, values and patterns either promotes or blocks the realization of social justice. A concept of culture broad enough to include practice and social justice is needed. The definition from the Brazilian sociologist, Marcello De Carvalho Azevedo, manages to do just that by going to a level prior to a symbolic-practical difference.[2] The practical is "the activities and ways of conduct of social life, tools and techniques, customs, forms of apprenticeship and instruction, etc. In one word, the social practice."[3] The symbolic, on the other hand, encompasses "all that transmits meanings (be they conscious or unconscious) and representations between the members or the generations of a society: rites, traditions, myths, language, etc."[4] But in light of the fact that two societies can use the same social practices and symbols yet diverge in the meanings expressed, Azevedo concludes to something prior to practice and symbol. Culture is that depth of meaning and value prior to both symbol and social practice. He defines "culture" as

> the set of meanings, values and patterns which underlie the perceptible phenomena of a concrete society, whether they are recognizable on the level of social practice . . . or whether they are carriers of signs, symbols, meanings and representations, conceptions and feelings that consciously or unconsciously pass from generation to generation."[5]

Azevedo preserves the difference between the practical and the symbolic, while indicating their common source. His concept of culture as prior to, yet manifest in, symbol and practice allows for a meaningful practice because practice embodies culture.

This concept admittedly lacks clarity on how practice in its turn can affect culture and not just social practice. Azevedo, though, conceives culture as changing because it is both human self-realization and the humanization of the world. Nor does Azevelo clearly enough explain how culture is not a Platonic realm of Ideas, though he presents culture as the meaning of perceptible phenomena. It may be that Azevedo's concept of culture can be adjusted so that the underlying set of meanings, values and patterns can be seen to reside in a people's language. Their language would then be the actual repository of that depth prior to social practice and (formal) symbolic life. His tripartite analysis (practice/symbol/ culture) is valuable even if not thoroughly worked out. It will be followed here.

According to Azevedo's definition of culture as "the set of mean- ings, values and patterns which underlie the perceptible phenomena of a concrete society," culture is the common source for social practice and for the symbol-system. The activities of United States' citizens acting out of solidarity with the poor and oppressed for the sake of social justice, accordingly, belongs to what Azevedo calls "social practice." As such it manifests culture and expresses the "values, meanings, and pat- terns which underlie" and come to light in practice. Practice, therefore, belongs to the concept of culture no less than does a society's symbol-system.

Everything Murray summed up in terms of the American Proposi- tion and American Experiment (charter documents; "public philosophy" held in "public consensus" supporting constitutional democracy and self-governance; First Amendment religion clauses; institutions, struc- tures and agencies of democratic government) belongs to American "cul- ture." The political organization of society derives from and conserves that culture by sustaining the "social practice" with which the United States acts to govern itself for the sake of a common good.

The First Amendment religion clauses, in particular, are social prac- tice drawing upon, while at the same time manifesting and sustaining, American culture. Participation by any and all citizens in a social practice informed by the First Amendment is activity that is cultural. American Catholic participation in what Murray designated the American Proposi- tion, especially the First Amendment, has been and is, therefore, a rela- tion between Catholic faith and American culture. Likewise, a new prac- tice arising within that relation will also be a cultural reality not solely a matter of compartmentalized economic or political decisions or techniques.

The importance of acknowledging the cultural depth of economic, political and social oppression can be learned from the reality of racism in the United States. The admirable legal advances toward full civil rights since the mid-1960s, together with a growing black middle-class and increasingly prominent black leadership in the political sphere have not by themselves eliminated white racism. Legal, economic, and political changes in structures have left undisturbed, that is, the cultural reality of racism. Racism remains, perhaps somewhat diminished, as a grave, uncivilized flaw in American, probably western, meanings and values prior to social practice and symbolism. Who, for example, was and is the "we" in "We the People" at the level of culture, as distinguished (but never separated) from laws? Where do native Americans fit in culture? Culture is the wellspring of social practice.

Joe Holland, coauthor of *Social Analysis: Linking Faith with Justice*, stated that his "focus has shifted from 'society' to 'civilization' " in order to take account of "the question of culture, and within it religion, which reveals, I believe, the most radical dimension of our social crisis in advanced industrial capitalism."[6] He criticized the "classical secular Left" for letting a correct perception of the destructive drive within industrial civilization lead to cutting itself off from "divine creativity." He found the opposite defect in the "classic religious Right," which objects to secularization as loss of contact with the divine but construes the divine without admitting the "prophetic side of the divine" and ends up retrieving "an authoritarian, patriarchal, militaristic society tied this time to powerful modern technology."[7] Only linking the energies of faith to those of justice overcomes both these one-sided nonsolutions to the crisis in western civilization.

His recognition of a cultural depth in society as the key to social justice involved taking account of cultural differences between, at least, advanced industrial societies and the Third World. His analysis implies that cultural pluralism is the actual condition for both injustice and the transformation of societies. J. Fitzpatrick had approached this theme in arguing that "the heart of the problem of justice is culture"[8] because judgments on an acceptable amount of food, the way to dress, and decent dwelling-places have a cultural aspect. Customs, manners, relationships, attitudes toward family, work, and the future all have cultural meanings and values. In regard to economic arrangements, therefore, it becomes necessary to ask, "[w]hat do they mean in terms of human interests, in terms of human destiny, in terms of what human life means?"[9]

For example, he observes, the social reality of a poor person in a Latin American culture does not lack altogether for a sense of one's *dignidad de la persona* because this does not correlate with "how high one is on the socioeconomic scale."[10] By contrast, in the United States the values of upward mobility, education, conspicuous consumption, etc., militate against a poor person's having any sense of personal dignity, because poverty can be interpreted as an outward sign of inward vices, or in the Puritan vein, of a negative divine judgment. American culture, that is, tends to rob the American poor of any basis for their sense of personal dignity. Fitzpatrick counsels, as a result, a determined, methodical readiness to ask the question, "What do things mean?" and "what is the arrangement that will mean for these people justice or peace...?"[11] Although this line of questioning could be misappropriated to serve monological, paternalistic kinds of development schemes, its merit consists in pointing out that social transformation is also cultural change, that culture is more intimate and profound than institutional structures, and that change in culture reaches deeply into persons.

Just social and economic practice cannot become effective in the United States except upon realization that practice itself, as Azevado argues, partially expresses a set of meanings, values and patterns, the culture of our society. Movement toward a just social and economic order involves a cultural transition. This takes place in Catholic Americans too. Such a transition unsettles and then resettles the traditional synthesis Murray analyzed. Social transformation depends upon cultural transition; cultural transition activates an otherwise passive or customary religio-cultural synthesis. Forming and changing the synthesis so that transformation of social and economic structures is sustained by culture and faith is to have entered upon a new moment in the faith-culture combination, not only a "new American experiment" in political and economic matters.[12]

Inculturation of a Universal Value

Inculturation is a theological version of what Gadamer describes as "application" in the symbiosis of everyday understanding/interpretation/application.[13] True, the *sui generis* reality of Christ, church and gospel means that the dynamic of their self-communication in a new cultural context shares in their reality as mysteries of faith and so is not reducible to being simply a specimen of "application." Nonetheless, Gadamer's concept identifies aspects of ecclesial inculturation that are analogous to universally human aspects of knowledge and interpretation. Application is practical knowledge inseparable from every understanding or interpretation because a concept emerges as a moment in self-understanding and opens onto an anticipation of the future. A universal, whether it be a text's meaning as a whole or a particular aspect of being human, like courage, intersects with the becoming of the knower. Gadamer proposes that ethical study of the virtue of *phronesis* highlights something present but inconspicuous in all knowing: a codetermination between universal and particular in a situation already forming the knower through tradition.

Inculturation[14] is the action, the process, of engaging all that Christianity essentially is and does with the cultural reality of a local (regional, linguistic, or national) church. In this the traditional forms of Christianity are the universals in the midst of codetermining application by a local church coming to know the universal while already formed by a local or national culture. The immanent objective consists in working out a new way of living (and communicating) the one gospel of Christ.

Theological reflection on inculturation entered a new phase after Vatican II. Missiology broke away from a triumphalist concept of evangelization by formally and methodologically adhering to a principle of respect for non-western religions and cultures and for so-called local (indigenous) churches in India, Africa, and Asia. Reflection on inculturation has broadened and deepened the creative missionary's search for a distinction between what is western and what is essential Christianity so that the fullest measure of respect can be accorded to non-western peoples. The sensibility in such research is pained by colonialist tendencies associated with some past missionary work. The new approach is equivalent to foregoing a monologue through which the predefined universal determined everything about its application, admitting little or nothing from the local churches into the mode of its reception.

Despite the arcane name, inculturation is not, in the first instance, a specialized precinct in theological research; its primary mode of existence is as the lived experience of a local church. The process of inculturation does not make its appearance as a religious technique fully determined in advance by theologians and so cannot be considered as a deformation of practice into technique. Robert J. Schreiter insists on the priority of a community's activity to tasks of professional theologians:

> The role of the whole community is often one of raising the questions, of providing the experience of having lived with those questions and struggled with different answers, and of recognizing which solutions are indeed genuine, authentic, and commensurate with their own experience.[15]

A local church develops a local theology primarily by means of an existential discernment directed to ecclesial life, not by applying a professionally wrought, official theology of their culture. Inculturation is not punctilious execution of a fully detailed, premeditated central plan settling in advance how gospel and culture are to relate. Theology can examine and interpret the local way of being Christian in light of the larger tradition of the church and with the benefit of wisdom from other local churches, past and present.

Conciliar and postconciliar affirmation of inculturation, moreover, involves adjusting ecclesiology and not just missiology. Reconceiving relations between local, non-western churches and their Indian, African or Asian milieux brings deepened understanding of the whole church. Inculturation operates with an understanding of the church universal as a communion of local churches. Each local church, like those addressed by the Pauline letters to Thessalonika, Corinth or Rome, and like the original church in Jerusalem, realizes all that the church is, including communion with other churches, with successors to the apostles, and with the Bishop of Rome.

Each local church, no less than the universal communion of churches, has a mission and mandate to renew all creation. Pope Paul VI taught in *Evangelii Nuntiandi*[16] that evangelization comprehends the whole relation between the local church and the culture of its people and takes place with fullest respect for religious liberty and for the uniqueness of a people's heritage. This presupposes the obsolescence of a classicist humanism whose uniform norms could quickly judge what in any culture successfully manifested genuinely human attributes. Inculturation relies on, if not an agreed concept of culture, at least the kind of empirical approach to cultures taken by Vatican II's "Pastoral Constitution on the Church in the Modern World." When understood as inculturation, the mission of a local church is seen as, "the integration of the Christian experience of a local church into the culture of its people."[17]

This "integration" goes beyond incorporation of folkloric self-expression into liturgies and seeks to place the culture's fundamental meanings and values in dialogue with the gospel. The goal is recessive in the sense that inculturation is a continuous process which is identical to the mission of the local church. Differentiation of inculturation into three successive stages (translation, assimilation, transformation) clarifies the ongoing nature of that mission.[18] These stages do not arrive according to calendrical computation nor by decree. They are moments in a free dialogue between the gospel and a culture, not precisely scheduled steps determined by force of custom or history.

Inculturation is a way of understanding the mission of the church, evangelization, as a process comprehending all that the church is and does in dialogue with a culture in all that it is and does. Inculturation distances itself from the model of evangelization which seeks to realize the church's mission exclusively through preaching and baptizing. That would be to act as if the Christian way of life were confined to personal, spiritual conversion only, as if the act of faith left other, everyday activities and relationships untouched by the grace of Christ. The concept of inculturation emphasizes, finally, how faith, gospel and church affect culture along with their saving effect in souls. This involves conceiving the mission of Christ as divine renewal of creation rather than as the salvation of asocial, acultural, apolitical, Cartesian *res cogitantes.*

Inculturation is universal. It pertains to local churches everywhere, not only in Asia, Africa and India. It returns to the west to relativize western modes of Christianity by placing them in reference to alternatives. It assists in the creative development of western modes of relating gospel to culture by justifying attention to national or regional variations in western culture as the situation of dialogue with the gospel. Consequently, it is possible to conceive the already actualized and still future relation between Catholicism and American culture as a process of inculturation.[19]

Because this inculturation has been underway for so long a time and with some unique features, it cannot suffice simply to transplant Latin American liberation theology into a North American cultural, social, economic, political and ecclesial context. This does not mean liberation theologies have little to teach North Americans. It does mean that they do not by themselves remove responsibility for what Dennis P. McCann and Charles R. Strain describe as a "genuinely open dialogue in which North American Christians can question themselves in light of political and liberation theologies while recognizing that neither is sufficiently adapted to the North American reality."[20] For example, there has been a history of social theology in American Protestantism from Rauschenbusch's social gospel through Reinhold Niebuhr, and in American Catholicism from John Ryan and John Courtney Murray to Virgil Michel. It is not chauvinism but sociological analysis that compels John Coleman to conclude that in North America,

> ... the institutions have also been unique: Here Church and state are legally separated. Religious pluralism and the tradition of denominational voluntarism create a special climate for the Church's strategy to influence reform movements, from the abolition movement in the nineteenth century to the rise of the labor movement and the civil rights and anti-Vietnam movements.[21]

This, along with other factors, leads him to the judgment that American Catholicism needs to develop a regional strategic theology of justice and peace "appropriate to our own context."[22] In the first instance this means that an American Catholic option for the poor and orientation to social justice has to be formed in and by its context before it can hope to influence North American social and cultural reality. This formation, especially on the pretheoretical level, touches the internal, Catholic-American synthesis as well as practice and ministry on the basis of an ecclesial strategy. So a further consequence from recognition of inculturation is that the universal value in the option for the poor needs codetermination by the particular situation of American Catholicism.

Murray's Texts Enter a New Moment in Inculturation

Murray's texts exemplify not only *phronesis* (practical wisdom) in a philosophical sense but theological inculturation as well. They are reflections on and expositions of principles in an American inculturation of Catholicism. Though not the primary mode of that inculturation, they have the proportions of a major contribution to understanding a major element in a living exchange between gospel and American culture. However, the texts refer to, rely on, and explain an assimilative moment in inculturation. After a moment in which, usually, missionaries translate scriptures into a new language, and a people teach emissaries from elsewhere the values of their culture, there follows an assimilation in which a local church leadership emerges and the new faith makes an impact on the culture's mores while assimilating what is compatible with the gospel. The first phase may have no reality in the history of American religion apart from missions to the native peoples.[23] The phase of assimilation, indications are, ended for Catholicism at the time of Vatican II.

Murray went to Vatican II from an American Catholicism closing the chapter on an assimilative mode of inculturation. He came back to the beginnings of a transformative phase in which conscientious corporate resistance to an American war was thinkable. To a large extent, an assimilative accent on harmonies between Catholicism and American democracy serves to ward off uninformed charges of a fundamental conflict between being Catholic and being American. But this does not yet amount to guidance for a local church in its struggle to define and realize a social mission in terms of an option for the poor. Murray need not be counted among those who would oppose the prospect of social transformation in service of justice. In fact, his distinctive contribution originated within the "social Catholicism" of the 1930s and 1940s.[24] But the phase of transformation had accumulated too little pretheoretical substance before Murray's death in 1967 for him to do more than recognize its advent.

Murray expected that the futures of "The Declaration on Religious Liberty" and of American Catholicism would converge to carry the doctrine of religious liberty into the life and structures of the church. He looked for a distinctively American Catholic contribution to a "pastoral theology of freedom."[25] Though a prominent theme in theology, the latter has by no means monopolized the struggle to interpret and to modify the gospel-American culture relationship. It could possibly be that the phase of transformation will pivot on the "social question," in the form of an option for the poor. If it does not, the sheer weight of human suffering outside the church will make a one-sided focus on internal ecclesial freedom an excess of ecclesiocentrism. Yet, the question of freedom in the church cannot be separated from commitment to liberation from economic or social oppression, because in both tasks the dignity of the person, now possessed as emergent consciousness, theological theme, and magisterial norm, is essential.

Interpreting Murray in light of *Economic Justice for All* helps link an option for the poor to the lasting gains acquired by Catholic self-understanding in an earlier, assimilative relation to American culture. That interpretation, in turn, opens up new meaning in Murray's contribution and helps form an option for the poor in accord with American Catholic identity.

Interpreting Church-State Norms for Transformative Inculturation: General Principles

a) From Principles Applied to Tradition Appropriated

Murray taught four perennial principles for church-state relations[26]: a) an irreducible difference between Church and state;[27] b) an effective primacy in dignity of the spiritual;[28] c) the independence of the political;[29] d) the finality of church-state relations toward a practical cooperation for the good of the believer-citizen[30] who, as a person, is the source, agent and end of sociopolitical structures.[31] These principles are aspects of the church's self-realization[32] in relation to a people's social self-actualization in the political order. They are also norms for ecclesial conduct in church-state relations, whether "church" be "spiritual authority," "people of God," local church, diocese, family, parish or individual believer. They are norms, too, for what the church expects from a state and so are norms for states in relating to the church. They can be recapitulated in the single principle of the church's freedom to exercise her mission. As principles and as norms, they have entered into the American Catholic synthesis. But what do they mean in that synthesis when it shifts toward a readiness to challenge and perhaps in some respects to seek to transform social and economic institutions under the impulse of an option for the poor?

First, they can be shifted into a hermeneutical framework and interpreted as formative upon American Catholic identity. That is, they can be considered as principles internal to self-understanding and not solely as precepts for conduct that remain extrinsic. They are a basic moment in the dialogue between Catholic faith and American culture. In that context, our problematic becomes how to appropriate them within our situation, different as it is from Murray's.

The first act of interpretation has to do with their meaning, not simply with extending deliberations by which they can be applied in light of new facts to well-known First Amendment issues in already defined zones of church-state contact. More precisely, the task is to understand Murray's church-state teaching as a moment in transformative rather than assimilative inculturation. The meaning, truth and value in his version of the traditional principles is to be understood from within a modified and modifying relation to American culture.

This gives practice an expanded role. When inculturation is grasped as appropriation of Christian mission and tradition in a new context, then a renewed meaning, truth and value in traditional church-state principles can be sought in practice by believer-citizens. Inculturation takes place primarily in daily lives and secondarily in officially instituted ways of proceeding. Practice relates knowledge and a particular situation. For example, Catholics in America knew a universal value (the dignity of the person; a spiritual-temporal difference between church and state) in a particular cultural context (life guided by the First Amendment religion clauses).

When the situation changes from, say, seeking to maximize harmony between Catholic faith and American culture, to, for instance, a summons to an option for the poor, then the way the universal is known also changes. It changes from being the ground for affirming a fundamental affinity and harmony between Catholic tradition and the First Amendment, to being a ground for hoping for changes in social and economic structures favorable to those most in need. In appropriation of any universal, knowing and the being of the knower mesh.[33] But, and to accept Richard J. Bernstein's extension of Gadamer's analysis,[34] that link can be expressed in prereflective, pretheoretical but meaningful practice which in effect correlates American democratic procedures with Catholic tradition. The policy recommendations flowing from an option for the poor receive an overall orientation and staying power, not from each detail of eradicating unemployment, but from the practice of an option for the poor. That root of practice, and perhaps much of its impact, is consistent with a profound religio-moral and cultural heritage but does not implement it after the manner of technique.[35] And its political side may be eventual and instrumental, rather than a programmatic hastening of some inevitable goal.

For example, an interior sense about the meaning of Christianity gradually could arise within the practice of a businessperson whose modifications, however slight, in the direction of greater respect for the dignity of those needing employment might occasion at the same time a questioning, resisting attitude toward practices treating them as instruments of production purely and simply. It would not be out of place to attach a new readiness to seek joint public/private support out of an awakened insight into relevant political measures toward a common social good. This could occur without reading a particular book or document and might find expression in a new habit of feeling, thought, language, and relationship. This would ordinarily be considered spiritual growth or a deepened grasp of the businessperson's own humanity. The point here is simply that this new way of being did not derive from a preformed theory but emerged in practice. Nor is this to deny an influence from conversations, books, friends, public speakers, preaching, etc. But it is to disengage for examination the person's practical originality: the person's own grasp and word is irreplaceably unique.

Reception of Catholic tradition can be located in deeds and ordinary conversations; it need not be sought exclusively in formal, reflective thought or in prepared remarks. Therefore, to learn how American Catholics after Murray have continued to link their Catholicism and their American reality in general and in regard to the First Amendment in particular, inquiry can proceed to their performed synthesis and to modifications in it. Though detailed investigation of that performed synthesis lies outside the scope of this book, and more in the domains of a history and a sociology of American Catholicism, it receives here the formal role of a principle correlative to theoretical interpretation of Murray's contribution. Scholarship on Murray that seeks to develop and to apply his practical wisdom needs to incorporate recognition of a performed or practiced interpretation of the Catholic-American democracy synthesis. As chapter 4 argued, Murray's subject matter had historical and interpretative priority to his theoretical concept of it. There is no reason to think that this priority does not still obtain. And, that practice would be seen to be indissociable from everyday language about its content.

The consequence is that, according to hermeneutics and a theology of inculturation, reflective application of his principles needs openness to initiatives in practice as what may well contain meaning, truth and value essential to developing Murray's reflection. What Catholic-American synthesis do the career and speeches of former Congressman Rev. Robert Drinan imply? Or of Governors Mario Cuomo or Richard Daley? Or, the ministry and writings of the Center of Concern? The oral tradition of Network? The Hispanic Cultural Center? The Offices for Black Catholics established in many dioceses? The Kateri Tekakwitha Conference? National Right to Life? The United States Catholic Conference? Are there Catholic businesspeople discussing the meaning of their work and its way of building a common good? What do the First Amendment religion clauses and the principles in Catholic church-state teaching as well as in "The Declaration on Religious Liberty," mean in these social ministries? How do they speak about them?

Murray's teaching can be understood as clarifying the dialogue between Catholic and American practices. Now, an option for the poor is a preliminary moment in practice which seems to have more the character of a basic change in orientation than a conclusion from deliberation on familiar ethical propositions. Learning what Catholic tradition on church and state means for transformative inculturation can begin from participated or observed practice, move through a conceptual approximation of the enacted meaning or value, and arrive at a concept of the tradition in a new situation. Or, acquiring knowledge of the new condition of the Catholic-American synthesis can take place in the form of learning the meaning of texts on the new situation. One question can be addressed to both reflection and to practice: what changes in the general American Catholic identity does an option for the poor introduce? More particularly, what changes in American Catholic self-understanding on church and state does an option for the poor begin to effect?

Economic Justice for All, of course, could not and did not give extensive attention to the question of how ". . . the Christian perspective on the meaning of economic life must transform the lives of individuals, families, in fact, our whole culture."[36] But chapter 5, "A Commitment to the Future," may have meaning in addition to its presence as a predictable hortatory epilogue. It inserts "deeds for justice," for instance, into Vatican II's description of the church as sacrament.[37] It refers to the lay vocation to holiness "in the midst of the world, in family, in community, in friendships, in work, in leisure" and adds, "in citizenship."[38] What lies beyond the chapter's purview is how following the path presented would modify the familiar interpretations and syntheses of being Catholic and being American. The "new cultural consensus"[39] on the essential conditions for human dignity, that is, changes those holding it at the same time that it procures justice for those lacking it. For Catholics it is a new Catholic-American synthesis. And resistance to it runs deeper than disagreements over specific policy recommendations.

The challenge of learning from Murray for the sake of an authentically American option for the poor is not only a matter, then, of arguing the question, can *We Hold These Truths*, for example, support the social Catholicism of *Economic Justice for All*, or not? It is also a question of starting with recognition that appropriation, interpretation and understanding of church-state relations may be expected to emerge in actual practice by Catholics unfamiliar with either Murray's writings or church-state principles as concepts.

This is to accept the possibility that a new codetermination between Catholicism and the American Proposition can occur and to expect it in meaningful deeds as well as in formal interpretations of Murray's theory. This approach to Murray asks: Are there new codeterminations of being Catholic and being American that Murray's teaching must now account for? For instance, does an option for the poor evoke new meaning from such long-standing issues as whether or not taxes can, in justice and in respect for the no-establishment clause,[40] assist schools with ties of one sort or another to Catholic Americans when most students in some of them in inner cities affiliate, if at all, with Protestant denominations? Does an option for the poor include an option for their human and civil right to the free exercise of their religion? If so, how can that right be effectively protected if one of the free exercises of religion consists in a movement for social and economic transformation? Does economic injustice, finally, tend to inhibit the exercise of this, arguably, most basic human right?

Or, along another line, does a new synthesis, integrating a transformative relation to culture, occur when James and Kathleen McGinnis[41] commit their family life to social action? What have they to teach Murray and vice versa? What might an ecumenical, church-based community action organization such as the MICAH[42] project contain in the way of a rich, ecumenical but implicit reorientation of how Catholics can relate to American culture, especially to democratic government? Does the ministry of Christian social activists express unthematic or partially thematized practical redefinition of what Murray spoke of as the spiritual power of the church to affect the political order indirectly through believer-citizens? What if, as believers, they presuppose Vatican II's ecclesiology and liturgical renewal, and as citizens they feel something in common with E. J. Dionne, Jr.'s *Why Americans Hate Politics* and with Donald L. Barlett and James B. Steele's *America: What Went Wrong.*[43] That would not be an American Catholic synthesis Murray took for granted. Does postconciliar social ministry revise and reintegrate a Catholic church-state relation? Are several models simultaneously operative?

b) From Church-State to Gospel-Culture

Further, a hermeneutically sensitive idea of inculturation emphasizes the broad gospel-culture relation within which church-state norms are a highly visible, juridically precise element. After Vatican II, Murray came to see church-state relations as a specific part internal to larger, church-society interactions.[44] Hermeneutics, though, refocuses the whole problem. With that, the problems of religious liberty and church-state relationship leave the cloister of esoteric theologians and lawyers, cease being a recondite, though occasionally volatile, subsection of social ethics. They stand forth in their proper ordinariness as a basic dimension of the life of faith in a democracy. Because they are a *de facto* feature of ecclesial and personal lives across all manner of themes and activities, are in fact a constant, though seldom reflective, practice of interpretation, they pertain to the act and content of a believer-citizen's faith, hope and charity.

Equally, they are a usually unnoticed condition within which Catholic dioceses, parishes, schools of several sorts, hospitals, and believers maintain their corporate existence in America. Because a relation to the political order of democracy is interior to every believer who is also a United States citizen, it is not a sporadic, external link exercised only in voting, public office, etc. A person is not sometimes a believer, at other times a citizen, and on certain occasions a merger of the two. The relation arises from simultaneous participation in church and state. While both modes of communal existence are in effect and unrevoked, there is, as a result, a believer-citizen relation. It has a quality of interiority and constancy by which it is a partner to faith.

There is no Catholic faith or institution in the United States without a relation to democracy. Thus, the believer's relation to being a citizen cannot be segregated into social ethics. Rather, it expands across the full horizon of faith. And for that reason it becomes subject matter proper to systematic, fundamental and practical theologies.[45] By directing attention first and foremost to how tradition is appropriated in a new context, hermeneutics inquires into how believer-citizens interpret their correlation of religious and civic realities. Church-state relations find their new place as a significant element in the inculturation of Catholicism in America. This removes Murray's contribution out from under the exclusive title of social ethics, which is an aspect of it.[46]

American Catholic church-state relations and Murray's teaching on them are subject matter for systematic ecclesiology and missiology as well as for social ethics, because they enact and treat the gospel-culture relation essential to the church's existence and mission. In addition, insofar as church-state relations are the traditional faith/reason problematic writ large and operational, they fall in that respect to fundamental theology.[47] And to the extent that a believer's option for the poor affects participation in the life of the political community, church-state relations become a coordination of practices properly studied by practical theology.[48]

The principles Murray taught, then, are more than obligatory norms and have more than an ethical content. As their dispersal across the lines of systematic, fundamental and practical theologies indicates, they bring the act, content and light of faith as a whole into play. They make a difference in the way Americans are Catholic, they shape a Catholic way of being an American, and their provenance exceeds the confines of occasional, specific moral determinations about given items. Appropriating Murray's church-state norms need not be, and in the following reflections will not be, solely a task of deriving additional socio-ethical precepts from them. The aim, instead, will be to adumbrate their meaning as principles in the American Catholic identity, or self-understanding, which envelops, situates and lends a selected perspective to the admittedly valuable though difficult task of spelling-out their socio-ethical implications for a public theology.

c) Results from Hermeneutical Analysis of the Principles

Church-state relations inhere in a gospel-culture interaction. When that interaction undergoes a shift, so do they. When the culture changes in some area that affects how citizens participate in the state, this cannot but touch church-state relations. When believers change according to some part of the gospel that has public dimensions and involves social justice then, too, church-state relations may gradually acquire new definition. *Economic Justice for All* called Americans to an option for the poor from a scriptural basis and with reasonable arguments. That option represents a conversion (not a confirmation of a status quo on economic justice) in the believing community and in believers that has implications for the national common good and for civic responsibility to it. The kind of option outlined did not concern private charity but new policies and structures, some of which, like "fiscal and monetary policies,"[49] can only come from political decision and public policy. That is tantamount to encouraging and initiating a process of revising some parts of how believers see their civic responsibility to the common good.

And the first step is, according to the National Conference of Catholic Bishops, a new cultural consensus on what human dignity requires in general, for example, "that everyone has a right to employment."[50] That first step occurs precisely in the interaction between a local church and the ambient culture. The option is a new kind of connection between faith and a people's underlying set of meanings, values and patterns,

between hope and their primary language and interpretation of existence.[51] That is why the first step consists in a new cultural consensus. A
predominance of assimilation, with its typical emphasis on areas of faith/
culture agreements, has ended, structurally. A heritage of already actualized inculturation, especially a practical synthesis of Catholicism and the
meanings, values, institutions and mores of American democracy, en-
dures within a transformation. But that former mode of synthesis no
longer defines the Catholic faith-American culture relationship.

This adds up to a major transition from what Murray referred to in
passing as Catholics' "tradition of acceptance"[52] of the singular circumstances of American democracy to what may be called a "practice of
transformation" by which Catholics engage themselves to bring about
social and economic justice through that democracy. *Economic Justice for
All* created, by instigating a new cultural consensus among Catholics and
by proposing a way toward economic justice, a new interpretative situation for American Catholicism. Transition to a Catholicism aiming at
transformation of national policies and goals reopens dialogue between
Catholicism and American culture. The dialogue moves from, as it were,
one already recorded and major agreement between the two, which
Murray did not invent but did expound. Dialogue after *Economic Justice
for All* can proceed as if that agreement were grounds for a new round of
discussions. And yet, like any dialogue, the settled agreement comes into
play when entertaining new possibilities in the relationship and may be
seen in a new light or integrated into a new Catholic-American synthesis.

The harmonious nature of the relation, especially between Catholic
natural-law morality and American political structures, reflected harmony between *faith* (Catholic tradition on church and state) and *reason*
(American political values, ethos, institutions, agencies, activities), itself
signifying the nature/grace relation of nonidentity and inseparable fulfillment. The challenge from the new situation circles to a greater degree
around hope in tension with standard versions of the future of America.
A believer's relation to the state as citizen is also a correlation between
hope and that picture of the future projected formally and informally by,
especially, the highest levels of the executive, legislative and judicial
branches of government.

*d) From Anthropocentric to Pneumatological Inwardness of Church-State
Relations*

Interpreting Murray's principles in ensemble entails attention to
their inwardness. This is to move from Murray's concept of their presence in people as dual responsibilities in moral conscience, to a concept
of their presence as identity and as influenced by the Holy Spirit. He saw

that the primacy of citizens in self-government meant that the church encountered a democratic state in the conscience of the person who was simultaneously believer and citizen. A copresence of two kinds of obligations in the conscience of a person who was Christian and citizen was the new manner of church-state relation.

However, Murray tended to conceive the inwardness of church-state relations in terms of a conscientious, deductive inference from universal principles to particular cases. He gave full attention, to be sure, to the contingency of cases and he advocated historical research into them. Their application could be expected to undergo change in not fully predictable ways due to unforeseeable contingent circumstances. That application, nevertheless, once learned from studying past cases in which deed preceded doctrine, tended to be a deduction. He expressed admiration that "Political rulers acted, Popes acted; and then came the theologians . . . to think out a theology."[53] And yet, his historically conscious method did not install the precedence of deed as a principle in his formulation of the church's doctrine. Rather, he presented a movement from clear propositions stating church teaching through subtle analysis of prevailing circumstances to prudent decision and carefully taken act. There is inwardness of conscience here.

But the inwardness of church-state relations in a believer-citizen has more to it than this kind of conscientious deliberation. There is the inwardness of interpretation preceding deliberation. A dialogical co-determination of a universal (Catholic tradition on church and state in Pope Leo XIII's texts) and the particular (American government limited by a Constitution drawn up under divine sovereignty) precedes inward deliberations. Murray's ecclesiastical opponents could make inferences as well as he did. What they lacked was a first premise gained in an act of more profound interpretation.

Insofar as Murray's principles incited acts of deliberate inference toward prudent decision, they prescinded from a larger, more encompassing religious and cultural self-understanding existing as participation in tradition. The "who" that acts in conscience is also historically-effected consciousness dwelling within both Catholic and American traditions. This has nothing to do with Descartes' perspicuous ego and everything to do with that presence of tradition in a person's or community's language which is a way of being in the world.[54] Differences between Canadian and American traditions with regard to Britain, for example, produce a different historically-effected consciousness in citizens of Canada and of the United States.

The United States has no solid, institutionalized incorporation of more than one cultural and linguistic model into the national consensus.

The "melting pot" ideal in America lacked respect for diverse traditions, since anything from Europe was by definition baggage from an Old World. Hence, an American self-understanding tends to accept "the American way" as somehow normative, with an assurance of its superiority that appears as insufferably naive arrogance to Canadians. As a result of this kind of difference, "national unity" invokes themes and images in Canadians living by the British North America Act of 1867, divergent from those in the land of Abraham Lincoln's Gettysburg Address.[55]

This presence-to-self mediated by memory and the language of tradition was not absent from Murray's work. But he couched it in a vocabulary of staunch adhesion to America's once and future consensus on "these truths" announced in the Declaration of Independence. Indeed, his stated goal in *We Hold These Truths* was to shore up "America's understanding of itself."[56] There was an urgent, if not entirely desperate, air to "The Civilization of the Pluralist Society." Without clarity on self-understanding, which is "the necessary condition of a sense of self-identity and self-confidence, whether in the case of an individual or in the case of a people,"[57] there is confusion unto madness and destructive behavior. He found himself at a juncture in American experience when "these truths" were no longer held to be "self-evident."

So he took up the charge of helping Americans regain the truths defining their identity, from arguments constituting "other more reasoned grounds."[58] Otherwise, he cautioned, "the peril is great." For a nation as for an individual the "complete loss of one's identity is, with all propriety of theological definition, hell."[59] And neither identity exists in a vacuum. In the case of a powerful nation, it would be injurious to Americans and others were "the American giant to go lumbering about the world today, lost and mad."[60] The arguments and deliberations he offered, in service of a renewed national identity, entered into the quality of inwardness possessed by that identity. Nonetheless, the interiority of that identity exceeds the arguments at least to the extent that an identity can become a background to them once they are grasped.

Perhaps the strengthened American identity toward which Murray wrote could be said to be the noninferential touchstone by which the nation's purposes, policies and decisions could be continuously tested for their appropriateness. A weakened identity would still act in this capacity with but obscure and tenuous formation by the founding consensus. In either condition, Murray concentrated on the inward acts rather than on a presence-to-self linguistically mediated.

There is also a relation to the Holy Spirit in the inwardness of church-state relations. Postconciliar Catholicism, familiar with descriptions of Vatican II as a "new Pentecost,"[61] surprised by a "charismatic renewal," and grateful for renewed lay and religious commitment to spiritual life and theology, speaks more and differently about the Holy Spirit than did Murray. His theology of the Trinity[62] and of the church,[63] to be sure, affirmed a distinct mission of the Holy Spirit. The mission of the Spirit animated the corporate existence of the church. The Spirit was the "soul" of the mystical body and the ultimate principle of unity in the church. In this Murray looked to Pope Pius XII's *Mystici Corporis* as well as to the Greek fathers of the church. Vatican II renewed faith-understanding of the Holy Spirit by interpreting the mission as one of power for renewal and change.[64] This theology of the Spirit was not so prominent in Murray's ecclesiology and did not figure into his church-state teaching. He did not, of course, deny a life-giving and sanctifying work of the Spirit. His theology of Trinity and church easily absorbed the new emphasis. But he did not accentuate a power of the Spirit acting outside word, sacrament and the church to bring *aggiornamento* and renewal.

He saw divine action in history, conceived it as "providence,"[65] and interpreted a slow, progressive coming of age of the state in the west as providential. He did interpret the emergence of a common consciousness of the dignity of the human person as actualization of exigencies the creator had given to human nature and had nurtured with a gracious providence. Personal and political consciousness were "signs of the times."[66] He accepted truth and moral value outside the church, as J. Leon Hooper has pointed out.[67] He had an orientation toward Christian unity and interreligious cooperation from the outset of his career in the early 1940s. He, however, did not typically conceive divine action in history in terms of the mission of the Holy Spirit. He embraced the ecumenical movement without formally addressing the role of the Spirit moving it. That the Spirit was a hidden influence touching peoples' innermost hearts was not Murray's leading theme in the area of divine immanence in the world, skilled though he was in the area of spirituality.[68]

Vatican II deepened appreciation for the Person and mission of the Spirit. Not the least significant theme has been the Spirit in the church.[69] Post-Vatican II ecclesiology has a strong pneumatological dimension not confined to catechesis and theology pinpointing the content of the Third Article in the Creed.[70] The pneumatological renewal cannot be segregated from a spiritual renewal—more widespread than the charismatic renewal—in which the Spirit works within believers and not simply through the mediation of word, sacrament, and institutional structures. Faith comes to be seen as arising in the presence of the Spirit, and becomes, with baptism, a participation in the Spirit of Jesus. Grace has come to be understood as life in the Spirit. Hope is a matter of already having a preliminary share in the eschatological plenitude of the Spirit who raised Jesus.[71] Post-Vatican II American Catholics, "charismatic" or not, share an ecclesial self-understanding with a prominent pneumatological dimension. This may be manifest simply and in so ordinary a thing as readiness to listen respectfully to other believers, convinced that there is more to faith than its doctrines, however precious these are, too. This is to say that reverence for the Holy Spirit laboring in the interiority of believers is not unknown in American Catholicism and may be fairly common.[72] American Catholic self-understanding has gained a reflex of sensitivity to a pneumatological depth and dynamic. This dimension of inwardness envelops the operations of moral conscience and identity that were the inwardness to which Murray often adverted.

Consequently, pneumatology has affected the church side of church-state relations within believer-citizens. Besides assent to "faith and morals," and along with their self-understanding forming in freedom, there is a spiritual dynamic. Because of the Spirit, the "life of faith" is understood as a kind of discipleship that consists in deepening rather than simply observing adherence to the word of God. And the depths of life given by the Spirit are more than an empty infinity. The Spirit is the presence of the eschatological plenitude in preliminary measure. So believers relate to the divine future by more means than faith's belief in God's promises and hope's surety about their realization. They participate in the future's cause. The believer already shares in the not-yet. The believer-citizen, then, does not straddle a divide between a this-worldly "below" on earth and an other-worldly "above" in heaven, but lives simultaneously as a pilgrim on the way and a guest already, albeit obscurely, welcomed.

Church-state relations become, therefore, relations between Spirit-indwelt believers and their citizenship. Customarily, and for the sake of maximizing the contrast, Catholic tradition and Murray both used the language of "temporal" and "spiritual" ends of state and church, respectively. This can be revised in light of Vatican II's renewal in pneumatology. The church is the beacon, admittedly dim at times, for the earthly future of creation, not the jumping-off point for eternity conceived as "heaven above." This means that the church which Vatican II described as, ". . . in the nature of a sacrament—a sign and instrument, that is, of communion with God and of unity among all [people] . . . ,"[73] demonstrates our corporate destiny at least in our relations with God and the rest of humanity.

The believer lives some participation in the future of communion and as citizen lives a participation in its present condition. Life in the

Spirit encompasses, without overriding them, the secular structures of social and political existence. In one way, the church is a parable for the state because it is a fulfillment of the proximate future toward which the state labors: political life could read off from the life of the church lessons about what realizes, or frustrates, human dignity. The church exemplifies a future condition in which the meaning of our humanity has come to fullness. In this way, the church, while offering little, perhaps, in the line of particular political means, serves as a constant witness to human fulfillment and testifies in season and out about a fulfillment beyond that of the state. For church-state relations this implies that, with or without clear theoretical guidelines for every occasion and crisis, believers as citizens have access, through life in the Spirit, to a guide and criterion pertinent to concrete realities. Whereas Murray rightly insisted on the church's duty to learn from the secular history of religious freedom, and to incorporate whatever is appropriate into its own life, it is no less true that believers do not come to their citizenship empty-handed, begging sufferance from political organizations and leaders.

To the contrary, ecclesial life, if lived in more than a perfunctory way, is a resource for thoughtful citizenship. For example, few things are more needed in American political and social life than regaining the experience of a community in whose midst all voices are listened to.[74] The believer can bring the memory and experience of struggling to deal with community in the church, as Murray argued in his fashion, too, the basis for a common life is common truth and value. For this reason, the cultural foundations of American democracy are crucial for self-governance.[75] If sheer self-determination and spontaneous nationalism substitute for truth about the innate dignity of the human person, then America's freedom becomes an absence of constraint upon collective arbitrariness, and the Bill of Rights becomes protection for a self-indulgent majority contentedly living at the expense of a minority who, by definition, cannot do more than suffer majority rule while hearing that this is freedom and democracy.[76] Who, more than those belonging to a community oriented by the divine future, is in better position to uphold the innate dignity of all citizens and to demand recognition for this truth within the national consensus than believer-citizens?

The uniqueness of the divine, eschatological future, given in the Spirit, is that it fulfills what is known on the way to it. And for that reason believers can have an, as it were, intuitive sense of, a developed taste for, what genuinely will bring social justice. They already live with intimations of its fulfillment. These anticipations become a negative norm insofar as what negates them is recognized as contrary to human fulfillment. Racism, economism, and consumerism negate those anticipations. To the extent that state decisions, policies, plans imply such an error, to that extent believer-citizens see a need to change the state's way of proceeding. For example, when citizens, the first officers in a democracy, come to realize that the act of voting carries less influence in determining a national course of action than the unelected finagling of hired lobbies, then there is reason to think democracy is being betrayed from within. Believer-citizens can amplify and clarify that realization by recourse to the truth of the innate dignity of every person.

The Spirit is the foretaste, the down payment, the realization in advance, of eschatological plenitude. The absolute future in the presence of the Spirit relates to the proximate future within believers as citizens. The eschaton meets the state in believers' interiority. Church-state relations foreshadow full reconciliation of all creation in Christ and can be known as a way toward it. This means that Christian hope measures, relativizes, and situates every definite plan by which a state undertakes to serve its people.

Pneumatological self-understanding makes a difference in the practice of believer-citizens seeking social justice. Coleman identifies four elements in the difference. First, "the Spirit who is called 'comforter' is a source of hope in discouragement in struggles for God's justice."[77] Second, "Christians should never lose hope in the struggle for God's justice since the Spirit is the guarantee that justice will prevail and that, even now, it is breaking through in history."[78] Hope has grounds in the present labor of the Spirit in history and not only in the promised future. Third, the Holy Spirit bestows charisms whose diversity is irreducible yet conducive toward the one end which is the building up of the one, universal body of Christ. They have an effect of disposing people to counteract their own despising of the poor and of changes for their sake. The Spirit leads them to "partiality toward the most burdened, the poor and the voiceless in our midst."[79] Fourth, the Spirit "sets directions for the style of the church's engagement" in the practice of justice. For, the "ultimate goal of strategies of justice is true reconciliation and the building up of a unity based on justice and truth."[80] Bold confrontation may be an intermediate step, however. Even then, there will be respect for "the multiple gifts in the Church and freedom of conscience in the Spirit."[81] This rules out "heavy 'guilt trips' " and "coercion of members of the Church to one concrete strategy of pursuing justice as some 'new laws.' "[82] These implications of the mission of the Spirit are consonant with Murray's work but give invaluable new specification to what he had to say about believers fulfilling their duties as citizens.

Three further considerations can be added. First, believers are pilgrims. Along with access to the gospel's social values, their social ministry can learn from their inchoate, nontheoretical share in a future of eschatological plenitude. The believer as citizen, though, may be comfortable in forfeiting a pilgrim's status. Instead of pilgrim-citizen, they can become, like Gulliver in Lilliput, tied down. One temptation for American Catholics, and perhaps others, is to tighten a correlation between a proximate, American future and eschatological hope.[83] This resolves the tension and produces, of course, a hideous, nationalistic messianism which often has militaristic themes. Such blending of America's promises with God's promises, seems endemic in an unofficial, unreflective way because it is part of the logic by which civil religion reigns. An opposite reduction of the tension between eschaton and proximate future dissociates them. This is the secularization of time. It disconnects temporality from the incarnation and resurrection of Christ and his concern for the full well-being of all peoples. It leads to sanctioning an idea of time emptied of address by God, without finality in an eschaton, and incapable of receiving an incentive for justice from eschatological tension. This underwrites passive resignation to all kinds of injustice as simply "the way things are" and presumably "always will be."

White American Christians, Catholic or not, gave resignation an especially vicious twist by fostering passivity as the Christian response appropriate for African-Americans while at the same time holding quite another view for themselves and their children. White American Christians, that is, by and large supported passive resignation to racism by African-Americans suffering under racist structures arising from a racist culture. Then, the same white American Christians, having dissolved tension between their actual way of hoping and eschatological hope, could veer over to its opposite, the excitement of an active, nationalistic messianism for their own future. In both instances they suppressed eschatological tension: but in favor of resignation for the victims of injustice and in favor of prosperity, active management of global affairs, and agitated anticipation over the imminence of an American eschaton for those conniving in injustice. Martin Luther King, Jr., led all Americans out of that polarity of futures, one for victims of racism, another for business as usual. His message, despite blending descriptions of America's future with images drawn from biblical eschatology, measured the proximate American future by the ultimate biblical future rather than merged or confused the two. Better, he liberated America's vision of the future from many of the pretensions inherent in projecting America's future as a paradise which merely fulfilled a status quo burdened with injustice.

Second, the labor of the Spirit does not confine itself to biblical word and sacrament, to church doctrine and personal faith, to institutional structure or formally religious words and deeds. The Spirit also acts directly, immediately and obscurely in persons. Charisms for the good of the church sometimes erupt into ecclesial life.[84] The special vocations of Mother Teresa, Dorothy Day, Jean Vanier or the Salvadoran martyrs were nurtured in the church, but cannot be interpreted as if mandated in detail and in their dispositions of courage by anyone except the Lord through the Spirit. The election of Pope John XXIII was altogether according to established procedures but his convoking of Vatican II surprised all, and even dismayed some because it was an unexpected, charismatic deed that departed from conventional wisdom about an aging, short-term, caretaker Pope. In a less conspicuous manner, many believers are led along a route of unpredictable conversions which do more than prepare them for conformity to a cultural status quo supporting dubious social, economic and political arrangements. The Spirit, that is, equips believers with a capacity for nonconformity which can enter their citizenship as a restive force for justice.

Third, the direct presence and labor of the Spirit in believer-citizens means that Catholic social doctrine does not exist in them—presuming their familiarity with it!—as a monological, doctrinaire program handed down from the heights of church authority. Correlative to and, if need be, compensatory to an authoritarian treatment of the teaching is a sovereignty "from below," as it were, though really "from above" insofar as the Spirit, without asking permission or needing doctrinal mediation, prompts people toward solidarity with their own poverty.[85] Catholic social doctrine, with a preferential option for the poor, becomes a way in which someone with the already received gift of the Spirit finds access to a life in the Spirit insofar as this impinges on the common temporal good and the sociopolitical order. This means also that a practice of justice by believers can move from, and find a warrant in, a spiritual interiority which is open to free, unbidden promptings by the Holy Spirit. This liberates their practice from the role of an empty jar transporting social doctrine from church to marketplace or public square. Social doctrine is a guide to spiritual growth as well as to principles reflecting divine wisdom on the common good.

As a result, believers' practice of social justice can proceed in the absence of an exact, detailed and fully comprehensive knowledge of its outcome. This does not dispense from social analysis, careful research, reflection on strategy and planning or from utopian vision. It does mean that just policies and actions are justified in themselves and not only from their long-term goal. Accepting the work of the Spirit in believers means that a practice of social justice has premises other than a judgment that control over the future or manipulation of present tendencies is the key to social transformation. The mission of the Spirit warrants a practice of social justice simply by moving people to it, or in many cases, by enlightening and strengthening rational analyses of society. The practice of social justice does not depend, that is, on possession of either a picture of the ideal society or the ideal state, which Murray rightly regarded as irrelevant chimeras.

Rather, the mission of the Spirit enriches the practice of believers with a content not identical to their already possessed self-understanding. No one's self-understanding is thoroughly perspicuous or filled with certainty about the proximate future. In this condition there is a hidden influence the Spirit has upon human freedom. This means that practice by believers as citizens contains new direction and content insofar as their freedom is freed gently and perhaps imperceptibly by the Spirit for what freedom demands: solidarity from poverty of spirit with those to whom the Spirit of the Lord sent Jesus. This opposes and tends to eradicate whatever could be a pretext for divisions into superior and inferior humanity according to material or cultural possessions. That is, an option for the poor and commitment to social justice by believer-citizens has an inwardness open to a continuing education in divine things. Becoming alert to the promptings of the Holy Spirit (not without the church, scriptures, retreats, prayer) sours a taste for consumerism, militarism, and materialism while bringing delight in friendships, cultural differences, physical nature and creative art. This affects the cultural substratum on which self-government relies.

6 | Free Exercise of Religion: An Option for the Poor

The Church-State Difference and *Libertas Ecclesiae*

John Courtney Murray located the problem of freedom in American democracy outside political structures. He asserted that "Our 'free institutions,' in their procedural aspects, are working today as well as they ever have worked or ever will work."[1] True, he admitted, some "tinkering with them may be needed." But the "basic issues of our time concern the spiritual substance of a free society," not its institutional procedures, and touch the underlying social structure. At the heart of that "spiritual substance" was "the central Christian concept, *res sacra homo,* man is sacredness (only the abstract noun can render the Latin rightly)."[2]

This can also be translated as "humanity is sacred." This affirms that no person and no social reality can be defined fully through their political or even social realities. The sacredness of human nature is its creation by and orientation toward God, and restoration and elevation of that status by Christ. *Res sacra homo* proclaims, consequently, a sphere of humanity prior to any political structure or authority, any social structure. Murray argued that this is a truth grounding the social, civil and political freedom of societies and persons in western tradition. He emphasized that it arose, and gained an impulse toward expression, from the *libertas ecclesiae* (freedom of the church). The freedom of the church in public life preceded that freedom of individual conscience which "political modernity"[3] has installed as a secular substitute for "all that the Christian tradition has meant by the pregnant phrase, the 'freedom of the Church.' "[4] This freedom, along with the irreducible difference between church and state it presupposes, can be appropriated as an option for the poor.

Murray doubted that modern forgetfulness of Christian revelation of the sacredness of the person and of the freedom of the church was a solid basis for future respect for freedom and justice on the part of western nations. The following analysis will show that an option for the poor meets his concern about the future of western, political respect for human dignity and is a new exercise of the *libertas ecclesiae*.

134

Church-State Non-Identity and Ecclesial Freedom

The freedom of the church is part of its identity. The identity contains new reality, a new otherness from all civilization and states which humanity had built so laboriously and often with astounding ingenuity and knowledge. New Testament distinctions between a duty to God and another to Caesar gave moral force to a sociopolitical implication attendant upon accepting Jesus as messiah in a community identified with him. Pope Gelasius declared a formal division between two authorities, spiritual and temporal, as a consequence of a radical difference between the church and every human institution. Medieval doctrine on two societies carried this principle of difference into an analysis of structural purposes and principles. Modern papal teachings have held as a tenet of faith that a gratuitous abundance of truth and value in the missions of Christ and the Spirit are a world-changing newness whose reality transcends every civil order and state.

The church-state difference originates, then, in the advent of new reality, not in a new principle for dividing what had always been extant. The church did not divide the state's political power, but existed to represent another kind of reality, different from society and the state. An effect was that the origin, activity and purpose of the church exceeded, and consequently differed from, those of the state, which were not annulled. Another effect was that the state was liberated from a burden of false transcendence, was freed to be and to act as a finite reality, a creature.

Political institutions, authorities, activities and purposes derived, not from the missions of Son and Spirit but from the prior act and status of divine creation. The state arose in created human nature's need to organize society for the fulfilling of conditions conducive to familial, personal and social flourishing. Political reality was a matter of human practical reason. Its purpose lay in the temporal common good. Murray observed, in regard to the way Christianity affected the political order, that it was

> an historical commonplace to say that the essential political contribution of Christianity was to destroy the classical view of society as a single, homogenous structure, within which the political power stood forth as the representative of society both in its religious and in its political aspects.[5]

He hearkened back to a celebrated letter of Pope Gelasius I to Emperor Anastasius I as the classic statement on the Christian revolution. "Two there are, august Emperor," asserted Gelasius, "by which this world is ruled on title of original and sovereign right—the consecrated authority of the priesthood and the royal power."[6] Murray endorsed the view of A. Dempf that Gelasius' position was "the Magna Carta of the whole 'freedom of the Church' in medieval times."[7]

The Gelasian text was the "charter of a new freedom . . . with which man could not enfranchise himself."[8] The new freedom was, as Leo XIII taught, the freedom of the church and this is nothing less than "a participation in the freedom of the Incarnate Son of God, the God-Man Christ Jesus."[9] The church was and is sent by Christ with the "freedom to teach, to rule and to sanctify"[10] its members. The freedom of the church is for the mission of the church, is expressed in activities constituting that mission and has, therefore, a positive meaning. It is not "freedom from" in the first instance, but "freedom for" and "freedom in." If a local church enjoyed full negative freedom from outside interference yet neglected its self-realization in mission, it would not exercise the most basic *libertas ecclesiae*. This freedom belongs to the identity of every local church and of the communion of churches. The event of Vatican II was a dramatic expression of it.

Postconciliar options for the poor by diverse local churches are new specifications of mission and so are new expressions of the church's freedom and identity. An option for the poor proposed by *Economic Justice for All* is a free act which begins to define the way American Catholicism exercises its ministry in American society. The act of making this option is a matter of a fundamental freedom of a local church to express and make actual its identity as the newness of the missions of Christ and the Spirit.

Her positive freedom involves two modes of ministry that Murray presented through a familiar hierarchy/faithful disjunction. The first, by "divine commission endows her with the freedom to teach, to rule, and to sanctify, with all that these empowerments imply as necessary for their free exercise."[11] A second is "freedom to have access to the teaching of the Church, to obey her laws, to receive at her hands the sacramental ministry of grace, and to live within her fold an integral supernatural life."[12] These freedoms, to cause (teach, rule, sanctify) and to be affected (access to teaching, obedience, reception of sacraments) are understandable also in light of an ecclesiology of the church as communion.[13]

A local church revolves around celebration of the eucharist which links all bishops, the bishop of Rome, and all sharing the eucharist in *communio*. The difference between apostolic office and baptismal office does not disappear in the eucharist, but it does become secondary to the eucharistic Christ, the biblical word of God, the sanctifying Spirit and the mission of the eucharistic community. Free exercise of apostolic ministry and of baptismal ministry in the one mission of a eucharistic church manifests and realizes the freedom of Christ and of the Spirit. Freedom in ministry pertains to the whole church active in eucharistic celebration. It cannot be adequately portrayed, the way Murray often did, as freedom of clergy and hierarchy to act, and freedom of the laity to be acted upon. Bishop and lay person are acted on by the word of God; bishop and lay person act to realize faith and charism.

Consequently, the negative side of the freedom as immunities from interference by the state can be reconceived. The negative freedom of apostolic office is immunity from "all manner of politicization, through subordination to the state or enclosure within the state as *instrumentum regni*."[14] The negative freedom of the laity "requires that all the intrapolitical sacrednesses (*res sacra in temporalibus*) be assured of their immunity from politicization."[15] An option for the poor by a local eucharistic communion (e.g., Catholics in the United States; a diocese) exercises the mission of the church and so has a right to these immunities. The bishop cannot be prevented from ministering to those *res sacra in temporalibus* in American culture, society, economy and state forming a large part of lay existence and mission, not to mention the lives of fellow citizens. Often, in fact, the laity or other citizens are those who initially draw the attention of a successor to the apostles to particular issues or problems. Concern for the moral dimensions of public policy, i.e., the impact of social, economic and political policies upon the dignity of persons, belongs to episcopal ministry.[16] Efforts to define away this concern or to prevent its actualization are interference with the freedom of the church to realize its mission.

Likewise, efforts to stifle lay initiatives within an option for the poor (in obedience to conscience, gospel and bishops) violate the freedom of the church by subordinating the faith-understanding of persons and families to preestablished ideologies. Such violations of *libertas ecclesiae*, moreover, should they acquire anything of coercive power, would also fail to observe the free-exercise clause in the First Amendment. Any attitude, philosophy, theology or practice tending to define the ministry of Catholicism in America as essentially that of being an *instrumentum regni* falsifies the identity of the church, compromises her mission, and is probably an ideology of a partisan, political sort.

Ecclesial Freedom Can Liberate Society from Political Oppression

Ecclesial freedom is a spiritual reality that has had, indirectly, a liberating impact on society and state. First and most important, "the freedom of the Church as the spiritual authority served as the limiting principle of the power of government."[17] There was a check and balance offered by pope, bishops and clergy to the political establishment. Power checked and balanced could not run to extremes in controlling peoples' lives. The effect was that, in the "face of public power and of all the private powers" Christian people claimed for themselves the "corporate freedom"[18] of the church in informal self-affirmation and by more formal assertion of immunity from total authority on the part of a ruler. The consent of the governed in the Magna Carta reflected this liberating impact of ecclesial freedom.

A "corporate freedom" of the church in America was exercised by episcopal agreement to draft, circulate, revise, then authorize *Economic Justice for All* and its option for the poor. A remarkable novelty in this freedom was of proceeding according to a principle of dialogue. Dialogue has freedom as an internal dynamic which permits speakers to allow the subject matter to play itself out. The published version of the document invited readers to public dialogue on how to apply universal principles of the Christian faith to matters of economic policy in the United States. This is a summons to ecclesial self-realization in freedom and dialogue. The novelty in a formal principle of dialogue is also the appearance of a new kind of freedom in the mission of Catholics in American society.[19]

It installs freedom and dialogue as the kind of relation obtaining in consciousness between a person's belief and her civil life in American society. Belief speaks with a partner, civic concern within the believer-citizen. The nature of this interior dialogue, of course, is affected by the prior and ultimate dialogue between Trinity and humanity. Creation and the missions of Son and Spirit, as well as faith entering covenant with the Lord give special features to interior conversation between belief and civic duty. Belief, that is, is more comprehensive than its civil partner. Their dialogue is free because neither coerces the other. Yet equality in freedom is not parity in content or equivalence in relation to human destiny.

Incidentally, an option for the poor taking place in freedom and dialogue is not educated resignation to an iron law of history whose inflexible progress makes any further word superfluous. Flexibility, creativity, willingness to learn from experience and controversy, not heartless rigidity, characterize the option for the poor in *Economic Justice for All.*

Further, Murray pointed out that "the freedom of the Church as the 'people of God' furnished the ultimate directive principle of government."[20] The church, along with the university, mobilized "the moral consensus of the people" and enabled them to bring it "to bear upon the power, thus to insure that the king . . . would 'fight for justice and the freedom of the people' [John of Salisbury].[21] The bishops addressed *Economic Justice for All* to American Catholics precisely as Americans, part of "the people." They set themselves a large, unfinished task of helping to mobilize a "moral consensus" in favor of influencing, among other realities, public opinion which is how a cultural consensus can be brought to "bear upon the power."

One objective was to help political sovereignty, possessed by citizens, not a king, exert itself in a struggle for "justice and the freedom of the people." Chapter Four in *Economic Justice for All,* "A New American Experiment: Partnership for the Public Good," recommended ways to complete the "unfinished business of the American experiment."[22] This exemplifies the freedom of the church. The bishops appropriated that freedom for the "spiritual authority" by their analysis of moral aspects in economic policies. Clergy and faithful appropriate that freedom for "the people of God" by actualizing their identity in a mission for the sake of the poor, the unemployed, the victims of racism, sexism, and economic policies heedless of what happens to persons. The content of the church's freedom is commitment to, and self-realization in, a contemporary version of what John of Salisbury and Murray called a "fight for justice and the freedom of the people."

In a phase of transformative inculturation, and in some circumstances, believer-citizen nonidentity could be expressed by belief's negation of the ordinary duty of a citizen to obey political authority. Then, believer-citizen nonidentity becomes a believer's negation of a state's operative definition of a citizen. In these extreme situations, church-state nonidentity and the freedom of the church are appropriated in an unusual act of rejecting a particular leader, policy or action of the state, or even, of a particular state's legitimacy.

For example, Robert McAfee Brown describes a believer's "Yes" to God in Christian faith as containing a "no" to the state as an absolute.[23] McAfee Brown discusses a *status confessionis* for Christian faith and Christian churches when they can continue to confess their faith in Christ only by formally negating a governmental policy or action which violates human dignity and justice. Then, as with the Barmen Declaration against Nazism in 1934, or the 1982 World Alliance of Reformed Churches' denunciation of South African apartheid as heresy, the church keeps its identity only by spelling out that to which faith says, "No."

Murray, equally with McAfee Brown, objected to a tendency states have to inflate themselves into mortal deities ballooning over society. He pointed to many instances: postmedieval regal absolutism; totalitarian extension of state power to every moment in social life under Hitler and Stalin; tendencies toward absolutizing the majority will in modern democracies. All sought control over the church and so failed to heed the church-state difference. Each was a case of political authority rejecting the revolutionary, ever-precarious dyarchy introduced by Christianity. All regressed into an ever-attractive monism which had the effect of allowing a government to invest itself with sacrality, and then to monopolize authority in society and public life. But the church-state dyarchy, however strenuously the church had to oppose its obliteration, manifested nonidentity, not antithesis.

The First Amendment's no-establishment clauses, Murray held, was the state's official, constitutional definition of itself as different from, and incompetent in, religion. This was *de facto* recognition of church-state nonidentity. American government did not, in principle, make itself sacred. Murray did not presuppose or project a *status confessionis* for American Catholics. Yet principles he expounded do support that possibility. If, for example, the American government began to "regard the state as a moral end in itself, a self-justifying entity with its own self-determined spiritual substance"[24] it would step beyond the limited competence accepted in the First Amendment. This would be the state's arrogating to itself the task of interpreting peoples' existence and the means by which they can achieve their destiny.

If, more in particular, American democracy gradually and unofficially became what McAfee Brown refers to as a "national security state,"[25] then Murray's principle of church-state nonidentity could be appropriated only in negation of the state's abuse of authority. If the state became an end in itself, for whose goals the people and society were no more than instruments, and if its agenda demanded the churches' compliance, the church-state difference within the conscience of believer-citizens could be affirmed only in the free negation of the state's national security ideology, policies, agencies, and institutions. This would be a case of the state bringing about conditions which, for believers, became a *status confessionis*. Appropriation of ecclesial freedom in that situation would approximate what McAfee Brown describes as prophetic resistance to state absolutism.

The Church-State Dyarchy in an Option for the Poor: Eschatological Features

According to Murray, and Catholic tradition, instability and fragility in the temporal-spiritual dyarchy is not due to a spiritual compromise with the temporal, as if political reality were inherently evil. The Gelasian dyarchy was duality between two powers or authorities guiding the same people toward two kinds of life. In Murray's teaching on the dyarchy, the church tended toward eternal life and participation in it by all humanity. The state tended toward the common, temporal good of a particular society. An option for the poor opens up the eschatological dimension in this traditional distinction. An option for the poor rephrases the distinction into a difference between two relations to the future. The church exists to be and to promote the kingdom of God fully realized in the eschatological future. A state exists and acts for a common temporal good partially and incompletely moving toward that plenitude but subject to measurement by its standards and goals.

If an eschatological framework encompasses the eternal-temporal duality, then church-state relations become less a matter of faith-reason harmony charted at Vatican I and more than a faith-culture successor emerging from Vatican II. The relations are then between two futures and two kinds of hope. The church in solidarity with humanity, especially the poor and afflicted, is a sacrament of hope, a sign and instrument of the realization of union with God and among peoples. A community of hope does not simply happen. It comes about in and through graced freedom actualized in a relation to the future. Murray's dyarchy in an eschatological context becomes a "spiritual" community of Christian hope relating to a "temporal" American society whose culture suffers from no lack of anticipations for the future.

The internal freedom of the church in opting for the poor makes an indirect impact upon the political order by working from an alternative to the culturally dominant and politically established definition of the future of society. Here, the nonidentity of the church and state manifests itself as the nonidentity of anticipations. The church expands an American self-understanding by keeping it in dialogical engagement with the memory of Christ's resurrection, and with hope for changing social structures to manifest some (not all) of its truth about humanity—that we are not meant for oppression by death in any of its forms. The church as a community of hope heads toward social justice as a goal for America in a political order charged with the culture's many expectations.

Not all are congruent with eschatological hope convinced that God's kingdom begins on earth and respects freedom. There are cultural, social and political forces championing, for example, the priority of national security to national and international social justice. Hope grounded in the resurrection can liberate church members from the all-consuming fear of death and a resultant, fundamental state of anxiety. This permits them to see how unreasonable it is to imagine that full security (when is it adequate?) has to precede and prepare for justice.

Hope allows recognition that the reverse is true: social justice brings security and is, therefore, a prior goal, though national security can accompany it. As a community of transcendent hope looking toward the fulfillment of God's kingdom, the church knows that the goal of social justice cannot be identified with a comprehensive and radical overcoming of all evil, starting with death. Nonetheless, it has a mission in the temporal order. In its freedom and distinction from the state, the church has its own recourse to the underlying culture which social practice and symbolic life express.

This makes possible a dualistic, dialogical relation to the future rather than a monological one funded and controlled by an economic elite and a political oligarchy. The church has an obligation, in fact, to engage itself in dialogue with the ways the culture conceives the future and to present its vision of the American future open to all in justice as an alternative. This, to some extent, is a task of encouraging its own members to do what, it seems at times, the political order has lost the will to do but could do. Transformative dialogue, then, puts two futures into tension that are intrinsically ordered to one another as, in general, nature operating interior to and influenced by grace. To the extent that a state absolutizes the future conceived within political terms, it unofficially embraces the erroneous *natura pura* view of the human future. Christian hope can liberate the political process from that illusory goal.

In that kind of dialogue, more than a faith-reason harmony can be heard. Something occurs that Murray did not consider. The church-state difference becomes nonidentity between a community bearing a transcendent hope and American society acting from its version of the future. For believer-citizens, this brings out a nonidentity, perhaps at times a contrast, between *hope* (realization of divine promises whose down payment is the Holy Spirit poured out into the hearts of believers) and *American anticipations*.

Attitudes, practice and symbols oriented toward the future manifest underlying cultural meanings, values and patterns. Meanings, values and patterns with reference to the future underlie and reside in American social practice and symbolic life. Some degree of nonidentity between Christian hope and any cultural definition of the future belongs, of course, to the characteristic condition of a pilgrim church. Hope, however, turns toward justice and decides to work for transformation of a culture when the difference between two futures becomes, as Martin Luther King, Jr., perceived so acutely, a weight burdening some with oppression and dehumanizing others.

The Independence of the Political in an Option for the Poor

A third church-state norm recognized the independence of the political order from the church. Murray gave this hard-won realization new force by showing how the church could not, in principle, enlist political assistance for religious purposes. He upheld an independence inherent in the state against a renewal of an ecclesiastical tendency toward words and deeds reaching out for state leverage on religious goals. The independence of the political was implied by the primacy of the spiritual. The primacy of the spiritual was a spiritual, not political, primacy. The independence of the political demanded that the efficacy of the spiritual be carefully and clearly understood. Spiritual efficacy was spiritual in means as well as in goals.[26]

The church legitimately wanted temporal affairs to be for the human good and was free to enter temporal affairs as part of its mission. This much was simply reaffirmation of the sovereignty of Christ in conscience. However, intervention was "purely spiritual, since it takes the form simply of moral judgments on political affairs."[27] The church's leaders, therefore, could not try to direct the temporal agencies and structures of the state toward the church's spiritual goal, eternal life. That is, "nothing is here said about the execution of those moral judgments in terms of law, public policy, social action, etc."[28] The authors of *Economic Justice for All* gave this principle prominence by refusing to issue binding, authoritative judgments on public policy recommendations which, instead, illustrated how American Catholics can appropriate universal values from tradition. The bishops respected the independence of the political within believer-citizens.

And their respect showed that the principle of the "independence of the political" has formed their ministry. Acute sensitivity to the need for this respect demonstrates how American Catholics have formed their self-understanding and their appropriation of gospel values in an all but universal, yet informal, consensus on the "independence of the political." The citizen holds a position of independence in her dialogue with church authorities. Neither the state nor citizenship derives from, nor stands under, governance by ecclesiastical office. The believer's relation to the state is not under the jurisdiction of the church because that relation is political. But the believer's conscience rightly forms itself in dialogue with all that the church is and does. In matters of faith and morality, believers appropriate authorized teaching (in freedom of course). But bishops, on the basis of their apostolic authority, do not and cannot command a specific political practice from believers.

There is simply no direct link from church authority to a believer's political practice. And so, there is no basis for a mandate for episcopal jurisdiction over any political act. Nor, by the same token, is there any ground for objections to episcopal entrance into America's political process. An option for the poor can be brought before American Catholics, who can then hear it as a particular concentration of the gospel with which they have long familiarity. On that condition, they can receive an option for the poor. They can redefine their self-understanding around it, change their practice by taking it to themselves. But no American Catholic voter, no American Catholic elected or appointed official can be governed by her church on a civic practice according to it. Nor can legitimate apostolic authority exercised by bishops tie her conscience to determinate prescriptions for political practice serviceable to social justice. Her own voluntarism, in a relation to the state, belongs by definition and widely-acknowledged right to the "independence of the political."

The Finality Toward Cooperation in an Option for the Poor

Independence in political self-interpretation, political practice and democratic structures from church authority does not absolutize the state. John Coleman correctly remarks that "to carve out institutional spheres of life as 'sacrally secular' enclaves untouched by God's action and purpose is a species of idolatry."[29] The enclave might be an institution or it could be a precinct interior to self-interpretation. Coleman quoted Simone Weil on a tendency toward a dichotomy between religion and life. Weil observed that French Catholics—Coleman includes it because it is apposite to Americans no less—"resign themselves to being irreligious . . . in all that appertains to the secular side of their own lives. . . . In any case they set aside the proper function of religion, which is to suffuse with its light all secular life, public or private, without in any way dominating it."[30] American Catholicism has not been exempt from segregating religion away from one or more spheres of life, one of the chief errors to which Vatican II addressed itself.

The "independence of the political" does not remove political reality from all reference to, or judgment by, the church, "the spiritual" or the gospel. Coleman rightly stresses that, to the contrary, "Hebraeo-Christian commitment to a radical monotheism ascribes ultimate sovereignty to God over all nations, times, and institutions."[31] At various times, that principle led to versions of theocracy and in the church's history generated the view that "the Christian world—or at least the Catholic nation—was considered to be somehow enclosed within the Church."[32] The practice of a sacral state extended religious prerogatives to the political ruler who was seen as more than political. In the west, it handed over to a king "care of the religion of his subjects and a care of their religious unity as essential to their political unity."[33] This did not allow for religious liberty and did not embody a full church-state differ-ence. Whatever locating of the political under the divine may be needed today, neither a revived papal states nor abolition of the church-state difference is the solution.

The fourth norm in church-state relations helps in this matter. Church and state are distinct and independent from each other, both externally in their institutional magnitudes and in their respective finali-ties toward mutual cooperation for the sake of the good of those who participate in both at the same time. The distinction and independence are preconditions for cooperation.

Church-State "Harmony" in an Option for the Poor

The fourth norm in church-state relations affirms their finality to-ward harmony in the believer-citizen's conscience and identity. Their finality is an inherent tendency toward a condition of harmony within the person. Harmony is a deliberate, principled coordination of the be-liever's duty to God with the citizen's duty to the state in a single identity.

Pope Leo XIII had advanced, Murray pointed out, beyond a re-ceived version of the Gelasian, temporal-spiritual duality. Leo XIII had initiated an anthropocentric church-state relation. Leo, "by some man-ner of genius," gave a "special twist . . . to the Gelasian doctrine."[34] He grounded the necessity for an orderly relation between church and state in "the fact that *utriusque imperium est in eodem*, the rule of both is over the same one man."[35] Papal originality was evident in relocating church-state relations from a sphere of official contacts between representative authorities to a dualism of duties in the conscience of the person who was believer and citizen. That person's conscience was where church met state. And, Leo taught, that encounter had a tendency, a finality, an inner momentum, toward mutual coordination of those duties. God was author of both church and state, and the person fulfilled two kinds of obligations to God by carrying out the two kinds of duties. Personal coordination of the duties was the church-state harmony toward which church-state rela-tions tended. The result was harmony in identity.

This, rather than conflict or parallelism was the end or goal, because only harmony enabled the person precisely to perform what was due. If "there is conflict and not harmony between them, the conflict is felt in the depths of personal conscience which knows itself to be obligated to both of the powers which are from God."[36] Conflict in a person between her duty to God in faith and her duty to God through the state divided the person against herself. The resultant condition of inner division prevented a solid and decisive orientation in personal choices regarding church and state. This paralyzed a person who faced the need to make choices and begin to act. Therefore, interior harmony "is required by the unity and integrity of the human personality."[37] The goal and criterion for church-state relations, according to Leo, was anthropocentric, or person-centered, and included self-understanding.

Murray analyzed interior harmony in terms of a "dualism within the human person, who is both child of God, member of the church, and also a member of the human community, citizen of a state."[38] As a consequence, that person was "endowed in each capacity with a set of rights, which are of different origin."[39] Participation in the mystery of Christ as a member of the church endowed one with a believer's rights, while participation in the state as a citizen gave a distinct set of rights. The two, however, cannot exist in mutually oblivious parallelism. That would be to ignore or to violate the norm that the "principle of organization is the primacy of the spiritual aspect of his nature."[40] Primacy of the spiritual meant the two sets of duties and rights "must be organized into an organic whole."[41] Leonine doctrine was that the person had a right "to have the two powers to which he is subject in harmony with each other" for the sake of the "integrity of the human personality."[42]

Only when a person enjoyed "preservation of this integrity" was he able to be effectively and "truly 'free,' empowered to be in fullness what he is—citizen and Christian."[43] What produced inner integrity was a prior and external harmony between authoritative representatives from church and state. This was an institutional arrangement prior to believer-citizen conscience and choice. Spheres of responsibility coordinated by officials representing church and state brought about an ecclesiastical-political situation in which believer-citizens could act freely, and with integrity. Leonine anthropocentrism saw believer-citizens locked into position inside a larger, controlling framework of institutional relations. The believer-citizen needed integrity and interior freedom in order to obey two kinds of commands, from church and from state. This was a passive believer-citizen. Still, that person had, or ought to have, freedom to carry out known and harmonious duties.

Murray went a step farther. He drew out something implied by Leo's statements. He noticed that, "Leo XIII was implicitly saying that the human person by his action as Christian and citizen ought to be the instrument and agent of establishing this harmony in actual fact."[44] There was, that is, an institutional harmony antecedent to and productive of harmony in the believer-citizen's conscience. That was explicit in Leonine teaching. And there was, in addition, Murray argued, a consequent sociopolitical harmony of which "the Christian and citizen ought to be the instrument and agent."[45] This was more than a coordination of duties in conscience because that coordinating brought about "harmony in fact" not only in principle. This was what Leo only implied.

Murray analyzed the activity by which believer-citizens established that consequent harmony. He did so by reference to a principle not on hand for Leo XIII. Pope Pius XII later came to the concept of the person as source and end of social processes, as well as their beneficiary. Murray commented on Leonine teaching in light of Pius' emphasis on the activity, not passivity, of the believer-citizen. Pius defined the citizen "as a human person, the subject of inviolable rights and duties, and the root and end of social life."[46] The citizen was not, as Pope Leo XIII tended to teach, a passive element existing to carry out political duties prescribed by the benevolent authority of governing authorities. The citizen, taught Pius XII and Murray, was an "active agent and self-determining."

The activity consisted in "exercise of his rights as a citizen." That kind of activity gave the citizen "a share in the public power and therefore a responsibility to see to it that the processes of government . . . tend to their proper end, which is the freedom" of persons.[47] Pope Pius XII retaught Leo XIII's idea of the believer-citizen while redefining the citizen as actively participating in public power, not passively performing what an external authority determined was to be done. But Murray went beyond Pius by a singular emphasis on freedom as that central reality with which and for whose sake the citizen acted when exercising his rights and participating in self-governance.

He advanced beyond Pius XII also by assigning to believer-citizens, not to officials acting on their behalf, the primary responsibility in forming church-state relations. Their conscientious and free activity as believers who engaged themselves in civil tasks brought the primary contact between church and state. This principle, of course, undermined a view that favored, indeed, an active citizenry but one whose church-state relations were arranged for them, over their heads, by church representatives negotiating with the state. The end of paternalism brought the resolution of the ancient dyarchy into a new, concrete, operative form that was interior to believer-citizens. Believer-citizens not only engaged in self-governance politically, but also were the active front line along which church dealt with state. This was to have arrived at, not just an active political anthropocentrism, but an active and constructive ecclesiopolitical anthropocentrism.

Vatican II placed church-state relations within the broader church-world context.[48] That further developed this ecclesiopolitical anthropocentrism. Vatican II changed the understanding of the believer-citizen's active, constructive role. The nature of the person's activity became service or ministry. First, Murray noted, the "Declaration on Religious Liberty" embraced Pius XII's teaching that " 'the human person is the foundation, the goal, and the bearer of the whole social process' including the processes of government."[49] Then, the "Pastoral Constitution on the Church in the Modern World" reaffirmed harmony as the goal in church-state relations but described it as "cooperation."[50] And the "Pastoral Constitution" went on to define the cooperation as one between two kinds of service.

Murray drew attention to the fact that in the Constitution, church and state " 'stand in the service of the personal and social vocation of the same men.' "[51] Church and state did not rule over, or were not institutional containers shaped by their active inhabitants, but *served* persons participating in both. External, institutional church-state cooperation did not only manifest finality toward internal passive harmony in consciences (Leo XIII), or tend solely toward an active harmony in consciences and activities (Pius XII), or even toward actualization of freedom in formation of church-state relations (Murray in 1949). The finality toward harmony revealed the servant nature of church and state. Each was a servant (i.e., a means) for the person (i.e., an end, not a means to the institution's ends) in her personal and social vocation (i.e., her inmost tendency toward self-actualization in communities). Within her identity, her tendencies toward union with Christ (church) and toward contribution to the common temporal good (state) cooperate. There Murray left the matter. He bequeathed us a postinstitutionalist, person-centered but not individualist idea of church-state harmony.

What does his incipient development of tradition mean in an option for the poor? Church-state relations tend toward a person's integral self-realization. The principle of integration can be summed up as eschatologically energetic faith-hope marked by an option for the poor. The independent yet serviceable political facet of that person's self-realization has the signal feature of social justice. Their harmony is an integrating self-understanding whereby an evangelical, religious option for the poor gains efficacy in the citizen's political will to social justice. The harmony is not simply in coordinated principles but in practice embodying at once the ultimate horizon of Christian hope and the proximate horizon which is civil anticipation of a fulfilled common good.

The traditional church-state harmony can be reconceived as practical coordinating of two irreducible yet indissociable anticipations of the future. Coordinating does not mean contriving harmony at all costs, because the order in coordinating puts the eschatological hope foremost where it acts as a criterion for temporal anticipations. Use of that criterion produces a critique of the temporal hope, and of its distance from the eschatological hope. Eschatological hope also contains a positive, general directive for temporal expectations, though by no means does it supply what human experience, analysis, and political agency alone has the task of substantiating. Habitual, common church-state dissociation can be reconceived as a divorce of temporal anticipation from eschatological hope that leaves Christian citizens' expectations of the state enervated and prone to ideological captivity.

Notes

Introduction

[1] National Catholic Bishops Conference, *Economic Justice for All: Pastoral Letter on Catholic Social Teaching and the U.S. Economy* (Washington, DC.: United States Catholic Conference, 1986).

[2] *Ibid.*, nn. 53–5, pp. 29–30.

[3] George Gallup, Jr. and Jim Castelli, *The People's Religion: American Faith in the '90's* (New York: Macmillan, 1989), pp. 23–4. Andrew M. Greeley challenges the Gallup figures for being too high at 28%. The NORC numbers say 25% of Americans are Catholic, and that this has held for the last twenty-five years. Greeley considers, in contrast to Gallup, the data in the *Official Catholic Directory* to be too low, around 22%. Differing results come from differing ways of gathering and interpreting data. Andrew M. Greeley, *The Catholic Myth: The Behavior and Beliefs of American Catholics* (New York: Scribner's Sons, 1990), pp. 109ff.

[4] Figures from *Economic Justice for All*.

[5] Gallup and Castelli, *op. cit.*, pp. 26–7. But 36% of Americans under 30 identify "raised Catholic."

[6] Victor Ferkiss, "The Bishops' Letter and the Future," p. 147, in R. Bruce Douglass, editor, *The Deeper Meaning of Economic Life: Critical Essays on the U.S. Catholic Bishops Pastoral Letter on the Economy* (Washington, D.C.: Georgetown University Press, 1986), pp. 139–55.

[7] Greeley, *op. cit.*, p. 146.

[8] Figures from Gallup and Castelli, *op. cit.*, pp. 201–3. They comment that, "[w]hite Catholics are the least appreciated element of the Democratic Party base; they will bolt the party but do so reluctantly." Yet, they say, "[n]o Democrat can be elected President without something approaching 60% of the Catholic vote," p. 249.

[9] *Economic Justice for All*, n. 359ff., pp. 179–80.

[10] For a bibliography of John Courtney Murray's work, cf., J. Leon Hooper, *The Ethics of Discourse: The Social Philosophy of John Courtney*

Murray (Washington, D.C.: Georgetown University Press, 1986), pp. 256–65; Thomas Hughson, editor and Introduction, *Matthias Scheeben on Faith: The Doctoral Dissertation of John Courtney Murray* (Lewiston, N.Y.: The Edwin Mellen Press, 1987).

The Woodstock Theological Center has entrusted the Murray Archives to the Special Collection Room, Joseph Mark Lauinger Library, Georgetown University, Washington, D.C. Unpublished material from these Archives will be designated by their assigned File Number. For biographical information and a general introduction to Murray, cf. Donald E. Pelotte, *John Courtney Murray: Theologian in Conflict* (New York: Paulist Press, 1975), pp. 30–4, 39–41, 76–106ff.

[11] Martin E. Marty, *An Invitation to American Catholic History* (Chicago: Thomas More Press, 1986), p. 182.

[12] Cardinal Joseph Bernardin, "Religion and Politics: The Future Agenda" (lecture given Oct. 25, 1984 at Georgetown University), *Origins: NC Documentary Service* 14, 21 (November 8, 1984), p. 323.

[13] *Ibid.*

[14] *Economic Justice for All* adopted the phrase "option for the poor" and set itself within that kind of basic will to justice which gives practical priority to the needs of those presently lacking conditions with which to fulfill their dignity as persons in society. Cf. *ibid*, n. 87. p. 45. Also, Donal Dorr, *Option for the Poor: A Hundred Years of Vatican Social Teaching* (Dublin: Gill and Macmillan, 1983) and Michael Walsh and Brian Davies, editors, *Proclaiming Justice and Peace: Papal Documents from Rerum Novarum through Centesimus Annus* (Mystic, Connecticut: Twenty-third Publications, 1991). In *Rerum Novarum* Pope Leo XIII wrote that, ". . . the will of God seems to give preference to people who are particularly unfortunate. . . . Jesus Christ proclaims formally that the poor are blessed . . . most lovingly he invites all those who labour and mourn to come to him, the source of comfort . . . with loving care he clasps to himself the lowly and oppressed," *ibid.*, n. 23, p. 25–6. In a new context, and in view of structures of oppression, Pope John Paul II states, "By virtue of her own evangelical duty, the church feels called to take her stand beside the poor, to discern the justice of their requests and to help satisfy them, without losing sight of the good of groups in the context of the common good," *Sollicitudo Rei Socialis, ibid.*, n. 39, p. 421. He defines the option, as is well-known and often commented upon, as "an option or special form of primacy in the exercise of Christian charity," *ibid.*, n. 42, p. 424, and sees poverty in a variety of forms, including marginalization, refugees, migrants and the "victims of consumerism," *Centesimus Annus, ibid.*, n. 57, p. 475.

There seems to be no compelling reason to think that an option for the poor must be defined either as an act of justice or of charity, as if charity did not require justice (and complete it) and as if charity were not able to inform without displacing the specificity of justice. Cf. John A. Coleman, "Charity and the Nature of American Society," in *An American Strategic Theology* (New York: Paulist Press, 1982), pp. 200–8. The Latin American origin and field of reference for "option for the poor" makes it indissociable from analysis of, and strategies to change, institutional structures of oppression.

Cf. also, Anthony J. Tambasco, "Option for the Poor," in R. Bruce Douglass, editor, *op. cit.*, pp. 37–55; Thomas M. Gannon, editor, *Reflections on the U.S. Bishops' Pastoral Letter on Catholic Social Teaching and the U.S. Economy* (New York: Macmillan, 1987); William E. Murnion, "The 'Preferential Option for the Poor' in *Economic Justice For All: Theology or Ideology?*" in Bernard P. Prusak, editor, *Raising the Torch of Good News: Catholic Authority and Dialogue with the World*, Annual Publication of the College Theology Society (Lanham, Md.: 1986), pp. 203–37; "Early Reactions to *Economic Justice For All*: Catholic Social Teaching and the U.S. Economy," in *Horizons: The Journal of the College Theology Society*, 15 (Villanova, PA: Villanova University Press, 1988), pp. 141–53; Jon Sobrino, "Theology in a Suffering World: Theology as *Intellectus Amoris*," in Paul Knitter, editor, *Pluralism and Oppression: Theology in World Perspective*, Annual Publication of the College Theology Society, 34 (Lanham, Md.: University Press of America, 1988), pp. 153–77; John Pawlikowski and Donald Senior, editors, *Economic Justice: CTU's Pastoral Commentary on the Bishops' Letter on the Economy* (Washington, D.C.: The Pastoral Press, 1988); Phillip Berryman, *Our Unfinished Business: The U.S. Catholic Bishops' Letters on Peace and the Economy* (New York: Pantheon Books, 1989); Peter J. Henriot, *Opting For The Poor: A Challenge For North America* (Washington, D.C., The Center of Concern, 1990).

[15] John A. Coleman, "American Catholicism and Strategic Social Theology," in *An American Strategic Theology* (New York: Paulist Press, 1982), pp. 131–52. His judgment begins from affirmation of liberation theologies in their context, then insists on the contextual specificity of American Catholicism in itself and in its relation to pluralism and secularity. He also argues for an American Catholic option for the poor as the best route out of the "inevitable class bias" that comes with the fact that "the Catholic population almost perfectly mirrors the social class stratification of the nation," and as a result "many if not most of the Catholic population will be influenced as much by class interests, social location, and social class perspectives as by the religious factor," *op. cit.*, p. 250.

[16] Dennis P. McCann and Charles R. Strain, *Polity and Praxis: A*

Program for American Practical Theology (Minneapolis: Winston Press, 1985). Their "program for renewing practical theology" carries on the kind of theological initiative outlined by Coleman, and seeks to get beyond the "cultural estrangement" separating North American theology from its own social reality, p. 7. Their work is a provocative *vade mecum* and a touchstone invaluable for practical-theological reflection, even that following divergent lines. It is not always clear whether a logic of the subject matter guides their method, or a logic of inquiry.

[17] In a public, plenary address to the June, 1992, meeting of the Catholic Theological Society of America in Pittsburgh, for example, Gustavo Gutierrez summed up the role of theology as helping to open the unity between faith and witness by serving as the hermeneutic between orthodoxy and ortho-praxis.

[18] For recent discussion of Murray's concept of consensus, cf. J. Leon Hooper, *The Ethics of Discourse: The Social Philosophy of John Courtney Murray* (Washington, D.C.: Georgetown University Press, 1986) and Robert W. McElroy, *The Search for an American Public Theology: The Contribution of John Courtney Murray* (New York: Paulist Press, 1989).

[19] *Ibid.*, n. 83, p. 43.

[20] Cf. John A. Coleman, "Religious Liberty in America and Mediating Structures," in *op. cit.*, pp. 209–33.

[21] *Economic Justice For All*, n. 27, p. 13.

[22] Cf. William D. Byron, "The Bishops' Letter and Everyday Life," in Thomas M. Gannon, editor, *op. cit.*, pp. 246–55, and Charles R. Strain, "Civic Virtue, Solidarity and Justice in American Culture," in Charles R. Strain, editor, *Prophetic Visions and Economic Realities: Protestants, Jews & Catholics Confront the Bishops' Letter on the Economy* (Grand Rapids, Mich.: William B. Eerdmans Publishing, 1989), pp. 190–202.

[23] *Economic Justice for All*, n. 123, p. 61.

[24] Norman Birnbaum, "The Bishops in the Iron Cage: The Dilemmas of Advanced Industrial Society," p. 170, in Thomas M. Gannon, editor, *op. cit.*, pp. 153–78. Cf. also, Dennis P. McCann, "New Experiment in Democracy: Blueprint for Political Economy?" in Charles R. Strain, editor, *op. cit.*, pp. 203–15. McCann points to the bishops' objective of promoting productivity, not just redistribution.

[25] Gary J. Dorrien, *Reconstructing the Common Good: Theology and the Social Order* (Maryknoll, N.Y.: Orbis Books, 1990), p. 14.

[26] *Idem.*

[27] *Economic Justice for All*, n. 297, p. 146.

[28] Robert N. Bellah, Richard Madsen, William M. Sullivan, Ann Swidler and Steven M. Tipton, *Habits of the Heart: Individualism and Commitment in American Life* (Berkeley: University of California Press,

1985), pp. 200–3; *Community in America: The Challenge of Habits of the Heart*, edited by Charles H. Reynolds and Ralph V. Norman (Berkeley: University of California Press, 1988); *Toward a Retrieval of Moral Discourse in America*, edited by Donald L. Gelpi (Notre Dame, Indiana: University of Notre Dame Press, 1989).

²⁹ Cf. Hooper and McElroy, *opera citata*.

³⁰ Bellah, *op. cit.*, pp. 200–3.

³¹ Cf. Brian Tierney, "Aristotle, Aquinas and the Ideal Constitution," *Proceedings of the Patristic, Medieval, Renaissance Conference*—Augustinian Historical Institute—Villanova University; Vol. 4 (1979): i–iv; L. P. Fitzgerald, "St. Thomas Aquinas and the Two Powers," *Angelicum* (1979): 515–56; Edgar Scully, "Aquinas' State: A Tyrannical Household Writ Large?" *Science et Esprit*, xxxiii/3 (1981): 379–93; Edgar Scully, "The Place of the State in Society According to Thomas Aquinas," *The Thomist* 45 (1981): 407–29.

³² Ernest Barker, translator and editor, *The Politics of Aristotle* (Oxford: The Clarendon Press, 1961); cf. Books I and II.

³³ John Courtney Murray, *We Hold These Truths: Catholic Reflections on the American Proposition* (New York: Sheed and Ward, 1960).

³⁴ *Ibid.*, especially pp. 27–123.

³⁵ McElroy, *op. cit.*, p. 67.

³⁶ *Idem.*

³⁷ *Idem.*

³⁸ Hooper, *op. cit.*, pp. 116ff.

³⁹ Murray, *op. cit.*, pp. 111ff.

⁴⁰ Hooper, *op. cit.*, p. 117.

⁴¹ Murray, *op. cit.*, p. 123.

⁴² Hooper, *op. cit.*, p. 117.

⁴³ *Ibid.*, p. 118.

⁴⁴ *Idem.*

⁴⁵ Donald E. Pelotte, *op. cit.*, notes that in 1937 Murray "returned to Woodstock as a professor of theology specializing in the areas of grace and Trinity. He held this post until his death in 1967." For a list of his course offerings, cf. Thomas Hughson, editor, note 5, p. 41.

⁴⁶ Cf. note 10 above.

⁴⁷ On the influence of this principle in *Economic Justice For All*, cf., Anthony J. Tambasco, *op. cit.*

⁴⁸ His views can be found in, for example, "Governmental Repression of Heresy," *Proceedings of the Catholic Theological Society of America* (1948): 26–98; esp. pp. 74ff., and "Contemporary Orientations of Catholic Thought on Church and State in the Light of History," *Theological*

Studies 10 (June, 1949): 177–234; esp. pp. 222ff. His natural-law ethic, moreover, in its emphasis on reason and freedom, along with his humanism, was in the tradition of Aquinas' understanding of the person in a nature, with a modern focus on the social conditions for the possibility of exercising freedom.

⁴⁹ "Pastoral Constitution on the Church in the Modern World," Preface, n. 1, p. 903, in Austin Flannery, general editor, *Vatican Council II: The Conciliar and Post-Conciliar Documents* (Northport, N.Y.: Costello Publishing Co., 1988, revised edition).

⁵⁰ Cf. *The Road to Damascus: Kairos and Conversion: A document signed by Third World Christians from El Salvador, Guatemala, Korea, Namibia, Nicaragua, Philippines, South Africa* (London: Catholic Institute for International Relations, 1989).

⁵¹ John Courtney Murray, in *We Hold These Truths, op. cit.*, moved beyond a purely contemplative and post-classicist humanism in "Is It Basket Weaving?: The Question of Christianity and Human Values," by an "incarnational humanism" active in processes of democratic self-governance. He accepted the view, however, that "the American people as a whole possess, or has within reach, that minimum of material abundance which is necessary for the practice of virtue" sufficient to equip citizens for public life, *ibid.*, p. 179.

⁵² Murray, *ibid.*, pp. 175–96.

⁵³ Don S. Browning, editor, *Practical Theology: The Emerging Field in Theology, Church and World* (San Francisco: Harper and Row, 1983); Dennis P. McCann and Charles R. Strain, *op. cit.*; and Don S. Browning, *A Fundamental Practical Theology: Descriptive and Strategic Proposals* (Minneapolis: Fortress Press, 1991). In some ways, too, David Tracy's *Blessed Rage for Order: The New Pluralism in Theology* (New York: Seabury Press, 1975) and *The Analogical Imagination: Christian Theology and the Culture of Pluralism* (New York: Crossroad Books, 1981) pioneered in outlining possibilities for an American practical theology.

⁵⁴ Thomas T. Love, *John Courtney Murray: Contemporary Church-State Theory* (New York: Doubleday, 1965).

⁵⁵ Gerald P. Fogarty, *The Vatican and the American Hierarchy from 1870 to 1965* (Stuttgart: Anton Hirsemann, 1982).

⁵⁶ Charles E. Curran, *American Catholic Social Ethics: Twentieth Century Approaches* (Notre Dame, Ind.: University of Notre Dame Press, 1982).

⁵⁷ David Hollenbach, "Public Theology in America: Some Questions for Catholicism after John Courtney Murray," *Theological Studies* 37 (June 1976): 290–303; with Robin W. Lovin, John A. Coleman, and

J. Bryan Hehir, "Theology and Philosophy in Public: A Symposium on John Courtney Murray's Unfinished Agenda," *Theological Studies* 40 (December, 1979): 700–15.

[58] Todd David Whitmore, "From Religious Freedom to the Conditions for Witness: Developing the Heritage of John Courtney Murray," paper presented in the workshop, "American Catholic Social Ethics in the Murray Tradition: Possible Directions of Development," at the June, 1991, Catholic Theological Society of America meeting.

[59] Tracy, *The Analogical Imagination*, p. 57.

[60] McCann and Strain, *op. cit.*, p. 20.

[61] *Ibid.*, p. 3.

[62] *Ibid.*, Chapter Four, "Memory and Expectation: The Critical Hermeneutic of Practical Theology."

[63] *Ibid.*, pp. 69ff.

[64] *Ibid.*, Chapter Three, "Theory and Praxis: The Foundations of Practical Theory."

[65] *Ibid.*, Chapter Four.

[66] *Ibid.*, pp. 50ff.

1. Believer-Citizens: Identity and Texts

[1] *Economic Justice for All*, n. 24, p xiv; nn. 41–55, pp. 23–30; nn. 327–36, pp. 164–69.

[2] *Ibid.*, n. 254, p. 123.

[3] *Ibid.*, n. 83, p. 43.

[4] McElroy, *op. cit.*, p. 39.

[5] *Ibid.*, p. 40, quoting Murray, "The Construction of a Christian Culture: A Lecture Series at Loyola University in 1940" (Murray Archives I-2).

[6] Hooper, *op. cit.*, concentrates on the "consensus" as a principle, the "authorization principle," essential to democratic self-governance. The culture, though, exceeds its politically active, or indeed, morally operative consensus. Hooper opens the door to the cultural realities that may cross over into the realm of political prudence in an intriguing discussion of "Propositional Versus Symbolic Modes of Prudential Knowledge and Determination," *op. cit.*, pp. 205–09.

[7] In his essay "Leo XIII: Two Concepts of Government: II. Government and the Order of Culture," *Theological Studies* 15 (March, 1954): 1–33, he considered Leo's concept of a supervised culture and dealt with the question of government censorship. He took it up again in "Should There Be A Law?: The Question of Censorship," in *We Hold These Truths*, pp. 155–74.

[8] *Ibid.*, "*E Pluribus Unum:* The American Consensus," pp. 27–43.

[9] *Ibid.*, "The Civilization of the Pluralist Society," p. 10.
[10] *Idem.*
[11] *Idem.*
[12] *Idem.*
[13] *Ibid.*, p. 5.
[14] *Economic Justice for All*, n. 83, p. 43.
[15] *Idem.*
[16] *Ibid.*, n. 87, p. 45.
[17] *Ibid.*, n. 85, p. 44.
[18] *Ibid.*, n. 86, p. 44.
[19] William E. Murnion, in Bernard Prusak, editor, *op. cit.*
[20] *Ibid.*, p. 226.
[21] Dorrien, *op. cit.*, p. 4.
[22] Murnion, *op. cit.*, pp. 227–29.
[23] Henriot, *op. cit.*, p. 20.
[24] *Ibid.*, p. 42.
[25] Coleman, "American Catholicism and Strategic Social Theology," in *op. cit.*, p. 131.
[26] J. Bryan Hehir, "Church-State and Church-World," pp. 54–74, in *Proceedings*, Catholic Theological Society of America, 1986; p. 58.
[27] *Ibid.*, p. 58.
[28] *Ibid.*, pp. 60–1.
[29] Coleman, "Religious Liberty in American and Mediating Structures," *op. cit.*, p. 211.
[30] *Ibid.*, p. 212.
[31] *Idem.*
[32] For the ground on which to extend protection of the right of free exercise of religion to religious institutions as well as to individual citizens, and at the same time the debatable status of constitutional rights for church institutions, cf. Sharon L. Worthing, "Corporate Free Exercise: The Constitutional Rights of Religious Associations" in James E. Wood, Jr., editor, *Religion and the State: Essays in Honor of Leo Pfeffer* (Waco, Texas: Baylor University Press, 1985), pp. 167–81.
[33] Bishop James S. Rausch, "*Dignitatis Humanae:* The Unfinished Agenda," p. 42, in Walter Burghardt, editor, *Religious Freedom: 1965–1975* (New York: Paulist Press, 1977), pp. 39–51.
[34] *Idem.*, and p. 43.
[35] This is an inference from the general position given by J. Bryan Hehir, *op. cit.*, pp. 61–2.
[36] James E. Wood, Jr., "The Advocacy Role of Churches in the Body Politic," in Henry B. Clark II, editor, *Freedom of Religion in America: Historical Roots, Philosophical Concepts and Contemporary Problems* (Rutgers, N.J.: Transaction Books, 1982), p. 105.

158   *The Believer as Citizen*

37 *Ibid.*, as quoted by Woods, p. 106.

38 *Idem.* However, as Woods observes, some potential for governmental constraint exists in the 1934 Internal Revenue Code which provides that "tax exemption for a public charity may be denied if the charity devotes a 'substantial' part of its activities to attempting to influence legislation," p. 109. Because of this, he holds, "the IRS has, in effect, been able to say that organized religion may not speak out on public issues and at the same time enjoy tax exemption," *idem.* However, "the principle has yet to be tested in the courts by any religious denomination," *idem.*

39 "Declaration on Religious Liberty," in Austin Flannery, editor, *Vatican Council II*, p. 803.

40 Edwin S. Gaustad, reporting for a Workshop, "Conclusion: Historical Perspectives and Contemporary Problems" in Henry B. Clark II, *Freedom of Religion in America*, p. 112.

41 Francois-Xavier Dumortier, "John Courtney Murray revisité: La place de l'Eglise dans le débat public aux Etats-Unis?" in *Recherche de Science Religieuse* 76/4 (1988): 499–531; p. 514.

42 Hehir, *op. cit.*, p. 61.

43 David Hollenbach, "The Church's Social Mission in a Pluralistic Society," pp. 3–15 in *Justice, Peace and Human Rights: American Catholic Social Ethics in a Pluralistic World* (New York: Crossroad, 1990), p. 9.

44 Hollenbach, *op. cit.*, p. 9.

45 Hehir, *op. cit.*, p. 57.

46 A Murray critique of liberal individualism in the Lockean version, occurs in *We Hold These Truths*, pp. 302–36.

47 Murray, "Contemporary Orientations of Catholic Thought," p. 222.

48 *Idem.*

49 Murray, "St. Robert Bellarmine on the Indirect Power," *Theological Studies* 9 (December, 1948): 491–535.

50 Murray, "Contemporary Orientations of Catholic Thought," p. 222.

51 Love, *op. cit.*, p. 65.

52 *Idem.*

53 *Idem.*, quoting Murray, "Governmental Repression of Heresy," p. 64.

54 Love, *op. cit.*, p. 65.

55 *Ibid.*, p. 66.

56 Murray, "Contemporary Orientations of Catholic Thought," pp. 222ff.

[57] Murray, "Governmental Repression of Heresy," p. 80.
[58] Murray, "On the Structure of the Church-State Problem," in W. Gurian and M. A. Fitzsimmons, editors, *The Catholic Church in World Affairs* (Notre Dame, Ind.: University of Notre Dame Press, 1954), p. 31.
[59] *Economic Justice for All*, n/5, pp. vi–vii.
[60] *Ibid.*, n. 25, p. 12.
[61] *Ibid.*, nn. 119–24, pp. 59–62; nn. 156–69, pp. 78–83; nn. 186–215, pp. 92–105; nn. 239–47, pp. 116–19; nn. 264–70, pp. 128–31; nn. 312–23, pp. 155–60. Cf. Charles E. Curran, "Relating Religious-Ethical Inquiry to Economic Policy," in Thomas M. Gannon, editor, *op. cit.*, pp. 42–54; esp. pp. 51ff; also Pope John Paul II, *"Centesimus Annus,"* in Michael Walsh and Brian Davies, editors, *op. cit.*, nn. 15–16.1, pp. 443–44; n. 40, p. 463; nn. 44–52.2, pp. 466–73.
[62] *Economic Justice for All*, n. 123, p. 61.
[63] For Murray's role at Vatican II, cf., Donald E. Pelotte, *op. cit.*, pp. 77–101; also, Richard Regan, *Conflict and Consensus* (New York: Macmillan, 1967).
[64] For example, cf. *The Reception of Vatican II*, edited by Giuseppe Aberigo, Jean-Pierre Jossua, and Joseph Komonchak, translated by Matthew J. O'Connell (Washington, D.C.: Catholic University of America Press, 1987).
[65] Hans-Georg Gadamer, *Truth and Method* (New York: Crossroad, 1982), pp. 274–304. Cf. also, *Truth and Method*, translation revised by Joel Weinsheimer and Donald G. Marshall (New York: Crossroad, 1991), pp. 291–307.
[66] Murray, *We Hold These Truths*, pp. 221–47.
[67] *Economic Justice for All*, nn. 251–94, pp. 121–44.
[68] Cf., Murray, "Selective Conscientious Objection," published as a pamphlet by *Our Sunday Visitor* (1967), edited by James Finn, and later published as "War and Conscience," in *A Conflict of Conscience* (New York: Pegasus Press, 1968). This was given originally as an address at Western Maryland College, June 4, 1967.
[69] Murray, "Are There Two or One? The Question of the Future of Freedom," in *We Hold These Truths*, pp. 197–217.
[70] Murray, "The Church and Totalitarian Democracy," *Theological Studies* 13 (December, 1952): 525–63; cf. also, McElroy, *op. cit.*, pp. 105–10.
[71] Murray, *We Hold These Truths*, p. 210.
[72] *Economic Justice for All*, n. 7, p. 4.
[73] William Halsey, *The Survival of American Innocence* (Notre

Dame, Indiana: University of Notre Dame Press, 1980), p. 2. Cf. John A. Coleman, "The Fall from Innocence," in *An American Strategic Theology*, pp. 161–81.

[74] Halsey, *op. cit.*, p. 2.

[75] *Ibid.*, p. 5, quoting R. Handy.

[76] *Ibid.*, p. 6.

[77] *Ibid.*, pp. 178–79.

[78] *Ibid.*, p. 77.

[79] *Ibid.*, p. 77.

[80] Avery Dulles, *Models of the Church*, expanded edition (New York: Doubleday, 1987), p. 34.

[81] *Idem.*

[82] *Idem.*, Dulles quotes Bellarmine's *De Controversiis*, tom. 2, lib. 3, cap. 2 (Naples: Giuliano, 1857), vol. 2, p. 75.

[83] Hehir, *op. cit.*, pp. 67–70.

[84] Pope Pius XII, *Mystici Corporis Christi*, in Claudia Carlen IHM, *The Papal Encyclicals: 1939–1958* (United States: McGrath Publishing, 1981), pp. 37–63. (Original, N.C.W.C., 1943, pp. 3–52).

[85] *Ibid.*, pp. 49–53. Cf. also, Murray, "The Roman Catholic Church," in *The Annals of the American Academy of Political and Social Science* 256 (March, pp. 36–42), and ecclesiological passages and principles in church-state and religious liberty texts. Murray, "The Roman Catholic Church," p. 36: ". . . it is the Holy Spirit Himself, as given to the Church, dwelling in her as His temple, and by His presence and action making her the Body of Christ, whose members are united, not merely by the moral bond of love or by the juridical bond of law, but by the mystical bond of a common sharing in the one Holy Spirit."
Also, Murray, *The Problem of God* (New Haven: Yale University Press, 1964), p. 28: "There with us, Father and Son breathe into us the Holy Spirit, who is their Gift, now given to us. The Three are here as who they are mysteriously the one God, the Triunely Holy One" . . . [manifest in] "the new works of God in our midst, more wonderful than ever—the Son's ransoming deed of love, and the Spirit's ceaseless energizing in the Church."

[86] Thomas Hughson, editor, *op. cit.*, pp. 16–20 in the "Introduction"; and pp. 161–180 in Murray's dissertation.

[87] For instance, Joseph Komonchak, "Ministry and the Local Church," *Proceedings of the Catholic Theological Society of America*, 1981, pp. 56–82.

[88] *Economic Justice for All*, n. 122, p. 60.

[89] *Ibid.*, n. 120, p. 60.

[90] *Ibid.*, n. 121, p. 60.

[91] *Ibid.*, n. 122, pp. 60-1.
[92] *Ibid.*, n. 123, p. 61.
[93] As recalled in Walter J. Burghardt's "A Mind, A Manner, A Man: Elegy for John Courtney Murray," in Walter J. Burghardt, editor, *Tell the Next Generation: Homilies and New Homilies* (New York: Paulist Press, 1980): 211–15, p. 215. This unique, lyrical portrait of Murray is more than a source of information about Murray. It reveals, as few other texts do, the warmth and humanity of Murray, the friend and humanist.

2. Believers as Citizens: From Historical to Hermeneutical Analysis of Tradition

[1] Charles E. Curran, *American Catholic Social Ethics: Twentieth Century Approaches* (Notre Dame, Indiana: University of Notre Dame Press, 1982); Ch. 5, "John Courtney Murray," pp. 172–232.

[2] Francois-Xavier Dumortier, op. cit.

[3] Curran, *op. cit.*, accepts Gustavo Gutierrez's objection, in *A Theology of Liberation: History, Politics and Salvation,* translated and edited by Sister Caridad Inda and John Eagleson (Maryknoll, N.Y.: Orbis Books, 1973), pp. 53–8, to the dichotomy between temporal and spiritual planes of ecclesial life, activity and thought. For analysis of postconciliar struggles with the spiritual/temporal difference and unity, cf. also Leslie Griffin, "The Integration of Spiritual and Temporal: Contemporary Roman Catholic Church-State Theory," in *Theological Studies* 48 (1987): 225–51, Francis Schüssler-Fiorenza, *Foundational Theology: Jesus and the Church* (New York: Crossroad, 1985), pp. 197–245, and Avery Dulles, *The Reshaping of Catholicism: Current Challenges in the Theology of the Church* (San Francisco: Harper and Row, 1988), pp. 132–83.

[4] The Holocaust, as John Pawlikowski argues, has become a perspective for all Christian ethical deliberation and theory. John Pawlikowski, "Christian Ethics and the Holocaust: A Dialogue with Post-Auschwitz Judaism," in *Theological Studies* 49 (1988): 649–69.

[5] The term, of course, comes from trinitarian theology where it signifies a mysterious unity (literally, "dance") on the basis of personal distinctions.

[6] Gadamer points out in *Truth and Method*, p. 273:

Every encounter with tradition that takes place within historical consciousness involves the tension between the text and the present. . . . Historical consciousness is aware of its own otherness and hence distinguishes the horizon of tradition from its own. On the other hand, it is itself . . . only something laid over a continuing tradition, and hence it immediately recombines what it has distinguished in order, in the unity of the historical horizon that it thus acquires, to become again one with itself.

[7] His critique of the "prejudice against prejudice" is a rejection, of course, of a particular aspect of a Cartesian starting point, as well as of this Enlightenment theme. Instead, memory and prejudgments essential to thought are continually in a condition of being-tested. Some can emerge as worthy and as productive of further knowledge. Gadamer, *op. cit.*, pp. 238–53.

[8] The concept of "situation" "represents a standpoint that limits the possibility of vision" and is part of every finite present. The "hermeneutical situation is determined by the prejudices that we bring with us" which "constitute, then, the horizon of a particular present." Gadamer, *op. cit.*, pp. 269, 272.

[9] Cf. Donald E. Pelotte, pp. 3–72.

[10] Murray appreciated Vatican II's renewal of the principle that Christianity, like the Logos, embraced all that was human, including especially the unique gifts of every people. Cf. "Fairfield Commencement Address, 1966, pp. 2, 5":

There are, however, within each people "capacities and resources and traditional ways of life in which the genius of the people expresses itself. [*Vatican II*, "Dogmatic Constitution on the Church," n. 13] . . . The genius of America has perhaps chiefly revealed itself in a unique realization of the values of freedom, combined with a unique understanding of the uses of law."

[11] Murray, *The Problem of Religious Freedom*, Woodstock Papers, 7 (Westminster, Maryland: The Newman Press, 1965). Cf. especially, pp. 85ff. for his account of the clash between classicism and historical consciousness.

[12] Murray, *op. cit.*

[13] Murray, "The Two Views," in *The Problem of Religious Freedom*, pp. 7–45.

[14] *Ibid.*, p. 89.

[15] *Idem.*

[16] *Ibid.*, pp. 89, 32, 38–40, 47–84.

[17] Pelotte, *op. cit.*, pp. 120–22, 127–28, 131, 187–88.

[18] *Ibid.*, p. 128.

[19] These are structural and normative in relations between the church and any political order.

[20] Pelotte, *op. cit.*, p. 131.

[21] *Idem.*

[22] *Idem.*

[23] *Idem.*

[24] *Ibid.*, p. 120.

[25] *Ibid.*, p. 120.

[26] *Ibid.*, p. 118.

[27] *Ibid.*, p. 187.

[28] *Ibid.*, p. 188.

[29] Curran, *op. cit.*, Ch. 5, "John Courtney Murray."

[30] *Ibid.*, p. 185.

[31] *Ibid.*, p. 186.

[32] *Ibid.*, p. 223.

[33] *Ibid.*, p. 224.

[34] It is worth noting that his dissertation expounded the inseparability of natural and supernatural in the act of faith. Cf. *Matthias Scheeben on Faith*, pp. 29–37; 231–36.

[35] For example, *We Hold These Truths*, pp. 48–56, and *The Problem of Religious Freedom*, pp. 20–1.

[36] He mentions, for example, "the great sin of our times—carelessness and even contempt for the dignity of the human person and its birthright of freedom," *The Problem of Religious Freedom*, pp. 109–10.

[37] Curran, *op. cit.*, pp. 223ff.

[38] Murray, *The Problem of Religious Freedom*, p. 103.

[39] Curran, *op. cit.*, p. 227.

[40] *Ibid.*, p. 223.

[41] *Ibid.*, p. 229.

[42] *Ibid.*, p. 228. In "John Courtney Murray's Problematic Interpretation on Leo XIII and the American Founders," *The Thomist* (October, 1991): 598–613, Michael J. Schuck argues along similar lines against the validity of Murray's interpretation of Leonine texts. Schuck's interest lies in showing that Murray's own position, while correct in its defense of religious liberty and church-state separation, nonetheless errs in the argument for continuity with Leo XIII and harmony between Catholic social teaching in papal encyclicals and a common view of liberal democracy. Schuck has in view the worthwhile observation that Catholicism and American liberalism (an individualist model of self and society, an economic dynamic amplifying this model) conflict rather than harmonize on many fundamental principles. He charges Murray's interpretation of Leo XIII, and his argument for compatibility between Catholic and

American political thought, with complicity in producing the present "sanguine alignment in most Catholics' minds between American liberalism and Roman Catholicism," p. 610.

However, in one respect, Schuck's critique of Murray on Leo XIII is a variation on Eusebian archaism (cf. Murray, *The Problem of God*, pp. 46–51) in an insistence that true interpretation consists in reiterating given formulae or statements without consideration for deepening understanding of their truth or alteration of their cultural context. Murray's position, for instance, that "separation" of church and state meant one thing in Leo's text and immediate, historical context and another in Thomas Jefferson and American thought and law carries, apparently, no weight for Schuck. But this is to miss the richness of Murray's hermeneutic, which, apart from his animadversion on development, occurs as and in dialogue with tradition and its texts that contains moments of new appropriation (and deepening) of originally stated meaning and truth. Murray, for example, endorsed Leonine refutations of Continental liberalism's social and political monism which sprang, paradoxically, from a root in rationalist individualism. But Murray saw America's founding as something more original than a transplanting of principles from the French Enlightenment.

Schuck has a valid objection, though, to elements in an organic model of development of doctrine, at least in the version which (as in B. J. F. Lonergan's *On the Way to Nicea, The Dialectical Development of Trinitarian Theology*, translated by C. O'Donovan [Philadelphia: Westminster Press, 1976]) treats development as progress from mythos to logos from descriptive to explanatory. Still, the view that the alternative is an uneducable pluralism in Catholic social teaching seems doubtful.

Murray consistently opposed an individualist model of self, society, state and church. Yet he did not see the way American economic life incorporates and installs that model in the national consensus. Whether present Catholic comfort with individualism stems largely from Murray or not—Schuck does not show this link—objection to it is consistent with both social Catholicism and Murray's interpretation of Leo XIII.

[43] Gadamer, *op. cit.*, p. 263.

[44] *Idem.*

[45] Pope Leo XIII, *Cum Multa*, quoted by Murray in "Leo XIII: Separation of Church and State," p. 162, in *Theological Studies* 14 (June, 1953): 145–214.

[46] *Ibid.*, p. 163.

[47] Leo XIII, *Au milieu des solicitudes*, quoted by Murray in "Leo XIII: Separation of Church and State," p. 161.

⁴⁸ Leo XIII, *ibid.*, quoted by Murray, *ibid.*, p. 172.
⁴⁹ *Idem.*
⁵⁰ *Idem.*
⁵¹ *Idem.*
⁵² *Idem*, p. 173.
⁵³ Gadamer, *op. cit.*, p. 262.
⁵⁴ *Ibid.*, p. 263.
⁵⁵ Gadamer, *op. cit.*, p. 269.
⁵⁶ *Ibid.*, p. 270.
⁵⁷ Murray, "The Church and Totalitarian Democracy," p. 525, in *Theological Studies* 13 (December, 1952): 525–63.
⁵⁸ Murray, "Leo XIII: Separation of Church and State," p. 214.
⁵⁹ *Ibid.*, p. 153.
⁶⁰ *Idem.*
⁶¹ *Ibid.*, p. 185.
⁶² Gadamer, *op. cit.*, p. 270. He remarks that, "We think we understand when we see the past from an historical stand-point, i.e., place ourselves in the historical situation [of past agent, event text, culture, etc.] and seek to reconstruct the historical horizon," p. 270. This is to ignore our formation by traditions, and our "effective-historical consciousness." The second, revised edition and translation of *Truth and Method* renders "Wirkunggeschichtliches Bewusstsein," instead as "historically effected consciousness." This better expresses a double relation between consciousness and tradition: "at once 'affected' by history . . . and also itself brought into being—'effected'—by history, and conscious that it is so," Joel Weinsheimer and Donald G. Marshall, "Translators' Preface," in Hans-Georg Gadamer, *Truth and Method*, Second Revised Edition, translation revised by Joel Weinsheimer and Donald G. Marshall (New York: Crossroad, 1991), p. xv.
⁶³ Gadamer, *op. cit.*, p. 270.
⁶⁴ Murray, "The Church and Totalitarian Democracy," p. 550.
⁶⁵ *Idem.*
⁶⁶ *Idem.*
⁶⁷ This would have been to engage in Schleiermacher's psychological interpretation, "a divinatory process, a placing of oneself within the mind of the author, an apprehension of the 'inner origin' of the work . . . a reconstruction that starts from the vital moment of conception," Gadamer, *op. cit.*, p. 164.
⁶⁸ Gadamer, *op. cit.*, p. 263.
⁶⁹ *Idem.*
⁷⁰ Murray, "Leo XIII: Separation of Church and State," pp. 146–47.

[71] Cf. Murray, *We Hold These Truths*, pp. 63–76, 127–217, and "Leo XIII: The Separation of Church and State," pp. 148ff. and 187ff.

[72] Murray adopted the term from Christopher Dawson's *Beyond Politics* (New York: Sheed and Ward, 1939), where it referred to "the way in which the Jacobins anticipated practically all the characteristic features of the modern totalitarian regimes"; quoted by Murray in "The Church and Totalitarian Democracy", *Theological Studies* 13 (December, 1952), pp. 525–63.

[73] J. T. Talmon, *The Rise of Totalitarian Democracy* (Boston: Beacon Press, 1952), distinguished "totalitarian" from "liberal" democracy. The former issued from the French Revolution as a political messianism reducing all to the plane of political life, holding up an image of achievable happiness for all to be realized by the state guided by an elite, espousing a state-sponsored morality to which it educates all citizens.

[74] For example, "The Church and Totalitarian Democracy," throughout; "Leo XIII: Separation of Church and State," pp. 149, 154, 159, 163–66, 171–75, 188, 200, 207; "Leo XIII: Two Concepts of Government," pp. 556, 562; "Leo XIII: Two Concepts of Government: II. Government and the Order of Culture," pp. 5, 6, 20, 31.

[75] Gadamer, *op. cit.*, p. 258.

3. Beyond Dogmatism: Discovering the People Behind *We Hold These Truths*

[1] Hans-Georg Gadamer, "The Philosophical Foundations of the Twentieth Century" (1962), pp. 107–29, in *Philosophical Hermeneutics*, edited and translated by David E. Linge (Berkeley, California: University of California Press, 1976), p. 127.

[2] Donald E. Pelotte, *op. cit.*, pp. 27–73, covers this conflict and Murray's silencing. Cf. also, Richard J. Regan, *Conflict and Consensus: Religious Freedom and the Second Vatican Council* (New York: Macmillan, 1967); Gerald P. Fogarty, *op. cit.*, Ch. XIV and XV; J. Leon Hooper, *op. cit.*, pp. 51–81.

[3] Cf. Thomas T. Love, *op. cit.* pp. 88–143; Faith Burgess, *Ecclesia et Status: The Relationship between Church and State According to John Courtney Murray, S.J.* (Unpublished dissertation, University of Basle, 1971), Ch. II; Reinhold Sebott, *Religionsfreiheit und Verhältnis von Kirche und Staat: Der Beitrag John Courtney Murrays zu einer modernen Frage, Analecta Gregoriana*, 206; Rome: Gregorian University Press, 1977), Ch. 5.

[4] Gadamer, *Truth and Method*, pp. 310–25. Analyzing experience only as data for scientific understanding (Aristotle) leads to seeing it as a contribution to the formation of our concepts. This omits "its real char-

acter as a process," p. 316, and overlooks the negative aspect of that process. Gadamer accepts Hegel's analysis of "determinate negation" to correct the oversight. He remarks that, "If we have an experience of an object, this means that we have not seen the thing correctly hitherto and now know it better. Thus the negativity of experience has a curiously productive meaning. It is not simply a deception that we see through and hence make a correction, but a comprehensive knowledge that we acquire," p. 317. If church-state relations and the practice of religious intolerance are "objects" for experience, then Murray's description, in historical terms, of their progress toward constitutional nonidentity of church and state, and religious liberty, counts as an argument from "experience" as "determinate negation."

⁵ *Op. cit.*, n. 1, p. 903.

⁶ *Economic Justice for All*, n. 87, p. 45.

⁷ Cf. Matthew Lamb, "The Theory-Praxis Relationship in Contemporary Christian Theologies," in *Proceedings, Catholic Theological Society of America* (1976): 149–78; p. 151.

⁸ *Ibid.*, pp. 154–57.

⁹ Lamb, *ibid.*, p. 156:

> Although not a "professional" theologian but a Christian philosopher, Maritain is by far the best representative of this primacy of theory type. His *Degrees of Knowledge* is its finest expression, "accepting" the Aristotelian norm for scientific knowledge as necessary "irrefragable" intelligibility which "contrasts with the contingent, irreversible flux of the universe of existence."

Cf. Murray, *We Hold These Truths*, p. 107, for his contrast between experience as a "stream of successive 'facts' " on the level of contingent objects of knowledge and a "non-contingent element of thought, in terms of which the economic facts are transformed into issues that may be argued. . . ."

¹⁰ Lamb, *ibid.*, p. 157.

¹¹ *Idem*, Maritain's "historical ideal" of a "new Christendom," is what Gustavo Gutierrez rejects in *A Theology of Liberation*, pp. 53ff., as a pillar for the "Distinction of Planes Model" which liberation theology leaves behind. If Murray's doctrine, despite common themes with Maritain, does not subtend ecclesiastical power over the state and has emancipatory potential, there may be room for dialogue between Murray's contribution and liberation theology.

¹² Coleman, *op. cit.*, pp. 139–42.

[13] *Idem.*

[14] *Ibid.,* p. 141.

[15] *Idem.*

[16] *Idem.*

[17] *Ibid.,* p. 142. Maritain's thought may be more subtle and flexible than either Lamb's or Coleman's typologies disclose, however important their characterization of his leading themes. For example, Ralph McInerny explains that, although Maritain saw the "inner logic of capitalism" to be grounded in the principles of the fecundity of money, and the absolute primacy of individual profit, Americans did not follow its tendency to materialism and inhumanity. To the contrary, thought Maritain in his sojourns in America, "by a strange paradox, the people who lived and toiled under this structure . . . were keeping their own souls apart from it . . . their souls and vital energy, their dreams, their everyday effort, their idealism and generosity, were running against the grain of the logic of the super-imposed structure." *Art and Prudence: Studies in the Thought of Jacques Maritain* (Notre Dame, Indiana: University of Notre Dame Press, 1988), pp. 22–3. Could Maritain observe so paradoxical a situation in the 1990s, or has the "inner logic of capitalism" become also the inner form of people's lives?

[18] Cf. Gadamer, *Truth and Method,* pp. 278ff. On *phronesis* internal to practice, and "What Is Practice? The Conditions of Social Reason," "Hermeneutics as Practical Philosophy," and "Hermeneutics as a Theoretical and Practical Task," in *Reason in the Age of Science,* translated by Frederick G. Lawrence (Boston: MIT Press, 1986), on practice. Cf. also, Richard J. Bernstein, "From Hermeneutics to Praxis," in Robert Hollinger, *Hermeneutics and Praxis* (Notre Dame, IN.: University of Notre Dame Press, 1985).

[19] Cf. Gadamer, *Truth and Method,* pp. 91–119, on play.

[20] Gadamer, "Hermeneutics as a Theoretical and Practical Task," p. 114: "Thus hermeneutics is more than just a method of the sciences, or the distinctive feature of a certain group of sciences. Above all it refers to a native human capacity." Cf. Frederick G. Lawrence, "Translator's Introduction," to *Reason in the Age of Science:*

> . . . Gadamer has grounded his theory of human knowing/reading in a phenomenological thematization of the basic activity of life as human. Because human living at its most primordial is always a process of making sense. . . . this integrally interpretive structure of human life precludes and contextualizes the usual oppositions between the hermeneutics of suspicion . . . and the hermeneutics of recovery . . . ," pp. xix–xx.

[21] Richard J. Bernstein, quoting Gadamer's "The Problem of Historical Consciousness," in "From Hermeneutics to Praxis," *op. cit.*, p. 285. Gadamer's essay appears in *Interpretative Social Science: A Reader*, edited by P. Rabinow and W. M. Sullivan (Berkeley: University of California Press, 1979), pp. 135ff., p. 108.

[22] Gutierrez, *op. cit.*, p. 9.

[23] *Ibid.*, p. 10.

[24] Gadamer, "What Is Practice: The Conditions of Social Reason," in *Reason in the Age of Science, op. cit.*

[25] Gadamer, "Hermeneutics as Practical Philosophy," in *Reason in the Age of Science, op. cit.*

[26] Nicholas Lobkowicz, *Theory and Practice: History of a Concept from Aristotle to Marx* (Notre Dame, Indiana: University of Notre Dame Press, 1967), p. 11.

[27] Gadamer, "What is Practice?" pp. 71ff.

[28] From "The Declaration of Independence" in *American State Papers* (Chicago: Encyclopaedia Britannica, 1952), p. 1.

[29] The phrase and idea come from Abraham Lincoln's "Gettysburg Address." Cf. Michael J. Schuck, *op. cit.*, for comments on Garry Wills' *Inventing America: Jefferson's Declaration of Independence* (New York: Vintage Books, Random House, 1978). Schuck thinks that Murray repeated Lincoln's folly of imagining there was an "American Proposition" contained in the "Declaration of Independence." The subtitle of *We Hold These Truths* is *Catholic Reflections on the American Proposition*.

[30] Murray, *We Hold These Truths*, p. viii.

[31] *Idem.*

[32] *Ibid.*, p. 10.

[33] "The Declaration of Independence," *op. cit.*, p. 1.

[34] Murray, *We Hold These Truths*, p. ix.

[35] *Ibid.*, p. 42.

[36] *Ibid.*, p. vii.

[37] *Idem.*

[38] *Ibid.*, p. 10.

[39] Cf. Robert W. McElroy, *op. cit.*, pp. 116–42, for Murray's "vigorous effort to reconstruct the international order in the post-war era, not in an American image, but in a moral image," p. 116.

[40] McElroy, *op. cit.*, pp. 143–83, makes a persuasive case for a theistic natural-law method and substance capable of reopening our national consensus, discourse, and decisions to a moral order respecting the dignity and sacredness of the human person.

[41] Murray, *We Hold These Truths*, p. 221.

[42] *Ibid.*, p. 221.

[43] *Ibid.,* p. 273.
[44] *Ibid.,* p. 331.
[45] *Idem.*
[46] *Ibid.,* pp. 5–6.
[47] *Ibid.,* p. 6.
[48] *Ibid.,* p. 28.
[49] *Idem.*
[50] *Idem.*
[51] Like the first commandment in the Decalogue, and applying its affirmation of divine transcendence, this principle has the effect of identifying and prohibiting idolatry of a nation in the customs, laws, and practice of a people. The American interest is not the highest good of American citizens. Cf. *The Road to Damascus: Kairos and Conversion,* for analysis of modes of national idolatry.
[52] Murray, *We Hold These Truths,* p. 38.
[53] *Idem.*
[54] *Idem.*
[55] *Ibid.,* p. 36.
[56] *Ibid.,* for example, pp. 46–8, 63–72.
[57] *Ibid.,* for example, pp. 56–63.
[58] *Ibid.,* for example, pp. 67–71, pp. 74–6.
[59] *Ibid.,* for example, pp. 102–7.
[60] *Ibid.,* for example, pp. 16, 37–9, 63–6, 72–8.
[61] *Ibid.,* for example, pp. 27–43.
[62] *Ibid.,* p. 100. Adolf A. Berle, *Power Without Property: A New Development in American Political Economy* (New York: Harcourt and Brace, 1959).
[63] Murray, *We Hold These Truths,* p. 99.
[64] *Ibid.,* p. 100.
[65] *Idem.*
[66] *Idem.*
[67] *Idem.*
[68] *Idem.*
[69] Berle, *op. cit.,* quoted by Murray, *We Hold These Truths,* p. 101.
[70] Murray, *ibid.,* p. 103.
[71] Berle, quoted by Murray, *idem.*
[72] Murray, *ibid.,* p. 101.
[73] *Ibid.,* p. 103.
[74] *Ibid.,* p. 28.
[75] *Ibid.,* p. 30.
[76] *Ibid.,* p. 32.
[77] *Ibid.,* p. 33.

[78] *Ibid.,* p. 35.
[79] *Ibid.,* p. 36.
[80] *Ibid.,* p. 57.
[81] *Ibid.,* p. 64.
[82] *Ibid.,* p. 69.
[83] *Ibid.,* p. 76.
[84] *Ibid.,* p. 41.
[85] *Ibid.,* p. 27.
[86] *Idem.*

4. Remembering a Just Deed: The Maryland Experiment in Tolerance

[1] Murray, *We Hold These Truths,* p. 27.

[2] *Idem.*

[3] *Idem.*

[4] Cf. Patrick W. Carey, "American Catholics and the First Amendment," in *All Imaginable Liberties: The Religious Liberty Clauses of the First Amendment,* edited by Francis Graham Lee (Philadelphia: St. Joseph's University Press, 1990), pp. 101–29.

[5] Murray, *We Hold These Truths,* p. 28.

[6] Jay P. Dolan, *American Catholic Experience: A History from Colonial Times to the Present* (Garden City, N.Y.: Doubleday and Co., 1985), title for pp. 101–24.

[7] Cf. Thomas T. Love, *op. cit.,* pp. 19–31. John A. Ryan and the *American Ecclesiastical Review* staff defended, it is true, the thesis/hypothesis school of thought in its assertions for a Catholic State as the Catholic ideal, with a consequence of legal intolerance for some dimensions of non-Catholic religious life and practice. This need not be regarded, however, as an impulse toward establishing Catholicism in America; it was an attempt to hew to the logic of the church's *Jus Publicum Ecclesiasticum* with no expectation it would become reality, as John A. Ryan and Francis J. Boland admitted about their view:

> While all this is very true in logic and in theory, the evident of its practical realization in any State or country is so remote in time and in probability that no practical man will let it disturb his equanimity or affect his attitude toward those who differ from him in religious faith.

quoting Ryan and Boland from *Catholic Principles of Politics* (New York: The Macmillan Company, 1940), p. 320.

[8] Charles E. Curran, *American Catholic Social Ethics,* p. 176.

⁹ Donald E. Pelotte, *John Courtney Murray*, pp. 13–73.

¹⁰ Murray, *We Hold These Truths*, p. 63.

¹¹ *Ibid.*, p. 41.

¹² Dolan, *op. cit.*, p. 276ff.

¹³ *Ibid.*, p. 276.

¹⁴ *Ibid.*, p. 267.

¹⁵ Sydney E. Ahlstrom, *The Religious History of the American People* (New Haven: Yale University Press, 1972), p. 382.

¹⁶ Dolan, *op. cit.*, p. 277.

¹⁷ Ahlstrom, *op. cit.*, p. 382.

¹⁸ Dolan, *op. cit.*, p. 266.

¹⁹ "Americanism" is the topic for an enormous literature. Cf. Donald E. Pelotte, *op. cit.*, pp. 141–86; Gerald Fogarty, *op. cit.*, pp. 368–85.

²⁰ William L. Portier, "The Future of Americanism," pp. 49–51 in *Rising From History: U.S. Catholic Theology Looks to the Future*, Volume 30, Annual Publication of the College of Theology Society, edited by Robert J. Daly (Lanham, Md.: University Press of America, 1984), p. 49.

²¹ Ahlstrom, *op. cit.*, p. 828.

²² *Idem.*

²³ John Tracy Ellis, *American Catholicism*, Second Edition, Revised (Chicago: University of Chicago Press, 1969), p. 157.

²⁴ *Ibid.*, pp. 157–58. Elwyn Smith stated, "In reality, American Catholic Church-state policy underwent no unusual modification in the period of the Americanist controversy," in *Religious Liberty in the United States: The Development of Church-State Thought Since the Revolutionary Era* (Philadelphia: Fortress Press, 1972), p. 211.

²⁵ Thomas O'Brien Hanley, *Their Rights and Liberties: The Beginnings of Religious and Political Freedom in Maryland* (Chicago: Loyola University Press, 1984).

²⁶ Ahlstrom, *op. cit.*, p. 381.

²⁷ *Idem.*

²⁸ Dolan, *op. cit.*, pp. 106ff.

²⁹ *Ibid.*, p. 105.

³⁰ *Idem.*

³¹ *Idem*, p. 106.

³² *Ibid.*, p. 108.

³³ *Ibid.*, p. 109.

³⁴ Murray, *We Hold These Truths*, p. 48.

³⁵ Thomas J. Curry, *The First Freedoms: Church and State in America to the Passage of the First Amendment* (New York: Oxford University Press, 1986), p. 31.

³⁶ *Ibid.*, p. 52.

[37] John D. Krugler, " 'With Promise of Liberty in Religion': The Catholic Lords Baltimore and Toleration in Seventeenth-Century Maryland, 1634–1692," in *Maryland Historical Magazine* (Spring, 1984): 21–43, p. 40.

[38] *Ibid.*, p. 39.

[39] *Ibid.*, p. 21.

[40] *Idem.*

[41] *Ibid.*, p. 40.

[42] Dolan, *op. cit.*, p. 76.

[43] *Idem.*

[44] John D. Krugler, "Puritan and Papist: Politics and Religion in Massachusetts and Maryland Before the Restoration of Charles II" (unpublished dissertation, University of Illinois, 1971), p. 4.

[45] John D. Krugler, " 'With Promise of Liberty in Religion,' " pp. 23–4.

[46] John D. Krugler, "Lord Baltimore, Roman Catholics, and Toleration: Religious Policy in Maryland During the Early Catholic Years, 1634–1649," p. 55, in *Catholic Historical Review*, 65, 1 (January, 1979): 49–75.

[47] *Idem.*

[48] Dolan, *op. cit.*, p. 76, quoting Coleman Hall Clayton, editor, *Narratives of Early Maryland, 1633–1684* (New York: Scribner's Sons, 1910), p. 16.

[49] Dolan, *op. cit.*, p. 76.

[50] *Idem.*

[51] *Idem.*

[52] *Idem.*

[53] *Ibid.*, p. 77, quoting William Hand Browne, *et al.*, editors, *Archives of Maryland* (Baltimore: Maryland Historical Society, 1883–present), I, p. 246.

[54] Sydney E. Ahlstrom, *op. cit.*; John Tracy Ellis, *op. cit.*; James J. Hennesey, *American Catholics: A History of the Roman Catholic Community in the United States* (New York: Oxford University Press, 1981); Jay P. Dolan, *op. cit.*; Thomas O'Brien Hanley, *op. cit.*; John D. Krugler, *opera citata*; Thomas J. Curry, *op. cit.*

[55] Cf., Ahlstrom, *op. cit.*

[56] Cf., Hennesey; Krugler; Dolan; Ellis; all *opera citata.*

[57] Cf., Dolan, *op. cit.*

[58] Cf., Hanley, *op. cit.*

[59] Ahlstrom, *op. cit.*, p. 331.

[60] *Ibid.*, p. 332.

[61] *Idem.*

[62] *Ibid.*, pp. 332–33.
[63] Ellis, *op. cit.*, p. 23.
[64] *Idem.*
[65] Dolan, *op. cit.*, p. 64.
[66] *Ibid.*, p. 67.
[67] *Ibid.*, p. 74.
[68] *Idem.*
[69] *Ibid.*, p. 72.
[70] *Idem.*, quoting John D. Krugler, *op. cit.* (1971), p. 252.
[71] *Idem.*
[72] Curry, *op. cit.*, p. 36.
[73] Hennesey, *op. cit.*, p. 38.
[74] *Idem.*
[75] *Idem.*
[76] *Ibid.*, p. 41.
[77] Hanley, *op. cit.*, p. 77.
[78] *Idem.*
[79] *Ibid.*, Preface, ix.
[80] Krugler, " 'With Promise of Liberty in Religion,' " p. 27.
[81] *Ibid.*, p. 23.
[82] *Idem.*
[83] Krugler, "Lord Baltimore, Roman Catholics and Toleration," p. 59.
[84] *Idem.*
[85] *Ibid.*, p. 60.
[86] *Ibid.*, p. 58.
[87] Krugler, " 'With Promise of Liberty In Religion,' " p. 32.
[88] *Ibid.*, p. 33.
[89] *Ibid.*, p. 39.
[90] For example, Karl Rahner's theology opens up views on religion as a dimension of any activity, actualizing a person's tendency to know and to love. Cf. *The Foundations of Christian Faith* (London: Dartman, Longman and Todd, 1978).
[91] Francis Schüssler Fiorenza, *op. cit.*, pp. 214–25.
[92] *Ibid.*, p. 216.
[93] Thomas J. Curry, *op. cit.*, p. 33.
[94] *Ibid.*, p. 32.
[95] *Ibid.*, p. 31.
[96] *Ibid.*, p. 32.
[97] *Ibid.*, p. 33.
[98] *Ibid.*, p. 52.

⁹⁹ Gadamer, *Truth and Method*, pp. 289–305.
¹⁰⁰ *Ibid.*, p. 305.
¹⁰¹ Hanley, *op. cit.*, p. 67.
¹⁰² *Ibid.*
¹⁰³ Ahlstrom, *op. cit.*, p. 335.
¹⁰⁴ John Finnis, *Natural Law and Natural Right* (Oxford: The Clarendon Press, 1980), p. 276.
¹⁰⁵ *Idem.*
¹⁰⁶ *Idem*, and on discussions of the common good elsewhere in the book.
¹⁰⁷ *Idem.*
¹⁰⁸ *Idem.*
¹⁰⁹ *Idem.*
¹¹⁰ *Ibid.*, p. 277.
¹¹¹ *Ibid.*, 155.
¹¹² Hanley, *op. cit.*, p. 8.
¹¹³ Avery Dulles, *The Reshaping of Catholicism: Current Challenges in the Theology of the Church* (San Francisco: Harper and Row, 1988), pp. 83–6.
¹¹⁴ Richard J. Bernstein, *Beyond Objectivism and Relativism*, p. 225.
¹¹⁵ *Ibid.*, p. 226.

5. Identity Reinterpreted: Church-State Norms as Principles of Self-Understanding

¹ *Economic Justice for All* asked: "Who are the unemployed? Blacks, Hispanics, Native Americans, young adults, female heads of households and those who are inadequately educated are represented disproportionately among the ranks of the unemployed. . . . Among black teen-agers, unemployment reaches the scandalous rate of more than one in three," n. 140, pp. 70–71 (citing statistics from the U. S. Department of Labor, Bureau of Labor Statistics, *The Unemployment Situation: August 1985*). Little has changed.
² Marcello de Carvalho Azevedo, *Inculturation and the Challenges of Modernity* (Rome: Gregorian University Press, 1982).
³ *Ibid.*, p. 9.
⁴ *Idem.*
⁵ *Ibid.*, p. 10.
⁶ Joe Holland, *Social Analysis: Linking Faith and Justice* (Washington, D.C.: The Center of Concern, 1980; fifth printing Maryknoll, N.Y.: Orbis Books, 1988), p. xii.

⁷ *Ibid.*, p. xiv.

⁸ Joseph P. Fitzpatrick, "Justice as a Problem of Culture," in *Catholic Mind*, 76 (1978): 10–26; p. 10.

⁹ *Idem.*

¹⁰ *Ibid.*, p. 26.

¹¹ *Idem.*

¹² *Economic Justice for All*, Chapter 4, "A New American Experiment: Partnership for the Public Good," nn. 295–325, pp. 145–62.

¹³ Richard J. Bernstein considers that, "[o]ne of the most important and central claims in Hans-Georg Gadamer's philosophical hermeneutics is that all understanding involves not only interpretation but also application." "From Hermeneutics to Praxis," p. 272. And Gadamer approaches the integration of application into interpretation and understanding as "The Rediscovery of the Fundamental Hermeneutic Problem," in *Truth and Method*, pp. 274ff.

¹⁴ Cf. Ary Roest Von Crollius, "What Is So New About Inculturation?" and "Inculturation and the Meaning of Culture," in Ary Roest Von Crollius, editor, *What Is So New About Inculturation?* (Rome: Gregorian University Press, 1984).

¹⁵ Robert J. Schreiter, *Constructing Local Theologies* (Maryknoll, N.Y.: Orbis Books, 1985), p. 17.

¹⁶ Pope Paul VI, *Evangelii Nuntiandi: Apostolic exhortation of Pope Paul VI to the bishops, priests and faithful of the entire Catholic Church on evangelization in the modern world*, in Michael Walsh and Brian Davies, editors, *op. cit.*

¹⁷ Ary Roest Von Crollius, "What Is So New About Inculturation?" p. 16.

¹⁸ *Idem.*

¹⁹ Cf. Joseph A. Tetlow, "The Inculturation of Catholicism in the United States," in Ary Roest Von Crollius, editor, *On Being Church in a Modern Society* (Rome: Gregorian University Press, 1983), and Rodger Van Allen, "Catholicism in the United States: Some Elements of Creative Inculturation," in *Creative Inculturation and the Unity of Faith* (Rome: Gregorian University Press, 1986).

²⁰ Dennis P. McCann and Charles R. Strain, *op. cit.*, p. 7.

²¹ Coleman, *op. cit.*, p. 66.

²² *Ibid.*, p. 249.

²³ Tetlow, *op. cit.*, periodizes the phases as follows: translation, 1491–1921 (end of immigration); assimilation, 1921–1965; transformation, Vatican II and end of ghetto Catholicism in 1965 to the present. Van Allen, *op. cit.*, divides the phases otherwise: no phase of translation;

assimilation, 1776 to Kennedy presidency; transformation, 1963/65 to the present. Both, also, find the primary of gospel/culture encounter to occur in a practical, or in Tetlow's term, "pragmatic," mode by ordinary Catholic Americans.

[24] Social Catholicism is broader than Catholic social teaching insofar as it includes pastoral and lay initiatives in response to the "social question." Social Catholicism is the aspect of modern Catholicism which developed in response to the "social question." It "refers heuristically to Catholic responses to the industrialization process and its consequences in the social classes," in Paul Misner, *Social Catholicism in Europe: From the Onset of Industrialization to the First World War* (New York: Crossroad, 1991), p. 3. The "social question" itself, of course, has changed over time, can involve agricultural and other primary resources as well as industrialization, cannot be isolated from social and cultural realities, and has become global.

At least three of Murray's early essays defended Catholic cooperation with Protestants precisely in movements for social and economic justice: "Current Theology: Christian Co-operation" in *Theological Studies* 3 (1942): 413–31; "Current Theology: Christian Co-operation, Some Further Views," in *Theological Studies* 4 (1943): 100–11; "Current Theology: Intercredal Co-operation; Its Theory and Its Organization," in *Theological Studies* 4 (1943): 257–68. Robert McElroy notes that Murray's "initial interests in the question of public religion came from a desire to forge an inter-faith coalition for social justice in the 1940's," *op. cit.*, p. 5.

[25] In a commencement address at Fairfield University in June, 1966, Murray incited the graduates toward "the new Catholic task that confronts your generation in America." A new era had a task for men and women committed both "to the secular history of America . . . and to life of the people of God." They "will help develop a style of religious existence, which will likewise be authentically American." This primary mode of inculturation on the level of religious existence will benefit from theological reflection on: "a truly pastoral theology of Christian freedom and of the exercise of authority in the Church"; Jewish/ Christian relations and ecumenism; "clarification of the secular message of the Gospel . . . as the ferment of secular history"; the "fantastic phenomenon of the American economy" and "American presence in Asia." Unpublished paper (Murray Archives, File 547). *Economic Justice for All* can be seen to address in some way each of the theological topics he outlined, except for American presence in Asia.

[26] Murray summarized the trans-temporal principles variously and

not always comprehensively. Thomas T. Love, *op. cit.*, pp. 144–66 follows Murray's "The Problem of State Religion," *Theological Studies* 12 (June, 1951): 155–78 as does Charles E. Curran, *op. cit.*, pp. 202–7. Donald E. Pelotte, *op. cit.*, pp. 115–85 treats Murray's position in a more diffused fashion, as do J. Leon Hooper, *op. cit.*, pp. 65–81, and Robert W. McElroy, *op. cit.*, pp. 77–115.

[27] Samples of Murray's exposition of Pope Gelasius I's classic, bedrock formulation of this difference are in "Contemporary Orientations of Catholic Thought on Church and State in the Light of History," *op. cit.*, pp. 177–79, 195–202, 215–20, 225–27, 234; "Leo XIII: Separation of Church and State," *op. cit.*, pp. 187ff.; "On the Structure of the Church-State Problem," in W. Gurian and M. A. Fitzsimmons, editors, *op. cit.* 11–32; *We Hold These Truths*, pp. 63–5, 204–11.

[28] Cf. Murray, "Governmental Repression of Heresy," pp. 77–85; "Contemporary Orientations of Catholic Thought . . . ," pp. 202–4; "St. Robert Bellarmine on the Indirect Power"; "Leo XIII: Separation of Church and State," pp. 187 ff.; "The Issue of Church and State at Vatican II," pp. 581–606; *We Hold These Truths*, pp. ix, 69–71, 75.

[29] The affirmation that the church has spiritual power to affect the state indirectly makes spiritual primacy effective, but Murray's advance beyond St. Robert Bellarmine's concept of "indirect power" registers both Pope Leo XIII's and Murray's affirmation of the independence of the state in its sphere. Cf. "St. Robert Bellarmine on the Indirect Power"; "Governmental Repression of Heresy," pp. 54–65, 68–76; "Contemporary Orientations of Catholic Thought . . . ," pp. 198–202; "Leo XIII: Two Concepts of Government," *Theological Studies* 14 (December, 1953): 551–67; *We Hold These Truths*, pp. 189–96.

[30] This was also Pope Leo's renewal and relocation of the Gelasian dyarchy. Cf. Murray, "Contemporary Orientations of Catholic Thought . . . ," pp. 218–27; "Leo XIII: Separation of Church and State," pp. 193–212; "Leo XIII on Church and State: The General Structure of the Controversy," *Theological Studies* (March, 1953): pp. 17–8; "The Issue of Church and State at Vatican II," pp. 586–87, 602–4.

[31] Pope Leo had described a passive believer-citizen. It was Pope Pius XII who sought to explicate the active role of the believer-citizen and Murray incorporated the Pian principle. Cf. Murray, "Contemporary Orientations of Catholic Thought . . . ," pp. 221–27, 231–34; "The Church and Totalitarian Democracy," *Theological Studies* 13 (December, 1952), pp. 556–63; "The Issue of Church and State at Vatican II," pp. 586–90.

[32] Joseph Komonchak, "Ministry and the Local Church," *Proceedings, Catholic Theological Society of America* (1981): 56–82.

³³ Cf. Richard J. Bernstein, *Beyond Objectivism and Relativism: Science, Hermeneutics, and Praxis* (Philadelphia: University of Pennsylvania Press, 1983), pp. 144–50.

³⁴ Richard J. Bernstein, *ibid.*, pp. 156–65.

³⁵ Bernstein's immanent critique of Gadamer's hermeneutics rightly sustains Gadamer's insight into language and develops some implications for political life: dialogue in community that allows *phronesis* to flourish, suspicion of forces dominating a political community's language and conversations. But his question directed to Gadamer's oversight on conditions for the possibility of *phronesis* and dialogue (". . . the question of what material, social, and political conditions need to be concretely realized in order to encourage the flourishing of *phronesis* in all citizens," *ibid.*, pp. 157–58) implies how difficult it is to restrict *praxis* to the strictly political life, discourse, and community. A relation to democracy inheres in—or is rejected by—economic activities, too.

³⁶ *Economic Justice for All*, n. 327, p. 164.

³⁷ *Ibid.*, n. 331, p. 166.

³⁸ *Ibid.*, n. 332, p. 167.

³⁹ *Ibid.*, n. 83, p. 43.

⁴⁰ For Murray's case that public assistance to Catholic schools is a matter of seeking justice, not a concession, see *We Hold These Truths*, pp. 143–54. If he is correct, then Catholic Americans have learned to accommodate an injustice, which will not be a strong predisposition toward justice for others either.

⁴¹ James and Kathleen McGinnis, "Family as Domestic Church," in John A. Coleman, editor, *One Hundred Years of Catholic Social Thought: Celebration and Challenge* (Maryknoll, N.Y.: Orbis Books, 1991): 120–34.

⁴² Milwaukee Inner-City Churches Allied for Hope.

⁴³ E. J. Dionne, Jr., *Why Americans Hate Politics* (New York: Simon and Schuster, 1991); Donald L. Barlett and James B. Steele, *America: What Went Wrong?* (Kansas City: Andrews and McMeel, 1992).

⁴⁴ Murray, "The Issue of Church and State at Vatican II."

⁴⁵ For this understanding of theology, cf. David Tracy, *Blessed Rage for Order: The New Pluralism in Theology* and *The Analogical Imagination: Christian Theology and the Culture of Pluralism*. The division is, of course, agreeable. Cf. Dennis P. McCann and Charles R. Strain, *Polity and Praxis*, pp. 18ff. Cf. Francis Schüssler Fiorenza and John P. Galvin, editors, *Systematic Theology: Roman Catholic Perspectives* (Minneapolis: Fortress Press, 1991) 2 volumes.

⁴⁶ On the difference and complementarity between social ethics and practical theology, cf. McCann and Strain, *op. cit.*, pp. 145–78.

[47] For a conspectus on fundamental theology, cf. René Latourelle and Gerald O'Collins, editors, Matthew O. Connell, translator, *Problems and Perspectives in Fundamental Theology* (New York: Paulist Press, 1982).

[48] This has some resemblances to Matthew Lamb's category of "Critical Praxis Correlations" as a model of theory/praxis. A point of difference in emphasis with regard to the end of innocence about theory would be that *church-state relations* and theological reflection on them were not so much regarded as innocent of practical grounding, as innocent about the breadth and depth of the relations in practice and theory. Cf. Matthew Lamb, *Solidarity with Victims: Toward a Theology of Social Transformation* (New York: Crossroad, 1982), pp. 61–99.

[49] *Economic Justice for All*, n. 156. p. 78.

[50] *Ibid.*, n. 153, p. 77.

[51] Cf., Robert Bellah, et al., *Habits of the Heart*, on the ways a first language of individualism undermines society and self-governance.

[52] *We Hold These Truths*, p. 27.

[53] Murray, "Governmental Repression of Heresy," p. 35.

[54] Cf. Gadamer, "On the Problem of Self-Understanding," in *Philosophical Hermeneutics* (1962), pp. 44–58.

[55] Canadian novelists such as Margaret Atwood have explored the Canadian identity.

[56] *We Hold These Truths*, p. 5ff.

[57] *Ibid.*, p. 57.

[58] *Idem.*

[59] *Ibid.*, p. 6.

[60] *Idem.*

[61] Pope John XXIII, "Pope John Convokes the Council," in Walter Abbot, editor, translations directed by Joseph Gallagher, *The Documents of Vatican II* (New York: Herder and Herder, 1966): p. 709; cf. also, "Pope John's Opening Speech," *ibid.*, p. 717; cf. also, Pope John Paul II, *op. cit.*, p. 43: "In a certain sense, the Council has made the Spirit newly 'present' in our difficult age."

[62] Murray, "On the Most Blessed Trinity" (Murray Archives, File 506), and *The Problem of God*.

[63] Murray, "The Roman Catholic Church," *op. cit.;* "For the Freedom and Transcendence of the Church," *The American Ecclesiastical Review* 126 (January, 1952): 28–48; and "The Issue of Church and State at Vatican II."

[64] Cf. Pope John Paul II, *Lord and Giver of Life* (Washington, D.C.: United States Catholic Conference, 1986), especially pp. 39ff.

⁶⁵ Murray, "Contemporary Orientations of Catholic Thought," *op. cit.*, pp. 213–27; "Governmental Repression of Heresy," *op. cit.*, pp. 62–70; *The Problem of God., op. cit.*, Cf. also, J. Leon Hooper, pp. 209–13.

⁶⁶ Murray, *The Problem of God*, pp. 17–9, 86–7.

⁶⁷ Hooper, p. 172ff.

⁶⁸ For example, Murray, "The Danger of the Vows: An Encounter with Earth, Woman and the Spirit," in *Woodstock Letters* 116 (Fall, 1967): 421–27.

⁶⁹ One of the most fruitful remains Heribert Mühlen, *Una Mystica Persona. Die Kirche als das Mysterium der heilsgeschichtlichen Identität des heiligen Geistes in Christus und den Christen: Eine Person in vielen Personen* (München: Schöningh, 1968). On Mühlen's pneumatology in general, cf. Robert T. Sears, "Spirit, Divine and Human: The Theology of the Holy Spirit of Heribert Mühlen and its Relevance for Evaluating the Date of Psychotherapy" (unpublished dissertation, Fordham University, 1974), Thomas Hughson, "A Critical Study of the Analogy Central to the Pneumatology of Heribert Mühlen" (unpublished dissertation, University of St. Michael's College, 1981).

⁷⁰ Cf. Avery Dulles, "A Half-Century of Ecclesiology," in *Theological Studies* 50 (1989): 419–42; esp. pp. 434–35 on Mühlen. David M. Coffey, "A Proper Mission of the Holy Spirit," *Theological Studies* 49 (1988): 671–93 addresses ecclesiological aspects of pneumatology. Cf. Yves Congar, *I Believe in the Holy Spirit*, David Smith, translator, Volume II, 'He is Lord and Giver of Life' (London: Geoffrey Chapman, 1983), especially Part One "The Spirit Animates the Church," and Pope John Paul II, *op. cit.*, for pneumatological ecclesiology.

⁷¹ Chapter VII, "The Pilgrim Church," in "Dogmatic Constitution on the Church," *Vatican Council II, op. cit.*, pp. 407–13: "Already the final age of the world is with us; it is even anticipated in a certain real way, for the Church on earth is endowed already with a sanctity that is real though imperfect," n. 48, p. 408. And that sanctity has the Spirit as principle and the totality of the pilgrim way (including social mission) as content.

⁷² The National Conference of Catholic Bishops glanced at the process of preparing the letter: "The pastoral letter has been a work of careful inquiry, wide consultation, and prayerful discernment," n. 3, p. v. The authors then describe the church: "By faith and Baptism, we are fashioned into new creatures, filled with the Holy Spirit and with a love that compels us . . . ," n. 28, p. xv. Or, again: "Church is, thus, primarily a communion of people bonded by the Spirit with Christ as their Head,

sustaining one another in love, and acting as a sign or instrument in the world," n. 339, p. 170. That ecclesiology supports a readiness to consult and listen to the faithful as those who also are enlivened by the Spirit.

[73] "Dogmatic Constitution on the Church," *op. cit.*, n. 1, p. 350.

[74] Here, E. J. Dionne, *Why Americans Hate Politics*, revises things. Fragmentation of society, individualism, and withdrawal from political life are real. But the correction begins at the level of communities, mediating institutions, not at the political level of overcoming false polarities, though this, of course, merits our labors. Cf. Robert W. McElroy, *op. cit.*, pp. 42–76.

[75] Cf., Robert W. McElroy, pp. 60–76, on the cultural nature of the public consensus. Culture, as Azevedo's definition holds, is more than a moral reality, however. Pope John Paul II presents a profound analysis of culture through the personal vocation to work in common, in *Laborem Exercens* and *Sollicitudo Rei Socialis*, in *Proclaiming Justice and Peace*.

[76] Murray inveighed against divorcing freedom from truth, following Leo XIII on this. The truth at issue was *res sacra homo*. Pope John Paul II reads Leo XIII much as Murray did on this point:

> As has been mentioned, this error consists in an understanding of human freedom which detaches it from obedience to the truth and consequently from the duty to respect the rights of others. The essence of freedom then becomes self-love carried to the point of contempt for God and neighbor, a self-love which leads to an unbridled affirmation of self-interest and which refuses to be limited by any demand of justice.

(*Centesimus Annus*, n. 17.1, p. 445, in *Proclaiming Justice and Peace*, *op. cit.*). This truth means that those who err have rights.

[77] John A. Coleman, "The Church's Mission to Justice," in *An American Strategic Theology*, pp. 9–37; p. 18.

[78] *Idem.*

[79] *Idem.*

[80] *Ibid.*, p. 19.

[81] *Idem.*

[82] *Idem.*

[83] Jürgen Moltmann's incisive essay, "America as Dream," in M. Douglas Meeks, translator and editor, *On Human Dignity* (Philadelphia: Fortress Press, 1984), criticizes the de-Christianized and pragmatic messianism of America. His critique extends to "life as experiment," which detaches Americans from full life in the present. He comments, and it bears on the believer-citizen relation: "The hope which is born out

of the resurrection of Christ prepares one to live fully in the present and with ultimate love, that life which is once for all," p. 161.

[84] This is another way of describing the "supernatural existential" of Karl Rahner's theology, conceiving the universal divine addressing, sustaining, and fulfilling of humans as the mission of the Spirit.

[85] Cf. Johann B. Metz, *The Poverty of Spirit*, translated by John Drury (Glen Rock, N.J.: Newman Press, 1968).

6. Free Exercise of Religion: An Option for the Poor

[1] Murray, *We Hold These Truths*, p. 198.

[2] *Idem.*

[3] *Ibid.*, pp. 205–11.

[4] *Ibid.*, 201–5.

[5] *Idem* (from Chapter 9, titled "Are There Two or One?").

[6] *Idem.*

[7] Murray, *idem*, quoting Alois Dempf, *Sacrum Imperium.*

[8] Murray, *ibid.*, p. 202.

[9] *Idem.*

[10] *Ibid.*, p. 203.

[11] *Idem.*

[12] *Idem.*

[13] *Economic Justice for All* refers to the church in terms of being a messenger of the gospel, a servant of the poor, an institution, a community of disciples, a community of hope, a witness to the Word made flesh, a sacrament and in other ways. But, a direct statement on the nature of the church says:

> Church is, thus, primarily a communion of people bonded by the Spirit with Christ as their Head, sustaining one another in love, and acting as a sign or sacrament in the world (n. 339, p. 170).

Cf. also, Joseph Komonchak, *op. cit.*, and "Clergy, Laity and the Church's Mission in the World," *The Jurist* 41, 2 (1981): 422–47; Robert J. Schreiter, "Local Theologies in the Local Church: Issues and Methods," *Proceedings of the Catholic Theological Society of America* (1981): 96–112. The church as communion of local churches is an ecclesiological orientation, also, which places the Catholic Church in a positive relation to the visible unity sought by the ecumenical movement. If "[t]he one Church is to be envisioned as a conciliar fellowship of local churches which are themselves truly united," a communion ecclesiology of Catholicism lends itself to ecumenical dialogue on the nature of visible unity. William Lagerath, citing the Nairobi formula (1975) in Jeffrey Gros, editor, *The Search for Visible Unity: Baptism, Eucharist, Ministry* (New York: Pilgrim Press, 1984), p. 13.

[14] Murray, *ibid.*, p. 203.

[15] *Idem.*

[16] In its "Decree on the Pastoral Office of Bishops in the Church," *Vatican Council II, op. cit.*, pp. 564–90, the Council includes the following within the teaching duty of a bishop:

> They should expound likewise the principles governing the solution of those very grave problems concerning the possession, increase and just distribution of material goods, concerning peace and war, and the fraternal co-existence of all peoples (n. 12, p. 570).

[17] Murray, *ibid.*, p. 204.

[18] *Ibid.*, p. 205.

[19] *Economic Justice for All* formally incorporates two kinds of dialogue: one, in the consultations through which the document was drawn up (cf. n. 3, pp. v–vi); the other, on the specific policy recommendations (cf. n. 126, p. 63; n. 127–132, pp. 65–7; n. 135, p. 68; n. 360, pp. 179–80). The latter presupposes consensus on the moral vision outlined in chapters 1 and 2. Yet nothing indicates that the National Conference of Catholic Bishops wished to foreclose further dialogue on the *meaning* of chapters 1 and 2.

[20] Murray, *ibid.*, p. 205.

[21] *Idem.*

[22] *Economic Justice for All*, n. 286, p. 145.

[23] Robert McAfee Brown, *Saying Yes and Saying No: On Rendering to God and to Caesar* (Philadelphia: Westminster Press, 1986).

[24] Murray, *ibid.*, p. 209.

[25] McAfee Brown, *op. cit.*, pp. 58ff.

[26] Murray, "The Issue of Church and State at Vatican II," pp. 605ff.

[27] *Ibid.*, p. 604.

[28] *Idem.*

[29] Coleman, *op. cit.*, p. 20.

[30] *Ibid.*, p. 49.

[31] *Ibid.*, p. 31.

[32] Murray, "Contemporary Orientations of Catholic Thought," *op. cit.*, p. 220.

[33] *Idem.*

³⁴ Murray, "Contemporary Orientations of Catholic Thought," *op. cit.*, p. 220.

³⁵ *Idem.*

³⁶ *Idem.*

³⁷ *Idem.*

³⁸ *Ibid.*, p. 221.

³⁹ *Idem.*

⁴⁰ *Idem.*

⁴¹ *Idem.*

⁴² *Idem.*

⁴³ *Idem.*

⁴⁴ *Ibid.*, p. 222.

⁴⁵ *Idem.*

⁴⁶ *Idem.*

⁴⁷ *Idem.*

⁴⁸ Cf., J. Bryan Hehir, *op. cit.*

⁴⁹ Murray, "The Issue of Church and State at Vatican II," p. 586.

⁵⁰ *Ibid.*, p. 603.

⁵¹ *Idem*, quoting the "Pastoral Constitution on the Church in the Modern World," in *Vatican Council II, op. cit.*, n. 76, pp. 984–85.

ISAAC HECKER STUDIES IN RELIGION AND AMERICAN CULTURE

Other Books in the Series

IMAGE & LIKENESS: RELIGIOUS VISIONS IN AMERI-CAN FILM CLASSICS edited by John R. May

GOD'S FEDERAL REPUBLIC: RECONSTRUCTING OUR GOVERNING SYMBOL by William Johnson Everett

LANDSCAPES OF THE SACRED: GEOGRAPHY AND NARRATIVE IN AMERICAN SPIRITUALITY by Belden C. Lane

THE SECOND WAVE: HISPANIC MINISTRY AND THE EVANGELIZATION OF CULTURES by Allan Figueroa Deck, S.J.

FULLNESS OF FAITH: THE PUBLIC SIGNIFICANCE OF THEOLOGY by Michael J. Himes and Kenneth R. Himes, O.F.M.